FIGHTING FALSEHOODS

This book offers the reader tools to recognize, analyze, and fight back against the fake news, misinformation, and disinformation that come at us from every corner.
This volume:

- Uses real, lively examples to help readers detect fake news, false claims, suspicious information/data, biased reporting, and hate speech;
- Demonstrates through case studies where to look for information, what to look for, how to analyze the logic/illogic involved, and uncover the truth value of a story;
- Discusses fact-checking sites, what they examine, and their reliability;
- Provides examples and analyzes the components, purposes, and consequences of conspiracy theories;
- Illustrates the tricks of using numbers/data to mislead readers;
- Explains what to look for to help decide whether to believe the conclusions of stories based on surveys;
- Offers a range of concrete, effective responses to dangerous, exaggerated, distorted, and false narratives;
- Examines policy responses to fake news, disinformation, and misinformation across the world.

A key manual to negotiate the information age, this book will be essential reading for students, scholars, and professionals of journalism and mass communication, public policy, politics, and the social sciences. It will also be an indispensable handbook for the lay reader.

Irene Rubin is a retired professor from Northern Illinois University, U.S. Her BA is from Barnard College (Oriental Studies), and her MA is from Harvard (East Asian Studies). Her PhD is from the University of Chicago, in Sociology. She taught public budgeting, qualitative methods, and research design and has written many books.

Professor Rubin's research used many of the techniques outlined in this book. Her single-authored books include *Running in the Red, Balancing the Federal Budget: Trimming the Herds or Eating the Seed Corn, Class Tax and Power: Municipal Budgeting in the United States*, and *The Politics of Public Budgeting: Getting and Spending, Borrowing and Balancing*. She has also coauthored *Qualitative Interviewing: The Art of Hearing Data*. Her hobbies include traveling, reading Harry Potter in Spanish, and birdwatching.

FIGHTING FALSEHOODS

Suspicion, Analysis, and Response

Irene Rubin

LONDON AND NEW YORK

Cover image: Getty Images

First published 2022
by Routledge
4 Park Square, Milton Park, Abingdon, Oxon OX14 4RN

and by Routledge
605 Third Avenue, New York, NY 10158

Routledge is an imprint of the Taylor & Francis Group, an informa business

© 2022 Irene Rubin

The right of Irene Rubin to be identified as author of this work has been asserted in accordance with sections 77 and 78 of the Copyright, Designs and Patents Act 1988.

All rights reserved. No part of this book may be reprinted or reproduced or utilised in any form or by any electronic, mechanical, or other means, now known or hereafter invented, including photocopying and recording, or in any information storage or retrieval system, without permission in writing from the publishers.

Trademark notice: Product or corporate names may be trademarks or registered trademarks, and are used only for identification and explanation without intent to infringe.

British Library Cataloguing-in-Publication Data
A catalogue record for this book is available from the British Library

Library of Congress Cataloging-in-Publication Data
A catalog record has been requested for this book

ISBN: 978-1-032-15823-5 (hbk)
ISBN: 978-1-032-28780-5 (pbk)
ISBN: 978-1-003-29847-2 (ebk)

DOI: 10.4324/9781003298472

Typeset in Sabon
by Deanta Global Publishing Services, Chennai, India

TO ALL THOSE WHO HAVE BEEN THE VICTIMS OF FALSE OR MISLEADING INFORMATION.

MAY IT NEVER HAPPEN TO YOU AGAIN.

CONTENTS

	Acknowledgments	viii
1	Suspicion, Analysis, and Response	1
2	Recognizing Exaggerations, Distortions, and Lies	11
3	Quick Checks	35
4	Analysis: Logic and Completeness	55
5	Analysis by Comparison	70
6	What Does a Cited Source Actually Say?	87
7	Conspiracy Theories	104
8	Problems with Numbers	124
9	Surveys	137
10	Response: Fighting Back	157
	Afterword: The Responsibility Is Ours	175
	Index	190

ACKNOWLEDGMENTS

Every book is a collective activity, requiring the support of many, often invisible people, such as acquisition editors and copy editors, and computer programmers. I am especially indebted to the numerous advocacy organizations, news reporters, and fact-checkers who search for stories and data, validate them, and post them on the web. I stand on their shoulders, which is a good thing, since I am pretty short.

1
SUSPICION, ANALYSIS, AND RESPONSE

What Is the Problem? Exaggerations, Distortions, and Lies

John Adams, the second president of the U.S., observed that "Facts are stubborn things; and whatever may be our wishes, our inclinations, or the dictates of our passions, they cannot alter the state of facts and evidence." Adams was right when he claimed that facts are stubborn things, but he did not anticipate the extent to which we are pressured to ignore facts and evidence, to substitute instead "our wishes, our inclinations, or the dictates of our passions."[1]

On television and websites, in newspapers and magazines, in email and on billboards, and in ads and solicitations that come in the mail, companies, politicians, interest groups, and individuals try to convince us about something. They may want us to buy a computer or vote for them in the next election. They may advise us to buy their pills to lose weight or urge us not to vaccinate our children. They may tell us that global climate change is not occurring, or if it is, it is perfectly natural, and we should not take any steps to moderate it. They may warn us that the government is coming to take our guns, or that immigrants, artificial intelligence, or robots are after our jobs. Some of the many messages aimed at us are well intended, some are true, or at least not disprovable, while others are intentionally misleading.

Intentionally misleading material is becoming more common and efforts to combat it have not been able to keep up. The deceptions are becoming harder to detect. The threat to democracy has become apparent. On January 6, 2021, a group of Trump supporters, many armed, broke into the Capitol to stop the counting of electoral votes for Joe Biden, who had defeated Trump. The mob had accepted Trump's false claims that he had won the election, and that the Democrats had stolen it from him. The fundamental principle of democracy that leaders shall be chosen by free and fair elections was directly attacked by people who accepted a false claim.

The columnist, Margaret Sullivan, declared that America was not losing but rather had already lost the war against disinformation. She was referring to a viral video by a group of doctors endorsing misleading information about a treatment for covid-19. The doctors were promoting hydroxychloroquine, which had been shown in controlled studies to be ineffective. One of the doctors in this video had attributed various diseases to dreams, demon sperm, and alien DNA. Sullivan argued, "With nearly 150,000 dead from covid-19, we've not only lost the public-health war, we've lost the war for truth. Misinformation and lies have captured the castle."[2]

My opinion? We have not lost the war yet, only some of the preliminary skirmishes. But Sullivan is right that truth itself is being challenged.

The consequences of failure to fight back are almost unimaginably serious. How can we live in a society where there is no truth, where uninformed opinions substitute for evidence, where advertisers are free to make false claims, where candidates for office and public officials routinely mislead the public, and where there is no credible way of countering lies, misstatements, and exaggerations?

We need to arm ourselves and take action. In the play Cyrano de Bergerac, Cyrano had an imaginary sword with which to cut down lies. The goal of this book is to give readers some real weaponry and show you how to use it, so that recognizing and attacking falsehood becomes easy, automatic, and gratifying.

The Problem Is Serious

The frequency and impact of distorted information has been called "truth decay."[3] Truth decay occurs when the line between opinion and fact is blurred; when the volume and influence of opinion and personal experience are greater than that of facts and accumulated knowledge, and when trust in traditional sources of factual information erodes.

While false or misleading information is not new—President John Adams certainly recognized it—it has blossomed in recent years. The problem is not limited to political actors trying to influence an election or doctors endorsing an ineffective cure. Individuals publish their own unproven versions of events. They create believable but false evidence by distorting voices on recordings and altering pictures and videos. Search engines pick up altered or made-up stories, and news media repeat them. Some are even endorsed by the president. Fake news is cheap to produce, often financially rewarding, and abundant; by contrast, verifying information requires time and skill and doesn't earn a cent. But failure to recognize and combat false, misleading, or distorted stories hurts both individuals and society at large.

Threats to Individuals

For individuals, consequences of fake news can include embarrassment, loss of money to false advertising and fraud, loss of employment, illness, and even death.

Embarrassment

In its mildest form, failure to detect misleading claims can be embarrassing. I knew a woman who claimed that she had won a lottery because she received an advertising brochure from the Publishers Clearing House that said, "You may have already won ten million dollars!" She looked foolish to her friends who understood that what she had received was just an advertisement. The chance that she had won the sweepstakes was vanishingly small. People who have been taken in by scams often are too embarrassed to report the crime to the police.

Financial Loss

Failure to detect omitted evidence or missing steps in an argument can be expensive. If you buy a used car and fail to ask for certification that it has not been in a flood that ruined the vehicle, you may buy a lemon and waste your money. You may have to take the bus to work. Those who cannot recognize Ponzi schemes that promise unrealistic rates of return on an investment may lose their life savings.

Loss of Employment

Sometimes people who fall for false or misleading stories lose their jobs. A police officer in Louisiana read a statement falsely attributed to U.S. Representative Alexandria Ocasio-Cortez (AOC), "We pay soldiers too much." He became angry and posted on social media that AOC deserved a round [of bullets]. In the ensuing uproar, the officer was fired. The officer apparently never asked himself if the quotation might be false.[4]

Impact on Health

Failure to ask oneself whether a claim is true can have a serious impact on health, one's own, that of one's family, and that of one's neighbors and friends.

As long as there has been a vaccine to prevent the spread of disease, there have been anti-vaxxers. In recent years, the number of people who will not vaccinate their children has dramatically increased. Measles, which had been largely eradicated in the U.S. by 2000, returned with a major outbreak in 2019.[5] People who do not get vaccinated keep a disease alive, and spread it to others, including the young, the old, and those with compromised immune systems.

Advocates of the rice diet for weight loss failed to warn people that the more rice they ate, the more likely the diet would trigger diabetes. As recently as May 2017, Doctor Michael Greger defended the rice diet, arguing that it had saved tens of thousands of lives by lowering blood pressure and treating kidney failure. He failed to mention anything about the connection between eating too much rice, particularly white rice, and the development of diabetes.[6]

Possible Death

In the worst case, failure to question claims about cures for diseases can even lead to death. An article in *BBC Three*, in the United Kingdom, reported that a young woman's boyfriend, diagnosed with a return of his cancer, refused a second round of chemotherapy because of its side effects. He opted for alternative cancer treatments that had been touted on YouTube videos, in documentaries, and in speeches. They promised to cure cancer "naturally." The young man chose a vegan diet, with coffee enemas and cannabis oil. The proposed treatments came with a thermographic scan that was supposed to show if the cancer had returned but could not actually detect cancer. Thinking his disease was in remission because it did not show up on this test, the young man had no effective treatment and died at age 23.[7]

The young people, eager to latch on to some hope, never checked to see if what they were hearing, watching, and reading, was true.

Closer to home, in March of 2020, a man died, and his wife was in critical condition after taking chloroquine phosphate to prevent covid-19. In tests, the drug was associated with a risk of potentially deadly heart arrhythmias, but apparently the couple never checked.[8]

Threats to Society

For society at large, false or misleading information can result in the failure to deal with health or environmental crises, can cause the erosion of democracy, and can increase divisiveness and violence. Researchers who produce false or misleading results and those who circulate those studies influence, support, or obstruct critical policy decisions.

Climate change has already begun to increase the intensity of storms and the frequency of floods and droughts. Life-threatening heat waves are occurring more often, glaciers are melting, raising sea levels, threatening low-lying islands and cities along the coasts. Climate change is contributing to reduced harvests, creating pressure on food supplies. Wildfires in California have increased in frequency and area, an increase attributed to climate change.[9] A handful of scientists who deny the existence or importance of global climate change reinforce political decisions to take no action to moderate its effects.

The social costs of failure to see through false claims include going to war on false pretenses. For example, unjustified claims of a linkage between Iraq and Al Qaeda contributed to the rationale for the U.S. to go to war against Iraq. Claims that Saddam Hussein was creating weapons of mass destruction were questionable and were later disproved.[10]

False news can stir up hatreds and fears between groups, and can even be the impetus for killing sprees, as occurred in India when nationalists were subjected to false news about Muslims killing sacred cows.[11]

Democracy is threatened by false news when it is used for political advantage. If citizens cannot distinguish between what is true and what is false, they cannot monitor and control government policy and implementation. They would not know for whom to vote, or what policies to approve or oppose; they would not know what programs were successful in solving public problems, and which ones were failing, costly, wasteful, or corrupt.

Believing Nothing Is Not an Option

If you realize how much of what you hear and read is false or exaggerated, it is easy to fall into thinking that nothing is true. No one wants to fall for a made-up story told by a panhandler to get a bit of money or a fraud perpetrated by a scam artist. But the alternative, not accepting any story or any claim, means that you also turn away the genuinely destitute and let them freeze or starve, or send them back into situations in which they are likely to be murdered. If you believe that government programs are riddled with errors and overpayments, you oppose all programs that help people in need.

If you assume all candidates are liars, you will not vote, instead letting others less knowledgeable than you choose the president. Your choice probably would have been better than theirs, not just for you, but for your city, your state, and your country. If many people throw up their hands and withdraw from political participation, if they do not vote, if they pay no attention to politics, democracy dies, without a bang or a whimper.

When there is a real danger, and government or private agencies warn you about it, you do not flee from the hurricane or tornado because you do not believe the warning. You do not wear a mask to prevent the spread of covid-19 because you think the danger is greatly exaggerated. Then you or your family get sick.

Opting out, assuming everything is a lie, while tempting, is not a realistic option. The consequences of not using your judgment are too severe. The only sensible response to the barrage of false and misleading information is to learn how to recognize, analyze, and oppose exaggerations, distortions, and lies.

Obstacles to Truth Seeking

Perpetrators of false, distorted, or exaggerated stories do not want you to penetrate their lies and half-truths, and so try to make it impossible for you to do so. They encourage you to trust no source of news, no matter how neutral it looks, and to just believe them instead.

Legitimate and fact-checked news is called false, while actual false news is legitimated. When asked why he continually attacked the press, President Trump reportedly answered, "you know why I do it? I do it to discredit you all and demean you all, so when you write negative stories about me no one will believe you."[12]

President Trump called the press the enemy of the people. He went further, arguing that you cannot believe what you read or even what you see. He urged the public to disbelieve their own eyes if what they saw contradicted what he said. In a speech in 2018, Trump said, "And just remember: What you're seeing and what you're reading is not what's happening."[13]

Some politicians have explicitly promoted the idea that truth is subjective, that one person's opinion is as good as anyone else's, and have cast doubt on the legitimacy of any intellectual efforts to investigate and find a truth outside their own opinions.

The idea that evidence is not required, that any statement is as good or true as any other, has been articulated by Trump's advisers. Kellyanne Conway, defending Press Secretary Sean Spicer's false statement about the numbers in attendance at Trump's inauguration, argued that Spicer's statements were not false, merely alternative facts.[14] When questioned about the evidence for one of her claims about former President Obama eavesdropping on the president's campaign, she responded "I am not in the job of having evidence."[15] Evidence was irrelevant; she could say whatever she wanted or whatever she was told to say.

President Trump's attorney, Rudy Giuliani, added to the confusion by arguing in another famous quotation that truth isn't always truth, it is somebody's version of it.[16] Thus, there is no reality, only people's opinion of what is happening. Rather than assume that one version or claim was truer than another, or that both or multiple versions were equally acceptable, Giuliani argued that none of those versions is true, there were only different opinions.

The attack on truth makes it difficult for readers or listeners to find out if what is claimed is true. One easy way to test a statement for truth value is to consult some reliable fact-checkers, so some have attacked the fact-checkers. Such attacks are not against particular fact-checks with which the author disagrees, or against some specific fact-checker, but against the whole industry. The critics charge that the fact-checkers just recycle the opinions of the left-wing press. There is no objective information, no independent research, so they cannot possibly test the truth.[17]

In a post-truth world, there are different versions of a story, a set of alternative facts, and no way to choose between them. In a world with no truth, evidence is irrelevant. There is no clarity, and presumably many mistakes if you pick the wrong opinion to believe and act on. Those mistakes can be serious, from being subject to fraud to taking actions on false premises. They can even be life threatening.

As this image of a world without truth comes closer, those of us who still believe there is a reality, and there are truths that describe it, or at least that there is a continuum of more and less truth, must figure out what to believe.

Overcoming the Obstacles: Sorting Truth from Fiction

Fortunately, figuring out where truth lies gets easier as one goes along. Learning to recognize and refute false and misleading efforts to persuade is engaging and sometimes even fun. And, if enough of us beat back the perpetrators and challenge the lies, we can reduce their role in society and return to a less crazy world. We can walk back through the looking glass.

It is our job, yours and mine, to prevent a world of truthlessness, where records disappear, where the description of reality is remade at will by those in power, and where there is no way to debunk false claims. Our motivation should be high. No one likes to be deceived, to be lured into a phony investment promising high returns. No one wants an implanted heart device that shorts out, or a hip replacement that sheds metal bits. No one wants to get sick because some people refused to have their children vaccinated or because someone didn't tell them that adopting a particular diet could cause diabetes. I hope that we as a nation are not ready to give up democratic control of government.

It does not seem likely that this barrage of big and little lies and distortions can be choked off without simultaneously curbing free speech and legitimate advertising; efforts to block or curtail false news and overt propaganda evoke shouts of censorship.

A recent survey by the Pew Foundation reported that 79 percent of Republicans and 78 percent of Democrats reported finding stories they guessed might be false and checked the facts in the stories themselves. But only about a third of those responding took further action to report to others the story they had identified as misleading or fake.[18]

While many people are aware that some news they encounter might be false or misleading, a Stanford University study found that many students were unable to distinguish fake news from the real thing.[19]

Moreover, as the Pew study pointed out, when people do discover something they think is biased, the majority don't let anyone else know; they do nothing to prevent its spread. So, there is work to do, there are things to learn and action to take. To this point, misleading advertisements and false or misleading news and quotations have outstripped our capacity to respond, but we can catch up.

What to Do: Be Aware, Analyze, and Answer Back

We can learn to recognize most exaggerated or false arguments, evaluate them, and if warranted, oppose them.

Develop Awareness

The first step is to cultivate a healthy skepticism, an awareness that something about a particular argument warrants further investigation. Many people accept arguments, even without sufficient evidence, if those arguments support their beliefs and opinions. If you encounter some argument and find yourself saying, "Whew, I knew that would be the case," you need to tell yourself instead, "I wish that were true, I wonder if it is."

More generally, we need to ask ourselves, is there something about this effort to persuade me that should rouse my concern? Is it coming from some source known to be self-interested or biased? Does it seem improbable, over the top, or too good to be true? If an advertisement promises that some pill can restore youthful energy, you probably should not take it at face value.

Does whatever you are hearing or reading play on your emotions, is it short on evidence, does it rely on stereotypes? Any title or headline that has exclamation points is probably trying to appeal to your emotions, not your reason or experience; any source that argues that others are trying to keep this information from you, but this source will tell you the truth, is probably not giving you information you can rely on. Does the credibility of the piece depend on authority, someone famous or important, rather than on evidence? Does it claim "everyone knows this" or "it is widely known that" without further specification?

Does it cite the source of its information? Missing or incorrect sources should rouse suspicion. How do the authors know what they claim? If there is no way to know, the authors are guessing, and likely overclaiming, which should rouse your suspicion.

Analyze

If your concern is roused, then the next step is to analyze the claim more carefully. You can examine the argument, pay attention to its flaws and shortcomings, find other articles or reports that provide a different perspective or contradict the first piece you looked at. You can look for websites that may have already fact-checked this argument.

Ask yourself, how logical is it, does it leave out steps or options? If what you are examining is a research report, how strong is the design of the study? If the argument is based on survey data, does the article or speech tell you all you need to know about who did the survey, when and how it was done, and whether the researchers followed standard protocols? Do the results depend on small or biased samples, or on misused or abused statistics? Does the argument rely on cherry picking, that is, citing studies that disagree with most of the rest of the literature or relying on selected cases or dates when other cases or longer time series would result in different conclusions? How does the argument compare to others you have read or heard on the same subject? Differences between arguments do not necessarily mean that the one you are considering is wrong but do suggest that you need to look into both or multiple sides of an argument and compare and weigh the evidence each presents.

Answer Back

If you determine that an argument is false, misleading, or grossly exaggerated, and possibly dangerous, then what? Where do you go with your conclusion? How can you answer back? If it is advertising, you can refuse to buy the product, and report the deception to government agencies and consumer watchdogs.

If it is a news story, you can report the story as biased to a public editor or to the publisher of the paper or website. You can frame contradictory evidence and try to publish it in newsletters. You can tweet it or blog it. You can contact your elected representatives; you can write letters to the editor. You can frame your story as newsworthy and get on talk shows to present your case.

You need to be very sure you are right, and then, if the misrepresentation is important enough, that is, affects a lot of people in a harmful way, go public. You can send your work to a factfinding organization and suggest they follow up and publish the results on their websites. If you discover a fraud, you can ask the local police or mayor to warn the public. You can even write and publish a book.

You may feel that the task is too big, and that you cannot reach the real opponents, that no one will listen, that money and power are all on the other side. If that kind of thinking prevents you from acting, you will have disempowered yourself. Just getting a counternarrative out there is important. If you put your argument up on the web, search engines may find it and make it available to others. Not everyone will respond to an evidence-based argument, even if it is convincingly stated, but some will. Most importantly, you will not be alone. There will be others alongside you doing the same thing, convincing others.

You can teach other people to ask the kinds of questions you have learned to ask. Is this threat real, has it happened before, what is the history here? What is the evidence? And how good is it? Is that evidence made up or misinterpreted? Each person you teach teaches others, and the truth, and truth seeking, goes viral.

You do not have to give up or give in, you don't have to accept all efforts to persuade you or reject them all. With a little practice, you should get good at sorting arguments into piles: probably true, maybe true, maybe not true, definitely not true. Then, if you get a hurricane warning, you will know whether you should pack up and leave or sit it out.

About This Book

The rest of this book is divided into four parts. The first part discusses how to recognize efforts to persuade that may be inaccurate, exaggerated, or in some way untrue. The second part is about ways to analyze arguments you suspect might not be reliable. The final section is about how to take arms against fiction sold as fact. An afterword describes how difficult it has been for governments to control false and misleading news, and the spotty efforts of social media companies to regulate themselves.

Notes

1 John Adams, " Argument in Defense of the Soldiers in the Boston Massacre Trials," December 1770, www.quotationspage.com/quotes/John_Adams/.
2 "This Was the Week America Lost the War on Misinformation," *The Washington Post*, July 30, 2020, www.washingtonpost.com/lifestyle/media/this-was-theweek

-america-lost-the-war-on-misinformation/2020/07/30/d8359e2e-d257-11ea-9038af089b63ac21_story.html.
3. Jennifer Kavanagh and Michael D. Rich, *Truth Decay: An Initial Exploration of the Diminishing Role of Facts and Analysis in American Public Life*, Santa Monica, CA: RAND Corporation, 2018. www.rand.org/pubs/research_reports/RR2314.html.
4. Neil Vigdor, "Louisiana Police Officer on Facebook Says Alexandria Ocasio-Cortez 'Needs a Round,'" *The New York Times*, July 21, 2019; Justin Wise, "Louisiana Police Officer Fired after Saying on Facebook that Ocasio-Cortez 'Needs a Round,'" *The Hill*, July 22, 2019.
5. Centers for Disease Control and Prevention, Measles Cases and Outbreaks, updated June 7, 2021, www.cdc.gov/measles/cases-outbreaks.html.
6. Michael Greger, "What Happened to the Rice Diet?" *Nutrition Facts.org*, May 18, 2017, https://nutritionfacts.org/2017/05/18/what-happened-to-the-rice-diet/.
7. Hannah Price, "I Lost My Boyfriend to Cancer 'Conspiracy Theories,'" *BBC Three*, July 20, 2020, www.bbc.co.uk/bbcthree/article/7239691747b0-4aac-856f-e213c3a0c3fa.
8. Scott Neuman, "Man Dies, Woman Hospitalized after Taking Form of Chloroquine to Prevent COVID-19," *NPR*, March 24, 2020.
9. Robinson Meyer, "California's Wildfires Are 500 Percent Larger Due to Climate Change," *The Atlantic*, July 16, 2019, www.theatlantic.com/science/archive/2019/07/climatechange-500-percent-increase-california-wildfires/594016/.
10. Glenn Kessler, "The Iraq War and WMDs; An Intelligence Failure or White House Spin?," *The Washington Post Fact Checker*, March 22, 2019, www.washingtonpost.com/politics/2019/03/22/iraq-warwmds-an-intelligence-failure-or-white-house-spin/.
11. Kai Schultz, "Murders of Religious Minorities in India Go Unpunished, Report Finds," *The New York Times*, February 18, 2019, www.nytimes.com/2019/02/18/world/asia/india-cowreligious-attacks.html.
12. Eli Rosenberg, "Trump Admitted He Attacks Press to Shield Himself from Negative Coverage, Lesley Stahl Says," *The Washington Post*, May 22, 2018, www.washingtonpost.com/news/thefix/wp/2018/05/22/trump-admitted-he-attacks-press-to-shield-himself-from-negative-coverage-60-minutes-reporter-says/.
13. Peter Wehner, "Trump's Sinister Assault on Truth," *The Atlantic*, June 18, 2018, www.theatlantic.com/ideas/archive/2019/06/donald-trumps-sinister-assault-truth/591925/
14. Rebecca Savransky, "'Alternative Facts' Tops List of 2017 Notable Quotes," *The Hill*, December 12, 2017, https://thehill.com/homenews/news/364414-alternative-facts-topslist-of-2017-notable-quotes.
15. Philip Bump, "Kellyanne Conway on Surveillance: 'I'm Not in the Job of Having Evidence,'" *The Washington Post*, March 13, 2017, www.washingtonpost.com/news/politics/wp/2017/03/13/kellyanne-conway-on-surveillance-im-not-in-the-job-of-having-evidence/.
16. Posted by Tim Hains, "Giuliani vs. Chuck Todd: Truth Isn't Always Truth, Comey's 'Truth' Different from Trump's 'Truth,'" *Real Clear Politics*, August 19, 2018, www.realclearpolitics.com/video/2018/08/19/giuliani_truth_isnt_truth.html.
17. Sharyl Attkisson, "Investigative Issues: The Troubling Fact Is That the Media's Fact-Checkers Tend to Lean ← Left," *RealClear Investigations*, August 4, 2020, www.realclearinvestigations.com/articles/2020/08/04/investigative_issues_the_troubling_fact_that_media_factcheckers_lean_left_124663.html.
18. David A. Graham, "Some Real News About Fake News," *The Atlantic*, June 7, 2019, www.theatlantic.com/ideas/archive/2019/06/fake-news-republicans-democrats/591211/.
19. Stanford History Education Group, "Evaluating Information: The Cornerstone of Civic Online Reasoning," November 22, 2016, https://stacks.stanford.edu/file/druid:fv751yt5934/SHEG%20Evaluating%20Information%20Online.pdf.

2
RECOGNIZING EXAGGERATIONS, DISTORTIONS, AND LIES

Clues That Something May Not Be Completely True

How can you recognize that what you are reading or hearing may be distorted, exaggerated, or just plain false? You can check out the source to see if it sometimes or often offers misleading material, and you can look for clues that the content may not be reliable.

The source of the story sometimes provides a hint that something in that story is wrong. Where did you find it? A source you know and trust, or somewhere else? Some websites, social media, and individuals often create or repeat fake news and hoaxes. Some of these sites are short lived and some individuals use a variety of names, which makes any list of them likely to be imperfect, but even so, such lists can be useful. Wikipedia offers one.[1]

Chapter 3 includes a description of how to figure out whether a site or an author often presents biased or bogus material to help you make your own list of questionable sources. If you don't know the source, or if the source mixes fake and real posts, you can look for clues that hint at possibly misleading content.

Words and Phrases Suggesting Bias

Sometimes a particular word or phrase can be a clue that a story is biased.

Weasel Words and Phrases

Weasel words and phrases muffle a message, giving the impression the authors have said something specific and provable when they haven't. Common examples include "may, might, can, could be, perhaps, possibly" and vague amounts, such as "some," "many," "as much as," or "almost" that don't tell you how much.

"To our knowledge" is a weasel phrase, meaning the speaker or writer doesn't know for sure. Secretary Alex Azar of the Department of Health and Human Services claimed "'to our knowledge' nobody in the U.S. has died because they didn't have access to a ventilator or a bed in an intensive care unit."[2] The reader or listener has no idea how thorough Azar's search was or whether he searched at all, which makes his claim vague.

Using phrases like "Many people say," "People think," or "Some say" allows the speaker to pass along conspiracies and innuendoes while denying doing so. President Trump, discussing his accusation that former President Obama doesn't understand radical Islam, said, "there are a lot of people that think maybe he doesn't want to get it. A lot of people think maybe he doesn't want to know about it. I happen to think that he just doesn't know what he's doing, but there are many people that think maybe he doesn't want to get it. He doesn't want to see what's really happening. And that could be."[3] President Trump implied that Obama sympathized with terrorists, without saying he personally believes that, but he also used the weasel word "could be." It was possible, he argued, that those who thought Obama sympathized with Islamic terrorists were correct.

Another common weasel phrase is "I'm just saying." The phrase "I'm just saying" is used to indicate that the speakers refuse to give reasons why what they have said is true.[4] This phrase simultaneously makes an accusation and denies making it. For example, in the case of accusations that covid-19 was a result of an escaped virus from a Chinese laboratory, Steven Mosher, a social scientist educated in China, argued in the right-leaning *New York Post*, "I'm not saying this has been genetically engineered to be a bioweapon that's escaped from the lab. ... I'm just saying that [China is] collecting dangerous pathogens, [and] they have a history of letting them escape from the lab."[5] The reader is supposed to conclude that China is guilty although no evidence is provided, just conjecture.

Color Words

Writers sometimes try to persuade by using color words, words that tell you how you should react emotionally to a story or argument, instead of presenting information you can analyze intellectually. Color words and phrases are often clues that you should check the truth value of a story or argument.

Daily Kos, on the left of the political spectrum, offers many examples of color words. One Kos post described Trump's rallies: "his hate engorged crowds salivate hungrily for someone to target with their relentless, thoughtless anger, all carefully ginned up by a master demagogue, who stands preening happily before his bubbling cauldron."[6] In addition to the color words such as "hate engorged," "salivate hungrily," "relentless, thoughtless anger," "preening happily," and "bubbling cauldron," the author refers to Trump as a demagogue, that is, a politician who appeals to emotions rather than reason.

One-sided Definitions

Sometimes selected words are taken over by one side or another of a political argument and used with specific emotionally laden meanings to steer the reader or listener in a particular direction. The word "patriotism," for example, has been taken by the political right to mean someone who supports the military and military spending instead of the more general meaning of loving one's country. If you oppose increases in military spending, according to this revised definition, you are unpatriotic, even if you love your country.

The word "reform" is often used to refer to a tax reduction instead of its broader meaning of improving some system that is not working well. Since reform is supposed to be good, calling a tax reduction a reform gives it cover, you are supposed to like it, even if its purpose is solely to reduce the tax burden on the well-to-do.

When the meaning of a term has been reassigned with the intent of telling you what is good or just and who or what is bad, you should look more carefully at the rest of the argument. Such definitions do not necessarily mean that the claim or argument is incorrect, only that someone is trying to move you to one side of an argument without evidence or context.

Dog Whistles

A dog whistle is a phrase that has particular meaning for one subgroup of voters and is used to motivate and activate their support. Sometimes the message seems innocuous to the broader public. Astute political commentator William Safire used as an example Bush's criticism in 2004 of the Supreme Court Dred Scott decision denying citizenship to any African American. To many people, that criticism would seem acceptable and about exactly what it claimed to be about, but to a smaller group it sent the message that Supreme Court decisions could be overturned, and that Bush as president would select court justices who would overturn Roe v. Wade, the court case which made abortions legal.[7] That coded message was intended to appeal to anti-abortionists, without a direct anti-abortion statement.

Senator Susan Collins used an anti-Semitic dog whistle. In fundraising letters, Collins referred to financial support of her opponent from Senate Minority Leader Chuck Schumer (D-N.Y.), George Soros, and Donald Sussman. Senator Schumer is Jewish, as are Soros and Sussman. "The demonization of Jewish donors to the Democratic Party is a tactic often employed as a dog whistle to the far right."[8]

Dog whistles often depend on the emotional context that surrounds a word or phrase. These terms continue to carry that emotion even when stripped of the context. Thus, opponents of Barack Obama pointedly referred to him as Barack *Hussein* Obama, suggesting that he was a Muslim (which he was not) and evoking the fear and hate that a subgroup of the population feels toward Muslims. For those with more experience, tolerance, knowledge, or understanding of Islam, the name would not carry the same emotional baggage.[9]

Memes

A meme is a brief description, often a short phrase with a visual image, packed with meaning. To be successful, a meme must be picked up and repeated by many people. While some memes are just intended to be funny or clever, many are meant to mock or tease, or to divide people into hostile groups. In politics, memes may delegitimize opponents. When used this way, they are efforts to persuade without providing evidence, and hence it is often worthwhile to take the time to unpack them, that is, make their meaning more explicit, and then check the contents for truth value.

Republican Dan Bishop labeled democratic progressives "clowns." "Clowns" is a general insult, but in Bishop's case, the word came with videos of blow-up clown dolls with faces of individual progressives. He played on the appearance of frightening clowns in literature and movies, promising to fight these scary clowns for you. He called national democratic figures like Alexandria Ocasio-Cortez, Nancy Pelosi, Elizabeth Warren, and Bernie Sanders "crazy liberal clowns" and wanted you to be afraid of them and their proposals.[10]

Democratic candidate Hillary Clinton described half of Trump's supporters as sexist, racist, homophobic, xenophobic, Islamophobic deplorables. She divided his followers into baskets, one of which was a "basket of deplorables" so someone created an illustration of a basket filled with deplorable people—a meme.[11]

Food memes are common and intended to divide people into us and them. Descriptors such as "Latte liberal," "goat's milk latte drinking insider's elite," and "the brie and Chablis set" are intended to suggest left-leaning upper-class snobs with enough money to indulge in expensive and sometimes foreign or bizarre food choices. The meme otherizes liberals, and delegitimizes them as hypocrites, people who are for the poor from the comfort of their fancy cars and large apartments.[12]

One meme that is widely used is "deep state." The term originally meant the hidden and powerful influence of big business but has morphed into a condemnation of the permanent bureaucracy (and professionalism) which is said to block the policy initiatives of elected officials. It is a shorthand for a conspiracy theory, "a secret cabal of government insiders hellbent on undermining the White House."[13]

Delegitimizing of Opponents

If the purpose of a story or argument is to delegitimize an adversary, you should be wary of its truth value. A number of clues can signal that the purpose is not to present a convincing argument, but rather to claim that an opponent has no authority, no expertise, no right to provide any opposition or criticize the speaker or writer. Maybe the author calls an opponent an outsider, or a newcomer lacking local knowledge, or as suggested above, an elite snob—anything that might imply the person has no right to speak.

Name Calling

One technique for delegitimizing opponents is to call them names. The purpose of name calling is to force others to disregard an opponent. For example, Representative Duncan Hunter called his opponent in the election a terrorist sympathizer. Trump has claimed Democrats are treasonous in their obstruction of his border security policy. Democrats have called Trump treasonous in his relaying of intelligence to Putin. Presidential candidate Beto O'Rourke labeled Trump's arguments "Fascist." Such terms are dismissive. Most likely, you would not think of voting for someone who was treasonous, a terrorist sympathizer, or a fascist.[14]

The names people use to delegitimize opponents can be colorful and descriptive. Republican Lindsay Graham called Trump "a race-baiting xenophobic religious bigot"[15] when he was running against him. He later changed his mind, or at least his rhetoric. As a result, Graham has been called a lickspittle for President Trump,[16] meaning a bootlicker, a toady, or a flatterer.

Democrats have called Republican Senator Mitch McConnell Moscow Mitch because he blocked legislation to protect our elections from Russian interference.[17] Moscow Mitch McTraitor trended on Twitter.[18] If McConnell could be linked to a pro-Moscow position, his legitimacy would evaporate.

Democratic Senator and military veteran Tammy Duckworth referred to President Trump as Cadet Bone Spurs, calling attention to the fact that Trump had avoided the draft by claiming bone spurs.[19] The name delegitimized the president, implying he had no right to run the military and make decisions about war and peace because he had never served in the armed forces.

Name calling sometimes calls attention to character flaws. President Trump has been a favorite target of this kind of attack. He has been called Cheeto Jesus, referring to his orangey hair color and habit of self-aggrandizing; he has also been called Angry Creamsicle, (a frozen treat with orange sherbet on the outside and white ice cream inside) because of his hair color and eagerness for revenge against anyone who crosses him.

Rather than criticism of character, name calling may reflect criticism of specific policies. For example, Speaker of the House Nancy Pelosi called President Trump Mr. Makes Matters Worse,[20] referring to Trump's dismissal of the seriousness of covid-19, his disdain for wearing a mask, and his endorsement of ineffective and dangerous treatments for the virus.

Nicknames can be a form of name calling. Continually referring to Binyamin Netanyahu as Bibi sounds like you are treating him not only informally, but almost as a child. An article in the *Atlantic* magazine argued:

> The infantilizing nickname that so many use when talking about him plays into the general idea that Netanyahu's warnings can be ignored or shunted aside, and that we have known him to play a certain character for so long that things he says should be taken with a grain of salt.[21]

Whenever you detect name calling, you should be suspicious that someone is trying to manipulate your opinions rather than convince you with reason and evidence.

Stereotypes

A negative stereotype is an unfavorable descriptive label improperly applied to a whole group of people. Even if some people in the group are described correctly, the label cannot possibly accurately describe everyone in the group.

Some doctors assume that fat people are weak willed and lazy—a negative stereotype.[22]

President Trump on the campaign trail called Mexican immigrants drug dealers, criminals, and rapists.[23]

Negative stereotypes sometimes serve as a rationalization for discrimination or a justification for punitive policies. Nazis during World War II referred to Jews as rats; this dehumanization preceded and bolstered a policy of so-called ethnic cleansing, that is, mass murder. Stereotyping Muslims as terrorists has been used as a justification for denying them visas to come to the U.S.

During rioting that took place after a Minneapolis police officer killed a black man by kneeling on his neck, President Trump tweeted that the protesters were "thugs." Such a stereotype seemed to justify a policy of armed repression, denying the legitimacy of protest, and removing any pressure to address the issue of police abuse of force.

When people evoke negative stereotypes in persuasive arguments, they are trying to get you to share their prejudices and approve of their policies. You should look out for statements that begin with "Blacks are," "young people today are," "rich people are," "cops are," or "protesters are." Even if the sentence ends with a compliment, such a generalization is not going to be true of everyone in the group, but if the sentence ends in an insult, you have found a negative stereotype.

Ad Hominem Attacks

Ad hominem is a Latin phrase that means attacks the speaker instead of the content of what he or she says. By attacking the person, the attacker hopes to deny the truth of anything the person has said or might say in the future without actually discussing any of those statements or charges.

Whistleblower Richard Bright, the federal government's director of advanced biomedical research during the covid-19 pandemic, was critical of the Trump administration. President Trump dismissed Bright's complaints, calling him an unhappy, disgruntled employee.[24] Trump's response qualifies as an ad hominem attack, an attempt to undermine anything Bright might say, without addressing any of Bright's charges.

When a former attorney of President Trump published a highly critical book about the president, Trump's press secretary responded by attacking the author's credibility. "Michael Cohen is a disgraced felon and disbarred lawyer, who lied to Congress. He has lost all credibility, and it's unsurprising to see his latest attempt to profit off of lies."[25] In other words, don't believe anything Cohen says.

Charges of Illegality

A little more sophisticated way of undercutting opponents or policies without engaging with their arguments is to deny them legal status. Authors claim that the opponents are illegal so their arguments do not have to be refuted, or their arguments have no legal base, and so should be ignored.

For example, one contemporary argument denies the legitimacy of the 14th and 15th amendments to the constitution granting equality before the law and voting rights to all those born in the U.S. That means that those born in the U.S. whose parents were not citizens have no right to vote and that there is no right to equality before the law. Whatever opinions such folks might have they cannot express through the ballot box. They and their claims are illegitimate.[26]

Arguments Based (Solely) on Authority

While some arguments aim to undermine the authority or legitimacy of people they oppose, without actually addressing their arguments or providing evidence against them, others are focused on increasing the appearance of authority of the author. Listen to me, believe me, because I am smart, important, famous, handsome, or rich, or because smart, famous, important, handsome, or rich people agree with me. The excellence or the appearance of excellence of the authority is intended to substitute for convincing evidence.

Of course, not everyone who poses as an expert really is one. For example, some people follow the advice of, and buy the products recommended by, famous and attractive actresses. Gwyneth Paltrow, the actress, is an example of a self-styled expert on diet, clothes, beauty, travel, and health. The breadth of the claim of expertise sounds exaggerated, which should alert you to possible self-promotion rather than credible expertise.

Paltrow claimed the $66 vaginal egg she was selling might help with increasing hormone levels, regulating menstrual cycles, or strengthening bladder control. It does not do these things. She had to pay a fine for false advertising.[27]

If you recognize an argument based on authority rather than reason, you should be cautious about accepting it, and investigate it in more detail.

Exaggeration

Exaggeration may be used to channel one's emotions. It is usually easy to recognize and is a good signal that one should look at the argument more carefully to see if there is any evidence behind it.

Iowa Rep. Steve King (R) claimed that "For every (undocumented immigrant) who's a valedictorian, there's another 100 out there who weigh 130 pounds. And they've got calves the size of cantaloupes because they're hauling 75 pounds of marijuana across the desert."[28]

A hundred to one, bad guys to good ones? How could King possibly know that? Moreover, a young male of 130 pounds would be slightly built; how could he have such large calves and be able to carry such heavy loads across a desert? These claims are clearly exaggerated and biased, invoking negative stereotypes.

Superlatives often signal exaggerated claims. The biggest myth about the gender gap, the best mayor New York has ever had, the most overrated general, and the greatest job producer are examples of superlatives. Similarly, words like perfect, flawless, faultless, infallible, unique, and pure often reflect overstatements. When President Trump claimed he had made a perfect phone call to the Ukrainian president urging him to investigate Trump's political rival, Trump was exaggerating about the quality of that phone call.[29]

Distortions

Exaggerations are one form of distortion. More broadly, distortions usually rely on some real evidence, but misinterpret it, slightly or extensively, to make a false claim. One way of misinterpreting data is to cherry pick.

If speakers or writers engage in cherry picking, their claims may be technically correct but misleading. Biased analysts sometimes pick a specific year or several years from a range if those years support a conclusion they favor, even though the long-term trend indicates the opposite. Another technique for cherry picking involves taking a conclusion from one report or part of a report that makes their case while ignoring the rest of the evidence that contradicts it.

Democrats attacking the republican tax cuts of 2018 engaged in cherry picking. They claimed that 83 percent of the tax cut went to the top 1 percent of earners. That was true only for one year, 2027, because tax breaks for middle class folks would have expired by then. Tax experts reported that the top one percent would get between 20 and 25 percent of the tax reduction, not 83 percent.[30] The Democrats' analysis was based on a single year, 2027. Why that year, why only that year, how does that year differ from any other year?

Another example of cherry picking occurred when one group of global warming deniers chose data that supported their case while ignoring the rest of the data. Those who claimed that global warming stopped in 1998 based their case on a temperature time series from the Hadley Center in the United Kingdom. That time series left out many of the spots where the fastest heating was occurring. These deniers also ignored the warming of the oceans. In a third bit of cherry picking, these global warming deniers chose individual years for comparison, rather than trend lines. Because weather varies somewhat from year to year, it is the trends over time that matter, not individual years.[31] The choice of one year, 1998, should make you curious, why that year, was it in some way different from years before and after it?

Sometimes it is the press that does the cherry picking. In October of 2015, the General Accountability Office released a report claiming that the Social Security Administration had overpaid recipients in the Disability Program $11 billion from 2005 to 2014. The report also included, but didn't emphasize, that all but $1.4 billion had been recovered.[32] News media cherry picked the results, headlining only the total overpayments.[33]

Lies

Some claims can be exaggerated or misleading, but others are just lies. The bolder ones are easy to detect.

Trump lied about who would pay for his wall along the Mexican border. He repeatedly claimed that Mexico would pay for it. However, Mexico insisted it would not pay for the wall. Confronted with the reality, Trump backed and filled. He argued that the Mexicans were going to pay for the wall indirectly, because the new trade deal that he backed would cost Mexico financially. However, even if the new trade deal cost Mexico money, that money would not end up in the U.S. treasury.[34]

Two clues in the Mexico-will-pay-for-the-wall story suggest a false claim. One is Mexico's vehement denial that it would pay for the wall; the second is the backing and filling when the president was caught in the falsehood.

He claimed the Mexicans would pay for the wall through the Trade Pact, a claim that made no sense.

In November of 2019, President Trump praised his daughter, Ivanka, for creating 14 million jobs. To that point, the entire economy had created six million jobs during the Trump administration. Ivanka had a fashion business; all its handbags, shoes, and dresses were made in other countries. How could she have created 14 million U.S. jobs? She didn't. She was helping to coordinate an effort to train people for existing jobs—not new ones.[35]

Hopefully, you would catch the false claim about Ivanka's job creation bonanza because she could not personally create more jobs than the entire economy had created. Even if you didn't think to look up the total number of jobs created, you might have wondered how someone who bought clothing manufactured abroad and sold it in the U.S. could create a massive numbers of jobs in the U.S. The claim was so illogical, it was unlikely to be true.

Some lies are transparent. Many stories are intended to catch the eye, and if they generate clicks, those who create and circulate the stories may get paid. As a result, such stories do not need to sound real, they only need to grab attention. Headlines that describe low-probability events or quotes that don't match the person to whom they are attributed suggest that you should be wary and check out the story or argument further.

The clickbait web blog, Political Ears, carried this story: "Germany has fallen to the Caliphate, with the blessing of Angela Merkel, the internationalist." The story attacks German Chancellor Merkel's welcoming of immigrants and tolerance of Islam and concludes that Germany accepted Islamic Sharia law governing families and marriages. The story was accompanied by a picture of young girls dressed in white, presumably marrying older men.

If you knew or looked up what a Caliphate was, a government under a religious ruler claiming succession from the Muslim Mohammad, you would be immediately suspicious about the claim that a Caliphate had taken over Germany. Had that happened, it would have been all over the news, and a war would have commenced to reclaim the country.[36]

Another story unlikely to be true stated that the Pope had just endorsed candidate Trump. The claim was unlikely because the Pope had previously described Trump as unchristian. Another clue that the story was improbable was that the claim appeared on the website WTOE 5 News, which describes itself as a fake news site.[37]

A different story with a low probability of being true had a quote attributed to George Soros, a thorn in the side of right-wingers for his support of democratic reforms around the world. In the made-up quote, Soros revealed his plan to bring down the U.S. by funding black hate groups. A wealthy humanitarian, Soros was highly unlikely to ever support such an action, let alone boast about it. If your curiosity had been pricked and you went to check the source of the quote, which was supposed to be a particular news interview, you would have found that the interview never took place.[38]

If you knew who George Soros was, you would have immediately felt that the quote was bogus, but if you didn't, you would recognize that someone was trying to frighten you, drawing up a nightmare of black violence, and then blaming a wealthy Jewish liberal. Those details should be enough to rouse your curiosity about the truth value of the quote and send you looking for the source.

While some lies are obvious because they are just unlikely to be true, others are obvious because they are too good to be true.

In the too-good-to-be-true category of lies, one major culprit is commercial advertising. One example came from Reebok, which in 2011 was ordered to refund $25 million to customers because it advertised its Easytone shoe as being able to tighten your butt and legs with every step. The company did not provide any evidence. Another example with a real wow factor was an ad for Dr. Clark's Zapper. The ad claimed it killed disease-causing parasites in the body with electricity and was effective in treating diseases like cancer and AIDS.[39]

When you see a claim that seems too good to be true, it should raise your suspicion, especially if no evidence is provided. In the case of the zapper, not only is the absence of evidence a clue, so is the claim that it kills all bacteria, since if it did that, it would kill the critically necessary bacteria as well as the harmful ones—not good for the patient.

A subset of "too good to be true" is the silver bullet. Originally, a silver bullet was a form of magic used to kill a monster, such as a werewolf. In its more recent usage, it is a proposal that offers a simple solution to a complicated and multi-stranded problem. Such solutions are often unrealistic.

An example of a silver bullet policy recommendation is the elimination of government regulations as a solution to homelessness. The argument is that with fewer regulations, construction will be less expensive, housing prices will come down, and there will be no more homelessness. Housing advocates have questioned that approach, one arguing that lower housing costs might help, but that reducing construction regulations would have no immediate effect. Other approaches need to be utilized as well, such as more rent subsidies, better and more effective shelters, and more mental health aid.[40]

President Trump has argued that a wall along the southern U.S. border will solve the drug problems of the U.S. Drug supply and abuse in the U.S. is a complicated problem that requires a set of different policy approaches and hence is unlikely to be solved just by building a wall. Moreover, the wall itself is of questionable utility. Newspaper photos show people climbing over the wall, and one can easily imagine a catapult tossing a package over the top. Smugglers have sawed through sections of the wall that have already been built. A retired border patrol agent argued "There's no one silver bullet, and we've done our best to try to explain that."[41]

Some economists have argued that a tax cut is a silver bullet for economic growth. Lower taxes are assumed to provide incentives to work harder because you get to keep more of your money.⁴² Lower taxes increase the incentive to work is a kind of shibboleth, an often repeated, taken-for-granted saying without convincing evidence behind it. Empirical research has come up with contradictory results.⁴³

Economic growth is complicated and requires a multi-pronged approach. As Joseph Minarik of the Committee for Economic Development has written, even if a tax break increased economic growth, it has the downside of increasing the deficit and debt. Further, he writes "The problem is that there is no neglected silver-bullet program to increase economic growth, nothing that we could pull out of the bag now to add to the GDP and the tax base and reduce the demand for government benefits and services."⁴⁴

You should question proposals for simple solutions to complicated problems. They are generally unrealistic. Someone may be pushing a given policy, not because it would work to solve the stated problem, but to gain some specific benefit or advantage, pretending it would benefit others in order to gain support for it. Getting rid of regulations is good for builders (possibly bad for renters or homeowners); lowering tax rates is good for people who have a lot of income and pay a lot of taxes but starves government of revenue needed to serve poorer folks. Pretending a wall along the southern border will keep out illegal drugs broadens support for anti-immigrant policies of the Trump administration.

Shibboleths

Shibboleths are sayings that are taken for granted as unquestionable truth, expressing and reinforcing some specific belief. If you recognize one in an argument, substituting for objective evidence, you should pause and think further about whether to believe the argument.

For example, "government should be run like a business" is a shibboleth, implying that business is efficient because it is disciplined by competition. Business failure is punished by bankruptcy so inefficient businesses fall out. Government, by contrast, is expected to be corrupt, inefficient, and weighed down by debt because it is often unable to declare bankruptcy. So, naturally, government should be run more like a business. Such a set of beliefs serves business interests.

The shibboleth that government should be run like a business is an attempt to persuade without evidence. If you think about it, much of government runs very well. Governments in the U.S. are more accountable and much more transparent than businesses. Some businesses have been inattentive to safety and privacy issues. Boeing airplanes crashed twice in recent years, killing all aboard, although the company had been warned that part of its automatic flight correction system was malfunctioning well before the accidents.⁴⁵

About 3.5 billion users have been affected by hacks of business organizations in recent years,[46] suggesting insufficient attention to security issues. Moreover, some private sector companies are debt ridden, fail to pay for their pensions, and avoid competition through mergers and acquisitions. Some raise prices when people are dependent on their products, such as insulin. Do we really want government to run like a business? At least we should specify which businesses are to be the models.

Another common shibboleth is "welfare makes people lazy." Though often repeated as if it were obviously true—why work if you can get an income without working—it turns out there is little evidence behind it. When programs are properly designed, they don't discourage work. For example, in the U.S., programs such as the Earned Income Tax Credit actually increase labor participation.[47]

When it comes to the presidency, one shibboleth claims that "Women are unelectable." This was a conclusion some people drew from Hillary Clinton's defeat at the hands of Donald Trump. This shibboleth is used against any female candidate for president, as if it were an unbreakable rule. Anything stated so broadly should rouse concern, especially because Hillary Clinton won the popular vote. One could easily come up with a different lesson from 2016.

There are shibboleths on the left and the right, and in the public and the private sector, in health and transportation, and nearly any other place you can think of. They persuade through repetition rather than reason, experience, or evidence. When you see one, you should probably look further into the argument and check it out. Whose interests do they serve? Though we often assume they are true, they may not be.

Blame Avoidance

People generally are uncomfortable with public blame and have developed a variety of responses to it. If you can see that blame is involved in a story, be wary that there may be distortions, exaggerations, or lies involved in the attempt to refute or duck the accusations.

Reversing the Charges

One response to blame is to argue that whatever politicians are accused of, the accuser has done.

When President Trump was lagging in the polls, his appointee to head the post office began removing sorting equipment and mailboxes and curtailed overtime hours, slowing down the mail, threatening mail-in ballots. His campaign reportedly discussed ways of changing the electors in the electoral college so that he would get votes that the citizens had given to Biden. Opponents declared that he was so afraid of losing he would do absolutely anything to prevent that from happening. Trump turned that criticism onto his opponent, Joe Biden. In a solicitation for funds, the Trump campaign wrote "The Democrats know that Joe Biden doesn't stand a chance against your President in November, so they will do anything they can to try to silence your voice and steal your vote."[48]

The strategy of reversing the charges works best if the countercharge is at least a little true. When the U.S. blamed China for reducing the independence of Hong Kong in order to put down political unrest, Chinese authorities responded, What about you and your response to rioting in Minneapolis after a policeman killed a black man? In other words, You can't criticize us for what you do, so pipe down.[49]

When Canada was about to call for an investigation of China's abuse of its Uyghur minority, China retaliated by asking what Canada had done to its own indigenous population.[50]

Blaming the Victim

Reversing the charges means accusing the accuser of what he or she is accusing you of. A related strategy is to shift blame to the victim. Whatever you did to victims, they brought it on themselves. The standard version of this approach is to blame a rape victim for dressing provocatively.

Richard Bright, a federal immunologist, lost his job after he accused the administration of not paying attention to his complaints about lack of protective gear for health workers during the covid-19 pandemic. Not long after Bright blew the whistle, making the matter public, Peter Navarro, the White House Trade Adviser, charged Bright with desertion for refusing the alternative and lesser job he was offered and for making his accusations public.[51] According to Navarro, it was Bright's fault he was fired; if he hadn't made the problem public, he would have been a team player, and would not have been fired. He should have taken his demotion quietly.

Diverting Blame Elsewhere

A different approach is to claim that someone or something other than the person making the charge or the victim is responsible rather than the person or thing being blamed. President Trump had been widely criticized for failures in testing for the novel coronavirus, so he blamed the Obama administration for the delay in testing. He claimed that his administration had inherited a broken testing system. In reality, there could not have been a test for covid-19 during Obama's term as president because the virus didn't exist until three years after the end of the Obama administration.[52]

After a spate of mass shootings that renewed calls for gun control, gun supporters swung into action, arguing that the guns were innocent, that the shootings were the fault of mental illness and video games. Ohio State

Representative Candice Keller blamed Obama, gay marriage, and "drag queen advocates." It was Obama's fault because he disrespected law enforcement. Gay marriage and drag queens were blamed for the breakdown of the American family, which presumably led directly to mass shootings.[53]

Evading Blame through Denialism

Denialism evades blame by claiming that what someone or some group is charged with didn't happen or if it did, it wasn't so bad. For example, Fox News host Bill O'Reilly has argued that slavery was not that bad, especially for the slaves who built the White House, since they were fed and sheltered.[54]

Some have denied the existence or severity of the Holocaust—the murder of six million Jews and five million others by Germans and their allies during World War II.[55] Despite the evidence that it did happen and painstakingly detailed documentation of its victims, some deny it because of guilt or blame avoidance; others deny it because they do not want to grant legitimacy to the existence of Israel, home to some of the survivors of the death camps.

Current denialism includes global warming. In this case, it is not individuals or nations trying to deny blame, but specific industries. If global warming isn't happening, the energy industry can continue to sell coal, gas, and oil. People can still drive large sport utility vehicles, the auto and truck industry can continue to build gas guzzlers, and dealers can keep on selling them.

Claiming the Victim Role

Another way of diverting blame is for the target of criticism to describe him or herself as the *real* victim in the situation. Those who are blaming you for something are actually out to get you so their charges can be discounted.

When the National Rifle Association was being criticized for its opposition to gun control after several mass shootings in a short period of time, the association head, Wayne LaPierre, responded that the real problem was not the folks with guns doing the killing, but the attacks on his organization. LaPierre thus tried to shift the focus from his organization as the perpetrator to his organization as the victim.[56]

President Trump had been promoting hydroxychloroquine as a preventative and cure for covid-19 infections. When a Veterans' Administration study showed that the medicine was not effective and was dangerous, Trump responded by criticizing the study, claiming it was a political attack against him. He was the victim, not the people who died taking a drug he recommended.[57]

Diffusing Blame

Yet another strategy for dealing with blame is to diffuse it. At times, the effort to avoid or divert blame is so strong that a variety of actors or causes are cited.

Flint's water supply was poisoned when officials failed to add a chemical that would prevent leaching and then made matters worse by changing the city's water source to a river that was saltier and more corrosive. As a result, lead from the city's water pipes seeped into the drinking water. Governor Rick Snyder diffused the blame, claiming that federal, state, and local government agencies all failed the public.[58]

During the rioting after a police officer killed a black man in police custody in Minneapolis, the Minnesota governor, Tim Walz, suggested right-wing white supremacists and possibly drug cartels were responsible. Minneapolis's mayor tried to diffuse blame among white supremacists, members of organized crime, out-of-state instigators, and possibly even foreign actors.[59]

Distracting from a Charge

When confronted with an accusation, politicians (and others) sometimes try to distract by mentioning something else. Recently, President Trump defended Giuliani, his attorney, from charges of election law violations, saying that the attorney had been the best mayor of New York ever.[60] Even if Giuliani had been the best mayor of New York City ever, that doesn't mean he didn't later violate election laws. One has nothing to do with the other.

Blaming China for the coronavirus pandemic is a distraction from the Trump administration's delays in responding to the coronavirus pandemic. Whatever mistakes the Chinese government made as the illness was spreading in that country have nothing to do with the U.S. response to the virus when President Trump was told about it.

When blame is being denied or diverted, it pays to be skeptical and look for more definitive and impartial information.

Credit Taking

The other side of blame avoidance is credit taking. Sometimes people take credit for things to which they have contributed extraordinarily little.

John Ratcliffe, nominated by the president to be the intelligence chief, claimed that he had arrested 300 illegal immigrants in one day. That number of arrests sounds exaggerated, so you might want to look more closely. He was a prosecutor at the time and prosecutors do not make arrests; the police do. The raid involved five states attorneys and the sweep was led by the Immigration and Customs Enforcement Agency, so Ratcliffe's claim that he was responsible for the arrests was overblown.[61]

President Trump took credit for a manufacturing plant in Pennsylvania and a liquified natural gas plant in Louisiana. Both plants predated Trump's presidency. Trump had nothing to do with the initial decisions by the companies or the awarding of state permits or state subsidies. The factfinder Politifact rated false the president's claim that neither project would have occurred without him.[62]

When you see a credit claim, you should ask yourself what the person actually did with regard to the claim and whether the credit should possibly go somewhere else.

Ruling Out Disliked Options

People who oppose some proposal often try to rule it out without discussing its pros and cons, without really considering it or allowing it to be considered. They use a variety of arguments to take an option off the table.

It Won't Solve the Whole Problem

Sometimes a proposed policy is rejected because it won't solve the whole problem. This type of argument is common when dealing with alternatives to carbon-based fuels. Those who opposed carbon sequestering claimed that it could not be scaled up sufficiently to help with global warming. They didn't say that carbon sequestering would not work.

Renewable energy sources won't solve the whole global warming crisis either. Solar panels depend on frequently sunny days and wind turbines depend on relatively steady winds, neither of which can be depended on, and do not occur throughout the country or throughout the world. So, the argument runs, since they won't solve the whole problem, let's not turn to renewable sources and away from carbon-based energy.

Consider the recent advice to shift away from the consumption of meat toward more vegetarian options. It is healthier and would probably be good for the planet, but it would not solve the whole problem of global warming. One author argued,

> If Americans' gave up meat and other animal products, would that solve our climate crisis? Research says no. In fact, it continues to demonstrate giving up meat would be a woefully inadequate solution to the problem of global warming and distracts us from more impactful mitigation opportunities.[63]

Eating less meat won't solve global warming all by itself, but it might help, and probably should not be ruled off the table as an option.

More generally, if authors suggest that proposals that don't solve the whole problem should be dismissed out of hand, you need to explore the proposals in more detail.

False Dichotomies

Another way of ruling out a disliked option is to use a false dichotomy. False dichotomies occur when an author or speaker frames an issue as involving only two possibilities, where the choices are loaded, in that one of the two is considered impossible or terrible and should be ruled out. That leaves only the author's preferred choice. In reality, there are nearly always more than two choices.

A common false dichotomy suggests that you are either anti-abortion or in favor of murdering babies. You are not granted a real choice there—who wants to be a baby murderer? But are there really only two choices? Could you be anti-abortion in some or most cases, but not all, for example? The phrasing of the question ignores some common options and forces the respondent to agree completely with one side of a debate.

President Trump recently argued that we cannot keep the country in lock-down forever because of the coronavirus, so we must open it up right away. He framed the issue as having only two alternatives, either we open up now, or we never open up. Since he ruled out "we never open up" as impossible, he left us with only the choice he preferred, open it up now. He ignored intermediate choices, such as opening up the country next week, next month, or six months from now, or opening it up gradually.[64]

One recent opinion piece offered a dichotomy between pension funding and infrastructure funding. If you wanted potholes filled, bridges repaired, and functioning mass transit, you have to cut pensions. The author ruled out other possible sources of funding. The disliked policy option was spending money on retirees.[65]

False dichotomies are used on the left as well as the right. Adam Schiff defended the Inspector General who passed a whistleblower's complaint to Congress: "In a democracy, public servants owe their loyalty to the Constitution and the rule of law, not to the President's personal, political interests."[66] Given the phrasing of this dichotomy, loyalty to the president did not stand a chance.

As a rhetorical device, false dichotomies not only limit the field of options to two seemingly exclusive categories, but weigh the options differently, so one is not acceptable. You should work at recognizing false dichotomies; they are a clue that writers or speakers are trying to rule out some policy option they don't want you to consider or analyze.

Distraction

You might also want to watch out for efforts to distract from a disliked option by offering other alternatives. Arguments of the form "what about X" where X is a different proposal from the one under consideration should make you curious about what, if anything, is wrong with the original proposal and why the writer or speaker wants you to look away from the proposal on the table.

When gun control was being considered to protect children from mass shooters in schools, an opinion writer asked, Want to Save Teens? Driving restrictions could save at least as many lives as gun control.[67] The argument is intended to distract from proposals for gun control. It may be true that driving restrictions would save teens' lives, but that does not mean that gun control would not save teens' lives as well.

Some of those people wishing to distract from Black Lives Matter protests against police violence ask, what about black-on-black violent crime. "You can't talk about the Black Lives Matter movement without discussing the homicide epidemic happening in Black communities."[68]

Slippery Slope

Another way of rejecting a proposal out of hand is to use a slippery slope argument. Such arguments maintain that some proposal should not be adopted even if it seems reasonable because it (inevitably) leads to some other outcome that is undesirable.

Senator Ted Cruz recently criticized a Supreme Court decision about honoring old agreements with Native Americans: "Neil Gorsuch & the four liberal Justices just gave away half of Oklahoma, literally. Manhattan is next." In other words, the decision is a slippery slope, and will lead inevitably to yielding back other land that once belonged to Native Americans, including Manhattan, an outcome that would be unacceptable.[69] In reality, what the court said was that the Muskogee (Creek) reservation in Oklahoma had not been terminated by statehood, so whatever agreement was made with them still holds. That argument would not apply in Manhattan, which was not a reservation for Native Americans but was sold by a tribe to settlers. The judgment for Oklahoma thus had nothing whatsoever to do with Manhattan.

With slippery slope arguments, any modest form of gun control leads to gun confiscation, and thence to tyranny. If you take guns from people who have been in psychiatric facilities, then next you will take them from everyone else. Opponents of gay marriage argue that it inevitably leads to other consequences, such as polygamy, polyamory (multiple sexual relations with consent of all involved), and incest, because other folks will then demand the same kind of rights.

A recent article on the American Conservative website argued that unregulated fake news everywhere was preferable to government decisions about what was fake, because government determination of misinformation could end with restrictions on political speech later. Notably, the essay says that government controls over fake news would be the first step toward eliminating political dissent, but neither provides evidence to that effect nor suggests what the next steps might be and whether those steps are inevitable or can be controlled.[70]

One opponent of taking the confederacy flag out of the Mississippi flag where it is embedded argued that redesigning the flag to eliminate the symbol of the confederacy would challenge the founding values of the nation, and he warned that the American flag would be next.[71]

While some predicted consequences sound extreme or unlikely, one should not automatically dismiss all slippery slope arguments. Each one should be evaluated in terms of the mechanism assumed and the likelihood of the predicted consequences.[72] What we know when we see a slippery slope argument is that someone is trying to persuade us, feels strongly against some proposal, and that the argument needs further analysis.

Illogical Claims of Program Failure

Sometimes a proposal is rejected with a bit of illogic. Recently, an alderman opposed the idea of civilian oversight of police, claiming that such a board or commission would not reduce crime. True, but the purpose of civilian police review boards has nothing to do with reducing crime. Its purpose is to assure the public that complaints against the police for abuse of force are being heard, investigated, and dealt with appropriately. The form of this argument is proposal X should not be approved because it won't achieve Y, where Y is not the goal of proposal X. If you see an argument of that form, you should be wary.

Conclusion

This chapter offers some clues that something you are reading or hearing may be exaggerated, distorted, false, or intended to direct you or misdirect you to a single preset conclusion. These clues don't necessarily mean that what you are reading or hearing or watching is false, but they do suggest that you should not accept the argument on face value. You need to look further, for evidence, logic, and context, to test their truth value.

Notes

1 https://en.wikipedia.org/wiki/List_of_fake_news_websites.
2 Rebecca Klar, "HHS Secretary Points to 'Unhealthy Comorbidities' When Asked About High Coronavirus Death Rate in US," *The Hill*, May 17, 2020, https://thehill.com/homenews/administration/498192-hhs-secretary-points-to-unhealthy-comorbidities-when-asked-about-high.

3. Jenna Johnson, "Many People Are Saying: How Donald Trump Spreads Unproven Theories," *The Washington Post*, June 13, 2016, www.washingtonpost.com/politics/a-lot-of-people-aresaying-how-trump-spreads-conspiracies-andinnuendo/2016/06/13/b21e59de-317e-11e6-8ff7-7b6c1998b7a0_story.html.
4. www.urbandictionary.com/define.php?term=just%20saying.
5. Quotation from Emily Makowski, "Theory That Coronavirus Escaped from a Lab Lacks Evidence," *The Scientist*, March 5, 2020, www.the-scientist.com/news-opinion/theory-that-coronavirusescaped-from-a-lab-lacks-evidence-67229.
6. Dartagnon, "Trump Criticizes Own Security Staff for Not Roughing Up a Woman Protesting His Pennsylvania Rally," *Daily Kos*, December 11, 2019, www.dailykos.com/stories/2019/12/11/1904903/-Trumpcriticizes-his-own-security-guards-for-not-roughing-up-a-womanprotesting-at-his-PA-rally.
7. William Safire, *Safire's Political Dictionary*, New York, Oxford University Press, revised, 2008, p. 190.
8. Cara DeRose, "Despite Vowing to Pause Campaign, Collins Continues to Air Ads, Attack Gideon," *The MaineBeacon.com*, April 29, 2020, https://mainebeacon.com/despite-vowing-to-pause-campaign-collins-continues-to-air-ads-attack-gideon/.
9. Ian Olasov, "Offensive Political Dog Whistles: You Know Them When You Hear Them. Or Do You?," *Vox*, November 7, 2016, www.vox.com/the-big-idea/2016/11/7/13549154/dog-whistles-campaign-racism.
10. Jim Morrill, "First 9th District Republican Goes on Air, Mocking Democrats and Backing Trump," *The Charlotte Observer*, April 9, 2019, www.charlotteobserver.com/news/politics-government/election/article229010419.html.
11. Katie Reilly, "Read Hillary Clinton's 'Basket of Deplorables' Remarks about Donald Trump's Supporters," *Time Magazine*, September 10, 2016, https://time.com/4486502/hillary-clinton-basket-of-deplorables-transcript/.
12. Emily Heil, "Move Over, 'Latte Liberal.' A New GOP Insult Invokes Goat Milk and Avocado Toast," *The Washington Post*, November 15, 2019, www.washingtonpost.com/news/voraciously/wp/2019/11/15/move-over-latte-liberal-a-new-gop-insult-invokes-goat-milk-and-avocado-toast/.
13. Mike Lofgren, "The Real 'Deep State' Is About Corporate Power, Not Entrenched Bureaucrats," *The Washington Post*, November 15, 2019, www.washingtonpost.com/outlook/the-real-deep-state-is-about-corporate-power-not-bureaucrats/2019/11/15/9bd203d6-0701-11ea-ac12-3325d49eacaa_story.html.
14. Jennifer Steinhauer, "Duncan Hunter Airs Ad Suggesting Opponent Is Terrorist Sympathizer," *New York Times*, September 28, 2018; Chantal da Silva, "Donald Trump Says Democrats Are 'Treasonous' on Border and Their 'Horrible Laws' Stop Military Acting 'Rough,'" *Newsweek*, April 11, 2019; Mike Lillis, "Hoyer: Trump Committed 'Treason' in Helsinki," *The Hill*, July 17, 2018; Aris Folley, "O'Rourke Compares Trump to Nazi Leader," *The Hill*, October 23, 2019.
15. E.J. Montini, "Lindsey Graham (in 2015) Perfectly Sums Up the Trump/Biden Race," *Arizona Republic*, September 29, 2020.
16. Dana Milbank, "Could Lindsay Graham Be Any More Obsequious?," *The Washington Post*, October 24, 2019.
17. Carl Hulse, "'Moscow Mitch' Tag Enrages McConnell and Squeezes G.O.P. on Election Security," *The New York Times*, July 30, 2019.
18. Morgan Gstalter, "#Moscow Mitch McTreason Trends after McConnell Defends Blocking Election Security Bills," *The Hill*, July 30, 2019.
19. Maegan Vazquez, "Duckworth Calls Out 'Cadet Bone Spurs' after Trump's 'Treasonous' Remark," *CNN*, February 6, 2018.
20. Zack Budryk, "Pelosi Unveils New Nickname for Trump 'Mr. Make Matters Worse,'" *The Hill*, July 26, 2020.
21. Michael Koplow, "To 'Bibi' or Not to 'Bibi,'" *The Atlantic*, October 13, 2012, www.theatlantic.com/international/archive/2012/10/to-bibi-or-not-to-bibi/263568/.
22. John Whyte, "Media Portrayal of People Who Are Obese," *Medicine and Society, AMA Journal of Ethics*, April 2010, https://journalofethics.ama-assn.org/article/media-portrayal-people-who-are-obese/2010-04.

23 "'Drug Dealers, Criminals, Rapists': What Trump Thinks of Mexicans," *BBC News*, August 31, 2016, www.bbc.com/news/av/world-us-canada-37230916.
24 PBS News Hour, "Trump Says Virus Whistleblower Is a 'Disgruntled, Unhappy Person,'" May 14, 2020.
25 Ashley Parker and Rosalind S. Helderman, "In New Book, Former Trump Lawyer Michael Cohen Describes Alleged Episodes of Racism and Says President Likes How Putin Runs Russia," *The Washington Post*, September 5, 2020, www.washingtonpost.com/politics/cohen-trump-book/2020/09/05/235aa10a-ef96-11ea-ab4e-581edb849379_story.html.
26 Garrett Epps, "Constitutional Myth #8: The 14th Amendment Doesn't Exist," *The Atlantic*, July 13, 2011, www.theatlantic.com/national/archive/2011/07/constitutional-myth-8-the-14th-amendment-doesnt-exist/241858/; Mark Sumner, "Why Trump's Expected Supreme Court Nominee Believes All Civil Rights Legislation Is 'Illegitimate,'" Daily Kos, September 26, 2020, www.dailykos.com/stories/2020/9/26/1980903/-Why-Trump-s-expected-Supreme-Court-nominee-believes-all-Civil-Rights-legislation-is-illegitimate.
27 Hilary Brueck, "Gwyneth Paltrow's Goop Must Stop Making Bogus Claims About Its $66 'Vaginal Eggs' Because of a Legal Settlement. Here's the Real Science," *Business Insider*, September 5, 2018, www.businessinsider.com/what-is-a-vaginal-egg-goop-lawsuit-2018-9.
28 Gene Demby, "Steve King Doubles Down," *NPR*, July 26, 2013, www.npr.org/sections/codeswitch/2013/07/26/205885068/steve-king-doubles-down.
29 Jeremy Diamond, "Trump Focuses on 'Perfect' Ukraine Call Despite Allegations of Broader Pressure Campaign," *CNN*, November 4, 2019.
30 Lori Robertson, "Democrats' Misleading Tax Line," *Factcheck.org*, January 26, 2018, www.factcheck.org/2018/01/democrats-misleading-tax-line/.
31 John Cook, "3 Levels of Cherry Picking in a Single Argument," *Skeptical Science*, July 21, 2010, https://skepticalscience.com/3-levels-of-cherry-picking-in-a-single-argument.html.
32 "Disability Insurance: SSA Could Do More to Prevent Overpayments or Incorrect Waivers to Beneficiaries," *GAO-16-34*, October 29, 2015, www.gao.gov/products/gao-16-34.
33 Lisa Rein, "Disabled Workers Were Overpaid $11 Billion in Social Security over 9 Years, Watchdog Reports," *The Washington Post*, November 2, 2015, www.washingtonpost.com/news/federal-eye/wp/2015/11/02/watchdog-cash-benefit-program-overpaid-disabled-workers-by-11-billion-over-nine-years/.
34 Kevin Breuninger, "Trump Says He 'Never Meant Mexico Would Write a Check' for the Wall," CNBC, January 10, 2019, www.cnbc.com/2019/01/10/trump-says-mexico-is-not-going-to-write-a-check-for-the-wall-contradicting-campaign-pledge.html; Adam Behsudi, "Fact Check: Mexico Will 'Indirectly' Pay for a Border Wall through the New Trade Deal," January 10, 2019, www.politico.com/story/2019/01/10/fact-check-mexico-border-wall-1073928.
35 Niv Elis, "Trump Falsely Claims Ivanka 'Created 14 Million Jobs,'" *The Hill*, November 13, 2019, https://thehill.com/policy/finance/470291-trump-claims-ivanka-created-14-million-jobs.
36 Bethania Palma, "Did Germany 'Fold' to Sharia Law and Allow Child Marriages?," *Snopes*, November 28, 2016, www.snopes.com/factcheck/germany-allows-child-marriages/.
37 Sydney Schaedel, "Did the Pope Endorse Trump?," *Factcheck.org*, October 24, 2016, www.factcheck.org/2016/10/did-the-pope-endorse-trump/.
38 Dan Evon, "Did Soros Say: 'I'm Going to Bring Down the U.S. by Funding Black Hate Groups'?," *Snopes*, September 7, 2016, www.snopes.com/fact-check/george-soros-bring-down-us/.
39 Time.com, "Too Good to Be True Hall of Fame," October 6, 2011, http://business.time.com/2011/10/11/14-products-with-notoriously-misleading-advertising-claims/slide/a-long-history-of-misleading-advertising/.

40 Gary Warth, "White House Report Urges Deregulation to Reduce Homelessness," *San Diego Union-Tribune*, September 17, 2019, www.sandiegouniontribune.com/news/homelessness/story/2019-09-17/white-house-report-urges-deregulation-to-reduce-homelessness.

41 Nick Miroff, "Smugglers Are Sawing through New Sections of Trump's Border Wall," *The Washington Post*, November 2, 2019, www.washingtonpost.com/national/smugglers-are-sawing-through-new-sections-of-trumps-border-wall/2019/11/01/25bf8ce0-fa72-11e9-ac8c-8eced29ca6ef_story.html.

42 Roy Cordato, "How Do Tax Cuts Spur Economic Growth?," *John Locke Foundation*, September 17, 2019, www.johnlocke.org/update/how-do-tax-cuts-spur-economic-growth/.

43 Scott Rick, Gabriel Paolacci, and Katherine Alicia Burson, "Income Tax and the Motivation to Work (March 19, 2017)," Ross School of Business Paper No. 1285, https://ssrn.com/abstract=2655424 or http://dx.doi.org/10.2139/ssrn.2655424.

44 Joseph Minarik, "Fixing the Budget: What's In It for Us," Committee for Economic Development, no date, www.ced.org/blog/entry/fixing-the-budget-whats-in-it-for-us.

45 Kent German, "2 Years after Being Grounded, the Boeing 737 Max Is Flying Again," *c/net*, June 19, 2021.

46 Dan Swinhoe, "The 15 Biggest Data Breaches of the 21st Century," *CSO*, January 8, 2021, www.csoonline.com/article/2130877/the-biggest-data-breaches-of-the-21st-century.html.

47 Ryan Nunn, "Three Proposals to Give Americans a Tax Break, and Boost Labor Force Participation," *Real Clear Markets*, April 15, 2019, www.realclearmarkets.com/articles/2019/04/15/three_proposals_to_give_americans_a_tax_break_and_boost_labor_force_participation_103695.html.

48 Trump Fundraising Emails, Twitter, September 30, 2020, https://twitter.com/trumpemail/status/1311332895232065536.

49 Anna Fifield, "Trump Hammers China over Hong Kong, China Responds With: What about Minneapolis?," *The Washington Post*, May 30, 2020, www.washingtonpost.com/world/asia_pacific/china-trump-hong-kong/2020/05/30/37ad056e-a25a-11ea-9d96-c3f7c755fd6e_story.html.

50 Adam Taylor, "China Calls for Canada Human Rights Inquiry, Preempting Demand for Investigation into Abuse of Uyghurs," *The Washington Post*, June 6, 2021, www.washingtonpost.com/world/2021/06/22/china-canada-uighur-indigenous/.

51 Justine Coleman, "Navarro Says Whistleblower 'Deserted' in an 'American Tragedy,'" *The Hill*, May 17, 2020, https://thehill.com/homenews/sunday-talk-shows/498185-white-house-trade-adviser-says-whistleblower-deserted-in-an?rnd=1589724230.

52 Associated Press, "Fact-Check: Trump Falsely Blames Governors for Virus Test," *VOA*, April 19, 2020, www.voanews.com/covid-19-pandemic/fact-check-trump-falsely-blames-governors-virus-test.

53 Alex Horton, "Ohio Republican Blames Mass Shootings on 'Drag Queen Advocates', Colin Kaepernick and Obama," *The Washington Post*, August 5, 2019, www.washingtonpost.com/politics/2019/08/05/ohio-republican-blames-mass-shootings-drag-queen-advocates-colin-kaepernick-obama/.

54 DiversityInc Staff, "Slavery Wasn't Really That Bad for Some Slaves, Says Fox News' O'Reilly," *DiversityInc*, July 28, 2016, www.diversityinc.com/slavery-wasnt-really-bad-slaves-says-fox-news-oreilly/.

55 Emma Green, "The World Is Full of Holocaust Deniers," *The Atlantic*, May 14, 2014, www.theatlantic.com/international/archive/2014/05/the-world-is-full-of-holocaust-deniers/370870/.

56 Walter Einenkel, "NRA Responds to El Paso and Dayton Shootings: The Real Problem Is the 'Effort to Destroy the NRA,'" *Daily Kos*, August 15, 2019, www.dailykos.com/stories/2019/8/15/1879237/-NRA-responds-to-El-Paso-and-Dayton-shootings-the-real-problem-is-the-effort-to-destroy-the-NRA.

57 KHN, "Trump Defends Use of Dangerous Malaria Drug, Falsely Claims VA Study Was Biased Against Him," *Kaiser Health News*, May 20, 2020, https://khn.org/morning-breakout/trump-defends-use-of-dangerous-malaria-drug-falsely-claims-va-study-was-biased-against-him/.
58 Laura Wagner and Merrit Kennedy, "Michigan Gov. Rick Snyder: 'We All Failed the Families of Flint,'" *NPR*, March 17, 2016, www.npr.org/sections/thetwo-way/2016/03/17/470792212/watch-michigan-gov-rick-snyder-testifies-on-the-flint-water-crisis.
59 Shane Harris, "Officials Blame Outsiders for Violence in Minnesota but Contradict One Another on Who Is Responsible," *The Washington Post*, May 30, 2020, www.washingtonpost.com/national-security/officials-blame-outsiders-for-violence-in-minnesota-but-contradict-each-other-on-who-is-responsible/2020/05/30/d722e9d6-a2b1-11ea-b5c9-570a91917d8d_story.html.
60 Sonam Sheth, "Trump Suggests Rudy Giuliani's Crusade to Overturn the Election Results Is 'More Important' Than When Giuliani Led New York's 9/11 Response," *Business Insider*, December 7, 2020.
61 Robert O'Harrow Jr. and Shawn Boburg, "Trump's Pick to Lead U.S. Intelligence Claims He Arrested 300 Illegal Immigrants in a Single Day. He Didn't," *The Washington Post*, August 1, 2019, www.washingtonpost.com/investigations/trumps-pick-to-lead-us-intelligence-claims-he-arrested-300-illegal-immigrants-in-a-single-day-he-didnt/2019/08/01/12b958e4-b3b7-11e9-8e94-71a35969e4d8_story.html.
62 Jon Greenberg, "Trump Falsely Takes Credit for Two Large Industrial Projects in Louisiana and Pennsylvania," *Politifact*, August 16, 2019, www.politifact.com/factchecks/2019/aug/16/donaldtrump/trump-falsely-takes-credit-two-large-industrial-pr/.
63 Frank Mitloehner, "What if the United States Stopped Eating Meat?," *Clear Center*, December 4, 2020, https://clear.ucdavis.edu/blog/what-if-united-states-stopped-eating-meat.
64 Michael Gordon and Samy Amanatulla, "The Final Presidential Debate of 2020, Between Donald Trump and Joe Biden," *The Propwatch Project*, November 12, 2020, www.propwatch.org/article.php?id=264.
65 Nicole Gelinas, "Infrastructure Investments Won't Matter Until We Lower Retiree Cost," *Governing*, January 2019, www.governing.com/archive/gov-infrastructure-funding-retiree-costs-pensions-opeb.html.
66 Felicia Sonmez, John Wagner, and Colby Itkowitz, "Democrats Announce Eight Witnesses, Including Vindman, Sondland and Volker, for Next Week's Public Impeachment Hearings," *The Washington Post*, November 12, 2019, www.washingtonpost.com/politics/trump-impeachment-inquiry-live-updates/2019/11/12/229f5484-04de-11ea-8292-c46ee8cb3dce_story.html.
67 Charlie Dunlap, Jr., "Want to Save Teens? Driving Restrictions Could Save at Least as Many Lives as Gun Control," *The Hill*, March 3, 2018, https://thehill.com/opinion/civil-rights/376956-want-to-save-teens-driving-restrictions-could-save-at-least-as-many.
68 Judith C. Scott and Kendall G. Johnson, "'A Desperate Need': Black Homicide Epidemic Demands Prevention, Justice," *The Hill*, July 31, 2020, https://thehill.com/opinion/criminal-justice/510057-a-desperate-need-black-homicide-epidemic-demands-prevention-justice.
69 Twitter, July 9, 2020.
70 Clyde Wayne Crews and Jessica Melugin, "Embracing the Idea of Unregulated Fake News Everywhere," *The American Conservative*, May 30, 2020, www.theamericanconservative.com/articles/embracing-the-idea-of-unregulated-fake-news-everywhere/.
71 Brittany Shammas, "Mississippi Lawmakers Pass Resolution Paving Way to Remove Confederate Symbol from State Flag," *The Washington Post*, June 27, 2020, www.washingtonpost.com/nation/2020/06/27/mississippi-flag-vote/.
72 Eugene Volokh, "Same Sex Marriage and Slippery Slopes," *Hofstra Law Review*, 33, October 5, 2005, pp. 1155–1201, www2.law.ucla.edu/volokh/marriage.pdf.

3
QUICK CHECKS

Once you have an essay or opinion piece in front of you that has roused your curiosity about its truth value, what do you do with it? You can make some first pass checks that do not require knowledge of the subject matter or the research design and data collection. You can look for reliable fact-checkers, who may have done the work for you, and you can also check out the reliability of the publishers and the authors.

Using Fact-checkers

Fact-checkers are people whose job it is to determine whether a public statement or claim is true or false, or somewhere in between. Given the increase in false or distorted information in recent years, fact-checkers are playing an increasingly important role in society. As a result, those who deal in false or exaggerated information often try to discredit fact-checkers who expose them.

Though the motives of the critics are questionable, some fact-checkers could be biased. Before you rely on fact-checkers, you should be confident that the ones you are going to use are accurate most of the time and make corrections quickly when they make mistakes.

Are Fact-checkers Biased?

Critics claim fact-checkers are biased against them, do sloppy work, and make black-and-white decisions when more subtle judgments are required. One criticism of fact-checkers has been that they disproportionately attack conservatives. A second charge is that they rely on investigative reports from left-oriented news sites and those left-wing sites get their news from the fact-checkers in a closed circle. Those charges are easy to test.

One of the most famous fact-checking sites is Snopes. Snopes has been criticized as biased against the left and also as biased against the right, suggesting that it has no consistent bias. Snopes fact-checks statements on the left as well as on the right. In a typical fact-check, Snopes recently examined a claim by Social Security Works, a non-profit advocacy group to preserve Social Security. The group had argued that President Trump had pledged to end Social Security if reelected. Snopes found the claim partly true, partly false, not a black-and white-judgment. Trump had said that he would delay collection of the tax supporting Social Security, and if he was reelected, would eliminate that tax, but he didn't *actually* say he would eliminate the program. Later, in another press conference, Trump denied he was out to terminate Social Security, vaguely suggesting that he would, if reelected, substitute general fund revenue for the payroll tax.

The language of the fact-check was unemotional, the evidence presented was the president's own words, what he did and did not say. This evaluation by Snopes was neutral. Social Security Works had overstated its case.[1]

The *Florida Times Union* ran a story on the fact-checkers, examining various charges of bias against them. The article noted that claims that Snopes was owned and run by a flaming liberal in the tank for Obama were false. The owners are a man who had registered Republican in 2000 and had not registered a party affiliation in 2008; his wife was a Canadian citizen who could not vote in the U.S. or contribute to a political campaign. The owners did not hide their identities, despite claims to the contrary. The Center for Responsive Politics, which tracks campaign contributions, has no record of any contribution to either party from the Mikkelsons, the owners of Snopes.[2]

What about some of the other major fact-checkers? Consider PolitiFact.com, a non-profit operated by the Poynter Institute in St. Petersburg, Florida. It, too, has been attacked as being biased against both the right and the left. The charge that fact-checkers do a superficial job of research and rely on left-biased news sources doesn't hold up in the case of Politifact. This fact-checker lists the sources it uses for each case it examines. For Kamala Harris's charge that Trump was undermining Social Security and Medicare, Politifact listed the following sources:

Kamala Harris, Instagram post, Aug. 9, 2020
White House, Memorandum on Deferring Payroll Tax Obligations in Light of the Ongoing COVID-19 Disaster, Aug. 8, 2020
White House, Remarks by President Trump in Press Briefing, Aug. 8, 2020
Legal Information Institute, 26 U.S. Code §3101.Rate of tax, accessed Aug. 12, 2020
Congressional Research Service, Payroll Tax Cuts as Economic Stimulus: Past Experience and Economic Considerations, Aug. 23, 2019
U.S. Congress, Tax relief, unemployment insurance reauthorization, and Job Creation Act of 2010, Dec. 17, 2020
Congressional Research Service, Social Security: Temporary Payroll Tax Reduction, May 7, 2012
Congressional Budget Office, Combined OASDI Trust Funds, March 2012

Social Security Administration, Cumulative combined OASI and DI income less cost (actuarial balance) for the long-range projection period 2019–2094, April 22, 2020

Committee for a Responsible Federal Budget, How Much Would President Trump's Executive Orders Cost, Aug. 8, 2020

Congressional Budget Office, The Federal Budget in 2019, April 2020

U.S. Joint Committee on Taxation, General Explanation of Tax Legislation Enacted in the 112th Congress, Feb. 25, 2013

Email exchange, G. William Hoagland, vice president, Bipartisan Policy Center, Aug. 12, 2020

Email exchange, Eugene Steuerle, cofounder, Urban-Brookings Tax Policy Center, Aug. 12, 202

Interview, Michael Gwin, spokesman, Biden for President, Aug. 12, 2020

In the text, reference is also made to the president's press conference on August 13, in which he mentioned his intent, if reelected and able to eliminate the payroll tax, to fund Social Security out of the general fund.

These sources include documents, transcripts of the president's news conferences, neutral sources such as the Congressional Research Service, and interviews with experts, both Democrats and Republicans. No media source from the left or right is cited. The list is both comprehensive and appropriate to the topic. The wording is analytical, clear, and balanced.[3]

Politifact fact-checks Republicans as well as Democrats. President Trump has been a frequent target. One recent post questioned Trump's claim that Democrats don't want to protect people from eviction. Politifact declared this claim false, because "Democrats have proposed and supported legislation to provide people with rental assistance and extend and expand the CARES Act's moratorium on evictions." The evidence was clear and strong behind the conclusion. The tone, despite the clear evidence of a false charge by the president, was neutral.[4]

While Politifact has rated more republican statements false than democratic ones, the Washington Post fact-checker evaluated both republican and democratic statements in equal measure, and the number of Pinocchio's (that is, ratings of false) was also about equally divided.[5]

One charge against the fact-checkers has been that republican statements are disproportionately declared false. One possibility is that with a president who is careless with the truth, there are more questionable statements on the right than on the left. But are correct statements by Republicans evaluated as false?

The *Washington Post* fact-checker examined an ad from a republican group called Restoration-PAC (political action committee). It described some of democratic presidential candidate Joe Biden's worst moments from an earlier failed run for president, including Biden's distortion of his educational achievements. The *Post*'s fact-checker concluded that Biden had really said what the ad claimed he had said, and the ad was neither distorted nor misleading.[6] Though the information was old, it was correct, and the *Washington Post* fact-checker said as much.

One can argue that the above examples are cherry picked and do not address the claim that, in general, fact-checkers rely on news stories as evidence for or against a claim. And if the news cited is typically from left-biased sources, that would account for the presumed bias against conservatives among fact-checkers.

A RealClearPolitics fact-check review (RealClearPolitics is moderately conservative) reported that "up to three quarters" (weasel words? what does up to three quarters mean?) of the fact-checks rely in part (more weasel words? what does in part mean?) on news coverage as "fact."[7]

While intended as evidence of a weakness in the system, this report does not say that the media reports that fact-checkers rely on are biased to the left (or to the right). Further, this critique notes that such news stories are only part of the evidence provided. Government reports, documents, academic studies, and interviews with experts are also included. If news stories from left-leaning sources were the only evidence cited in fact-checks, the fact-checks would indeed be biased, but even this attack on the fact-checkers was not able to show such bias. That many fact-checks used media reports, among other sources, is hardly a condemnation.

Many attacks on the fact-checking industry are unwarranted and unsupported, but not every fact-checking site is neutral. Some are rated slightly or greatly biased left or right. For example, Check Your Fact is rated as center right, high on factual content, but uses loaded words, stereotypes, and appeals to emotion to favor right-wing causes. Zebra Fact check is rated slightly right-center biased.[8] Media Matters for America is considered left leaning. Newsbusters is rated by Media Bias/Fact Check as extreme right biased and mixed on factual reporting. Newsbusters spends a lot of effort on attacking the *Washington Post* fact-checkers and Politifact.

With a few exceptions, fact-checkers are extremely careful in their work because their reputation for accuracy is what they have to offer. If they become known for mistakes, carelessness, or strong bias, they lose their audience. They might as well pack up and go home. As an industry, they police themselves, by setting standards for approval, by making awards for excellence, and by providing training for fact-checkers. The IFCN (International Factchecking Network at Poynter's) has set up standards of transparency, integrity, and non-partisanship. Fact-checkers have to agree to abide by these rules and be examined to demonstrate that they do adhere to them, including the provision of evidence for findings and a clear statement of ownership and financing of the fact-checking organization. Fact-checkers who meet the standards note this certification and are listed on the IFCN website.

Some Reliable Fact-checkers

While there are enough exceptions to warrant caution, there are many reliable fact-checkers online, including the above-mentioned Snopes and Politifact. Others are also reliable, such as Truthorfiction.com, AP Fact Check (https://apnews.com/hub/ap-fact-check), Washington Post Fact Checker, (washingtonpost.com/news/fact-checker), FactCheck.org (factcheck.org), and Fact Check: NPR (npr/sections/politics-fact-check). Also, the fact-checker Lead Stories gets a rating of least biased and very high on factual reporting from Media Bias/Fact Check (leadstories.com). If you have a question about the reliability of a fact-checker, you can look up its rating on Media Bias/Fact Check and look for Poynter's IFCN certification. (https://ifcncodeofprinciples.poynter.org/signatories).

Each fact-checking site has a little different coverage and offers slightly different information. Some focus on specific topics, such as politics, climate, or science; others focus on social media, rumors, and scams. Some deal with false news, others with the press more generally, including the talking heads, the pundits, and commentators of television. The amount of information they report on each fact-check varies. What follows are some examples of the coverage of a variety of fact-checkers.

Lead Stories

Lead Stories is a fact-checker with an intriguing feature. If you only want to look at fact-checks of the right, you can click on the blue feed tab; if you only want to look at fact-checks of the left, you can click on the red feed tab. The site includes a hoax alert and a section on the coronavirus. It posts prominently its own corrections when information changes or if it has made a mistake. The site monitors trends and debunks fake news before it goes viral.

A recent example of Lead Stories' fact-checking called false a claim by the founder of a conservative non-profit, Turning Point USA. Turning Point tweeted that the FBI said that military ballots for President Trump were found in a ditch in Pennsylvania. The tweet further claimed that this was voter fraud, and that Democrats were okay with it.

The FBI had never said anything about Pennsylvania ballots; a U.S. Attorney said that nine military ballots were found in a waste basket and said nothing about Democrats. The nine ballots got caught in confusion over a requirement that returned ballots be sealed in an internal envelope as well as an outer one. Two of the nine had been resealed in proper envelopes by officials. The fact-check is well documented, including the original charge and the full statement of the U.S. Attorney.[9]

QUICK CHECKS

Photo Checkers

With the increased number of faked photos and videos, you might want to check out photos with Apple's free Veracity app, available on iPhones and iPads, that searches for the image you are looking for and finds other instances of it, even if it has been cropped or edited. Or try Tineye, a reverse image web search service, meaning you use the possibly fake image you see as the input for a search. Tineye is free for up to 100 images a day for non-commercial users. Like Veracity, it will find other instances of a given image on the web, even if yours has been altered in some way. Google has a reverse image search as well (Google Images). Other highly rated reverse search engines include Yahoo Image Search, Bing Image Search, Pinterest Visual Search Tool, Picsearch, Flickr, and Getty Images. If you want to know if a photo or video has been faked, there are lots of programs that can help you check it out.

Factcheck.org

One of the most useful factchecking sites in terms of the range of topics covered and the depth of the explanations is Factcheck.org. The site doesn't come up with a single rating, true or false (or something in between), but discusses the ways in which a claim or article is false or misleading. A project of the Annenberg Public Policy Center, Factcheck.org also includes a range of more narrowly focused fact-checking groups, including misleading "political talking points," "viral spiral" on internet rumors, and "scicheck" that answers science questions. Factcheck.org takes questions from readers, which can be helpful if the site does not already post a fact-check on the topic you are examining. Taking advantage of volunteer labor on the web, Factcheck.org asks users of Facebook to report stories in their newsfeeds that they suspect are fake.

Examples from the Viral Spiral include viral attacks on Christine Blasey Ford, who charged President Trump's choice for Supreme Court with sexual transgressions. One of the unsubstantiated rumors was that "Ford had also made allegations of sexual misconduct against Associate Justice Neil Gorsuch, Trump's first Supreme Court pick."[10]

While many of the rumors that Viral Spiral looked into were political attacks on opponents, attempting to undermine their credibility and character, some of the rumors had more insidious intent to undermine the credibility of the fact-checkers themselves. If successful, this effort would make it easier to deceive many readers. The Viral Spiral reported that a meme falsely claimed that FactCheck.org had exposed the myth-busting website Snopes.com "as an extremely liberal propaganda site with an agenda to discredit anything that appears to be conservative." FactCheck.org had actually written "we found the site's work to be solid and well-documented," and that its articles appeared "utterly poker-faced when covering Democratic and Republican politicians."[11]

The Washington Post Fact-checker

The *Washington Post* fact-checker focuses primarily on national politics, policies, and politicians, covering a broad swath, from political ads to debates, from congressional testimony to claims made by members of Congress and the president. The site relies heavily on queries from readers. It rates claims with one to four Pinocchios, with four being the most egregiously false. It has created a bottomless Pinocchio, for the occasions on which a statement that has received a three or four Pinocchio rating is repeated at least 20 times.

The *Washington Post* fact-checker gave a rating of four Pinocchios to President Trump's claim that the server of the Democratic National Committee that had been hacked was in Ukraine and had been examined by a Ukrainian security company. The reality is that the server is on display in Washington, the security company is a U.S. company, and has no ties to Ukraine (one founder was a Russian-born U.S. citizen). The fact-checker noted that though the claim has been thoroughly debunked, the president continued to repeat it.[12]

While the *Washington Post* newspaper leans slightly to the left, its fact-checker finds fault with both Democrats and Republicans. The *Post* fact-checker critiqued Democratic Congressman Adam Schiff's claim that the whistleblower who started the impeachment investigation against Trump had a statutory right to anonymity;[13] the site also called attention to Democratic Senator Elizabeth Warren's underestimate of the burden of her proposed tax on the wealthiest.[14]

As for critiques of the political right, the site commented on President Trump's misleading spin on the border crisis,[15] and on an American Action network's [AAN self describes as center right] attack ad on freshman Representative Ocasio-Cortez.[16]

AP [Associated Press] Fact Check

In addition to fact-checking statements by political leaders, AP Fact Check includes a useful roundup of false rumors, called "not real news," spread on the internet. One recent claim that the fact-checker debunked was that Fox News Sunday host Chris Wallace responded to Trump's criticism of him that he would never be like his father Mike Wallace, saying that the president would not ever be like *his* father, Fred Trump, and that Trump was "a fraud. A charlatan. A thug. A loser. A trust fund baby. A punk. A serial adulterer." Someone was probably fantasizing about what Chris Wallace might have wished to have said, because the whole quote was made up.[17]

Politifact

Politifact focuses on political news, using the image of a truth-o-meter, to rank stories and claims as true, false, or somewhere in between. The site also includes a "pants on fire" list, stories and claims so wrong they earn the children's chant, "liar, liar, pants on fire." The discussions of stories on Politifact go much deeper than a single conclusion of true or false, explaining the ways in which a story is true, false, or misleading.

The site looks into statements by Trump, various Facebook posts, and viral images and arguments spread on social media. Many of these are memes, graphic images with a message attached. Politifact also has a section where it fact-checks bloggers. The site rates many of its fact-checks "pants on fire," that is, blatantly false. Politifact is a fact-checker for Facebook, and hence many of its fact-checks are on material posted there.

Two examples that evoked a rating of false dealt with a huge explosion in the port area of Beirut, Lebanon. One claimed that a video showed a missile attack in the explosion in Beirut; a second one claimed Israel had dropped a tactical nuclear weapon on the port of Beirut. Politifact concluded the video was a crude fake, and there was no evidence of a nuclear strike on Beirut.[18]

A recent fact-check that earned a rating of "pants on fire" examined a video circulated by Steve Scalise, a high-ranking republican representative. The fact-checker concluded that the video had been doctored to make it sound as if presidential candidate Biden supported defunding the police. Biden had made it very clear in many public statements that he did not support defunding the police. The fact-check was extensively sourced, including statements by Scalise, by Ady Barkan, whose speech was altered, and by Joe Biden. Scalise, when caught, restored the original video, so anyone could check the original against the doctored version and see what had been changed and to what effect.[19]

NPR (National Public Radio) Fact-checker

NPR's fact-check includes a range of U.S. national policies and statements by political figures, providing nuanced short essays about the topic and describing the ways in which such statements are misleading or oversimplified.

NPR also follows stories about fact-checkers and fact-checking, such as a story about why the only fact-finder in the Netherlands withdrew from a role in examining false news on Facebook. The answer, it turned out, was that the Netherland's fact-finder was focused on examining threats to democracy and taking them off Facebook, so Facebook's policy at the time of not examining politicians' claims made his work irrelevant.[20]

Truthorfiction

The name "Truthorfiction" makes it sound like the site just labels claims true or false, but in fact its judgments are much more sophisticated and complete. For example, one of its articles examined a claim that private prisons are suing states if the states don't keep the prisons full. In its analysis, Truthorfiction indicated that there were indeed some contracts that states had with private prisons that included guaranteed occupancy rates and financial penalties for failure to comply, but the fact-finder discovered only one instance in which a private company sued a state for failure to fulfill its contractual agreement. The article examined the circumstances of the one case that it found. In addition, the article examined the growth of the private prison industry, abuses, and scandals that had occurred, and what happened when states failed to keep their private prisons full. The result was a broader look at the implications of contract failures between states and private prison companies.[21] This is a good site if you want to learn about an issue, not just find out whether a claim is true.

Logically

Logically.ai (www.logically.ai) is a new fact-checking site in the U.S., although it has been operating in other countries for several years. It has a different approach to fact-checking that combines artificial intelligence with human fact-checking, covering over 100,000 news sites around the globe. It rates news sources (credibility high, medium, low) and individual articles (False, Misleading, or True). Using its massive database of trusted sources, it presents evidence on the topic at hand. The site promises to respond to individuals' requests to fact-check a story. Its goal is to put a stop to fake news, especially about elections, by informing people, as they read, about the credibility of what they are looking at. Presumably, people will be less likely to pass along a false story once it has been flagged for them. To accomplish this mission, Logically offers a browser extension and a mobile app for continuous fact-checking.

Fact-checking sites offer such interesting analyses that you might be tempted to look at them regularly, even when you are not examining a particular story or claim. Watching how the fact-checkers work can make you more sensitive to falsehoods, and more aware of the techniques involved in proving or disproving a claim. Some of the fact-checkers give you context and explain broader issues. They don't just play "gotcha."

The Poynter Institute lists 88 verified and active fact-checkers from around the world.[22] Like those based in the U.S., those from other countries vary in what they cover. A brief selection of reliable fact-checkers from countries other than the U.S. follows.

Mexico's Animal Político–El Sabueso, (Political Animal, The Bloodhound), offers broad coverage with an emphasis on background and explanation. Its stories are divided into four parts, a set of videos with stories of general interest, fact-checks of misleading stories, explanations of current topics, and identification of disinformation. The disinformation section monitors rumors spread on social media and identifies false or altered images.

One recent fact-check called false a pair of photos that were supposed to demonstrate that the president and the minister of health had received medals from the U.N. for their management of the covid-19 pandemic. One of the photos had been altered, and they had been taken in different years. Further, the fact-check reported, the U.N. doesn't give medals for managing pandemics.[23]

The Australian Associated Press fact-check adds a bit of humor by punning on some of its headlines describing the stories as it monitors social media for false news, rumors, and altered videos and photos. Examples include "Ginger treatment for lung conditions hasn't crystallized into evidence" and "Vaccine spike protein link to male infertility is a failed conception."[24]

In addition to the Australian Associated Press, The Conversation.com also covers Australia. It frequently fact-checks statements from elected officials. The fact-checking part of the website actively solicits suggestions from readers for statements to check. It relies on academic experts to check on what appear to be factual statements, and then adds another level of credibility to its research results, a blind review, which means that someone is asked to review the site's explanations and judgments without knowing who wrote it. The reviewer's comments are published along with the initial fact-checker's explanation.[25]

Demagog of the Czech Republic focuses on the speech, posts, and claims of public officials. Unlike fact-checkers who prominently display falsehoods, Demagog verifies claims most of the time. Recent fact-checks verified the claim that Israel notifies civilian occupants of buildings it plans to bomb, allowing them sufficient time to escape, and the claim that Czechoslovakia was Israel's oldest ally because it had provided weapons to Israel when Israel was fighting for its independence. Demagog also monitors the promises of politicians, listing which ones have been fulfilled and which ones have not.[26]

Fullfact.org, in the United Kingdom, provides the normal fact-checking, but also does research and is building automated fact-checking tools for use in newsrooms and by fact-checkers around the world. Their research includes not only the accurate version of false or misleading information, but also what interventions are likely to be most effective at reducing mis- and disinformation. They endorse the strategy of trying to get the person or people who state false claims to retract them, arguing that this has the most effect on changing minds[27] (Fullfact.org).

AFP Factcheck has a unique status under French law which mandates its complete independence and lack of bias. It is also certified by Poynter. It covers virtually the entire world, with a relatively heavy emphasis on uncovering fake or altered photos and videos. Its conclusions vary from judging something false to reporting something is misleading. Because of the emphasis on examining photos and videos, a common theme is where protests actually took place, but covid-19 misinformation is also prevalent.

Checking the Reliability of Authors and Publishers

In addition to checking out stories or claims you encounter by looking at the fact-checking sites, you can check out the locations in which suspicious stories occur. One shortcut to evaluating a source is looking at websites whose business it is to describe the degree and direction of bias for a broad range of news providers. If the source you are examining isn't included on one of these sites, you can do a few simple checks yourself.

Finding that a news source has a reputation of being biased one way or another doesn't mean that the story you are looking at is necessarily wrong. Even a site that often publishes false stories will sometimes post some true ones to maintain credibility. Similarly, authors who sometimes spin the truth don't necessarily falsify everything they write. Having said that, however, if you discover that a given site, author, or company often lies or distorts, you may be less inclined to believe the story in front of you and be more willing to track down the evidence that will confirm or disprove your concerns.

Websites

One clue that often means a claim or story is false is a fake website, that is, one that looks like or imitates a trustworthy site. Such sites come and go, so be aware that any given list of such sites is likely to be partly outdated. Many of them have names that sound or look a lot like legitimate sites, but with small differences.

One good list of false websites, called the List of Fake News Websites, has been compiled in Wikipedia.[28] Some of the sites mentioned claim to be satire or humor, but if you run across an argument repeated on other sites, you may not see the claim that it is intended to be humorous.

A site may be real, that is, doesn't pretend to be another site, but frequently publishes distorted or blatantly false stories. Factcheck.org has a useful annotated list of sites that have published bogus content. Some of these claim they are satirical sites, but others do not. Factcheck.org provides information about the founders, owners, or writers on the sites, paying particular attention to sites that have obscured the location and identity of the owner and noting which ones have included disclaimers in the "about" sections of the site concerning the truth value of the material they promote.

Factcheck.org's list is called the Misinformation Directory. It was last updated in November of 2018. A typical entry concerns Americasfreedomfighters.com. The site is registered with a company that hides the identity and location of the owner. Factcheck reports that the site is owned by a father and son in California, Dino Porrazzo Sr. and Jr., who write under the pseudonyms Dean James and Johnny Davis. The last time I checked, their site was still functioning.

Media Bias/Fact Check takes a little different approach, rating news sites in terms of whether they are biased to the left (left-center, left, extreme left), to the right (right center, right, extreme right), or are reasonably neutral.

For example, it lists The Bearded Patriot as extremely biased to the right, low on factual reporting, and a questionable source, recommending that each story The Bearded Patriot posts should be fact-checked.

In addition, Media Bias/Fact Check lists sites that are pro-science, and those that are conspiracy oriented or present pseudo-science. Media Bias also lists what it calls questionable sites and those that bill themselves as satire. It continually adds new sites and reanalyzes old ones using more stringent criteria. Though it does list a number of questionable sites, Media Bias is less focused on whether you should believe what a particular story tells you and more oriented to telling you what biases you might encounter in a given story on a particular news site. If you wish, you can click on the "least biased" button to get some news that has been prechecked by reliable fact-checkers.[29]

While Media Bias/Fact Check assumes there are degrees of bias and relative neutrality, Allsides assumes that there is no source without bias, so you should check out sources with different biases. The site locates major online news sources (distinguishing between editorial content and straight news) as either left, left leaning, center, right leaning or right. If you want to know whether the news source you are looking at is typically biased in one direction or another, this website is a good place to check. Their tag "center" does not mean unbiased, it means without a predictable and consistent bias in a given direction.

For some current stories, the site quotes from sources on the left, on the right, and from the center. For practice, you can read all three and compare them. One advantage is that you learn not only about the sites that are considered left, right, or center, but also quickly pick up the patterns of storytelling, the clues to bias from the left or right. When you are checking out an actual story that has raised your curiosity, if what you are reading is on one side, it can be useful to look for stories on the other side. If there are major differences between them, it suggests the need to investigate further.

Allsides works at helping readers recognize bias. In a recent story about the firing of a popular Canadian sports announcer, Allsides followed stories from left-leaning and from right-leaning sources. The sports announcer had criticized immigrants for not showing gratitude to veterans by buying and wearing a poppy on Remembrance Day. Allsides noted that left-leaning sources were more likely to condemn the TV personality with words like racist, divisive, derogatory, and insensitive, while a right-leaning source mocked the emotional response of the critics (the twitterverse was "losing its mind" over the announcer's comments) and reinterpreted the sportscasters comments to refer to all those who didn't wear poppies, not just immigrants.[30]

CBS news has a listing of news sites which have published fake news.[31] A more nuanced list that differentiates between false, misleading, click-baity, and satirical sources has been compiled by Merrimack College communications professor Melissa Zimdars.[32] At least one of the more egregious sites she listed has been suspended for violation of the terms of service. She has updated her original list but noted that many of the sites were no longer active, and in 2016, said she was not going to update the list again. At that point, she had listed hundreds of sites and rated them as conspiracy, hate, unreliable, biased, or just plain fake. Zimdars also wrote a list of steps to take to check out websites on your own.[33] (As of this writing, at least some of the sites Zimdars listed were still up and active although many had been taken down. While I would not recommend just clicking on the entries in this list unless you are certain that they would not put something undesirable on your computer or take something from your computer, if a story you run across can be traced to one of these sites, you would have a good reason to be skeptical and check the content further.)

You may run across sites that are not listed by fact-checkers and need to judge for yourself if they seem reliable. After you look at the name of the site and assure yourself that is it not a knockoff of a legitimate site, check the "about us" tab on the website; it should tell you something about the goals of the website, its founding, its funding sources, and its staff. It should tell you whether the selections presented are intended to be satirical or factual. There should be a "contact us" tab that tells the reader how to reach the editors and ask questions. If this information is missing, the site doesn't have much credibility. When it lists names, such as the founder or current owner or editor-in-chief, you can look them up in a quick web search.

When you look at the funders, you may recognize some names and their political views. If sources of funding are not mentioned, you might wonder who is funding the site and to what end, and why the funder would not want to be named. Some websites are funded by wealthy businesspeople or corporations who oppose unions and unionizing, favor small government and low taxes on corporations, and oppose government regulations. Other websites may be supported by unions, by organizations representing industries or interest groups, political PACs supporting individual candidates or party choices, or by donations from readers. If an organization is very dependent on one or two sources of funding, it may not have much freedom to depart from the ideology of those funders. The donors may influence or determine the research agenda and possibly even the conclusions drawn from studies.

On websites funded by businesses or wealthy individuals, nearly all the stories may say something bad about unions or attack any proposal that implies a tax increase or increased government regulation of businesses. For example, The Center for Union Facts (UNIONFACTS.com) is an anti-union interest group, funded by companies, trade organizations, and individuals, whom the organization has refused to name. The Center for Union Facts has been called a corporate-backed front group.

On the left, "Courier Newsroom is a clandestine political operation, publishing, among other things, positive stories about moderate Democrats who face difficult reelections in November." Courier is primarily funded by Acronym, a liberal dark-money group.[34] (Dark-money groups are non-profits who contribute money to influence elections without revealing their donors' names. They can be on the left or the right.)

Websites that depend largely on reader contributions or foundation grants may also be influenced by donors, but if they depend on a variety of sources of funding, they may have more freedom to call the shots as they see them.

A look at recent stories should tell you if they are all slanted in one direction, such as pro- or anti-Democrat, pro- or anti-Republican, anti-tax, pro- or anti-abortion, defensive of police or critical of police violence. This kind of quick test will not tell you if any particular article is partly or wholly false, but it should alert you to possible areas of bias and suggest when you should look for material from the opposite point of view to compare. If the stories are headlined with exclamation points or claim to reveal secrets that no one else will tell you, or that "THEY" are hiding from you, you should treat the stories with skepticism.

The fact-finder, Truthorfiction, has a section on how to discover if a website is likely to post false material. They note, in addition to missing information, that a search on names listed on the masthead often can tell you what you need to know. The site gives the example of Yournewswire.com, a site that often publishes false stories. If you didn't know that, and searched on the editor's name, you would get a large number of stories in major, respected outlets that condemn the site.[35] Poynter.org, which follows news stories about fake news, noted in July of 2018 that fact-checkers had debunked stories from Yournewswire at least 80 times and its posts were fact-checked as false through Facebook's fact-checking partnership at least 45 times.[36]

Another useful site is Newslit.org. This site not only examines some fake news stories, distorted rumors, memes, false claims, and faked photos and videos, but also works to give readers the tools to check out stories themselves, including information about sites that frequently publish false news. If you are going to check out a site about which you know nothing, and not much information is given on the site itself, Newslit suggests you use a tool called IP Whois, which provides registry information about websites. It will tell you who registered the website and where it is registered if you look up the domain name (the address where you found it on the internet). If IP Whois tells you the location is Veles, Macedonia, and you look that location up on the web, you would find that it is a hub of false news. For good measure, Newslit suggests you use Google Street View to look at the street address given for the website. There might not be such a street address, or it may be a factory or superstore.

The Authors

Besides the websites, you can also check out the authors of the articles or posts you are examining. Some have better reputations than others for scrupulous research and writing. Sometimes just a name search on Google or some other search engine will tell you what you need to know. Wikipedia can also be useful, as can the fact-checkers.

For example, John Solomon was a writer for years, with major stories against prominent Democrats. Media Matters for America tracked a number of his stories and explained what facts he started with, and how he distorted them.[37]

Solomon's writing became salient to the public when he promoted a conspiracy theory in *The Hill*, an online newspaper covering Washington, reportedly fed to him by Rudy Giuliani, President Trump's personal attorney, claiming that the Democrats not the Republicans colluded with a foreign power to influence the 2016 election. Further, he argued that former Vice President Joe Biden had worked hard to quash an investigation into his son's involvement with a Ukrainian gas company. There was no evidence for either claim. With such a history of distortions and anti-democratic bias, one should probably read or listen to his claims skeptically.

A biography might tell you where an author works, and where he or she has worked before. Sometimes those details give clues as to the author's perspective. If the author is working for an oil company and is writing against renewable resources, you would want to examine carefully the arguments posed. If the author is working for an organization known for defending the poor, you can probably figure out where bias might occur in the material you are examining. If the person formerly worked in a think tank or advocacy group on the left or the right, that is also a clue to treat a claim or argument with care.

Finding that the author has a marked point of view is not a guarantee that the material presented is false, but it does suggest where bias might creep in. If all the articles by a given author tend in one direction, with no offsetting articles or arguments that indicate a more nuanced view of a policy area, you should be able to see the goal of the author, even if the goal is not plainly stated.

For example, Ted Dabrowski is the founder of Wirepoints, a moderately right-wing online publication that opposes public worker pensions and health benefits, monitors outmigration from the state, blaming high taxes, and opposes a graduated income tax. Dabrowski formerly worked at the Illinois Policy Institute, which promoted many of the same issues.

Dabrowski and coauthor John Klingner argued

> Lightfoot [Chicago's mayor] should realize the debt burden on Chicagoans has already reached absurd levels. A Wirepoints analysis based on Moody's pension calculations shows Chicago households are each on the hook for $145,000 in combined local and state retirement debts. And that's the rosy scenario. Exclude the Chicagoans

that don't have the means to help pay down those debts and that per household amount jumps to an impossible $400,000 each.[38]

What is wrong with that analysis? First, one should be suspicious of any false dichotomy, in this case Dabrowski's solution, which is cut the pensions or accept a tax increase. Given this framing of the problem, cutting the pensions sounds like a more palatable option. There are many other options besides Dabrowski's favorite, but he has ruled them off the table. Second, Dabrowski has exaggerated the pension obligation in order to make his preferred solution seem urgent and inevitable.

Usually, economists measure the debt burden by dividing debt totals by total population to get debt per capita (per person). Dabrowski divided total pension debt by the number of households, instead of the total number of people. Since there are fewer households than there are people living in a state, the same amount of debt divided by fewer households is a bigger number. That Dabrowski was trying to make the debt look as large as possible is even clearer when he excluded poor households, saying they can't afford to pay. The same amount of debt spread over even fewer households yields an even bigger number. The exaggeration, as outlined in Chapter 2, should make you suspicious.

If you look further, his numbers bear little resemblance to reality. The business magazine *Forbes* reported on a Truth in Accounting study about cities' debt levels.[39] Truth in Accounting is a non-profit, one of whose aims is to attack and reduce public debt. It is not a left wing or labor-backed group with a goal of countering Wirepoint's arguments. Even so, their numbers thoroughly challenge the credibility of Ted Dabrowski.

Truth in Accounting reported that the debt per federal taxpayer in Chicago (close to the number of non-poor households used by Dabrowski) was $36,000; and of that 69 percent was due to pension debt, or $24,000. Even that is a high estimate, because it includes not only pensions, but also other post-employment benefits such as health insurance. So, the real figure for pension debt per federal taxpayer in Chicago (poor people don't pay federal taxes) is considerably less than $24,000.

To get to a higher figure, Dabrowski added all the teachers', the county's, and some of the state's post-retirement benefits. All that added together still would not get you to Dabrowski's figure of $145,000 per Chicago household. So, Dabrowski added something else. He adopted Moody's uniform discount rate, a figure Moody's uses to compare pension burdens across cities and states, making them seem uniform, although in reality it is possible that none of the cities or states use that particular estimate of interest rate return on investment. By using a lower estimated rate of return on investment, Dabrowski increased the official estimates of unfunded retirement benefits from $94.1 billion to $150.3 billion, and from $89,960 per household to $143,623 per household.

Dabrowski increased the numerator of total pension debt, and decreased the denominator, from individuals to households, making the amount of pension debt seem as large as possible. Each alteration seemed reasonable, but each of his choices all exaggerated the figure, to make it seem absolutely necessary to reduce pensions of existing retirees. This kind of exaggeration should make you skeptical of all of Dabrowski's analyses. There may be some truth to them, but then again, maybe not.

Dabrowski's themes and methods sound reasonable, until you look at them in more detail, but some authors don't care about sounding reasonable. One author has earned the title Godfather of Fake News: Christopher Blair. Though Blair describes his posts as satire, they are often picked up and repeated as fact, no matter how absurd they sound. He makes up stuff, including constitutional amendments and stories like "Clinton Foundation Ship Seized at Port of Baltimore Carrying Drugs, Guns and Sex Slaves." Anything written by Blair, under any of his pseudonyms, is likely to have nothing in common with the truth.[40] Other names Blair writes under include Ezekiel Wilekenmeyer, Christopher Lyman, Stryker, and Busta Troll. His identity was traced by PolitiFact.[41]

Punditfact, associated with Politifact, tracks the truth value of stories by or about people called pundits, people who offer opinions and analyses on politics and policies on radio, TV, or on blogs, that is, media personalities. Unlike many other fact-checking sites, Punditfact doesn't track elected officials or candidates for office (www.politifact.com/punditfact/). You can click on the name of the media personality and get back a series of statements by the person, all fact-checked. You can search the site by people, by television network, such as CNN, Fox News, or CBS, by radio, or by newspaper. If the pundit you are looking at has a whole long list of claims rated false, mostly false, or "pants on fire," you know that if you encounter that author again in another story, you should be highly skeptical.

Magazines, Journals, and Books

Not all sources of biased or false stories are on the web, television, or radio. Some of them are published in journals and magazines or printed in books. The fact-checkers listed above are generally less useful here, but a few simple clues may help you decide on the level of reliability of the source. The more reputable journals and book publishers have their own version of fact-checking, called blind peer review. When a manuscript is submitted to a book or journal publisher, the publisher sends the manuscript out for review to several experts in the field who are not told who submitted the manuscript (hence the term "blind"). Reviewers read the manuscript, critique it, and make recommendations to publish, revise, or reject it. Presumably if there is something radically wrong with it, if it is poorly written, if the study is poorly designed, or the article lacks evidence, the reviewers will catch these flaws. Reviewers do not always catch mistakes, lies, or distortions, but they do catch them more often than publishers who do not use a blind review process, or that lack fact-checking procedures.

Some journals and book publishers are just printing companies, where authors pay to have their material printed. In these cases, the companies have no interest in examining and rejecting manuscripts, as they get paid only for the ones they accept and print. Some authors want to see their material in print and are willing to pay for printing. The companies that print for a fee are sometimes called "vanity presses" for this reason. Another similar type of company is called a subsidy press, because the authors subsidize the expense of printing. The company doesn't expect to make back all its printing costs through sales. Some of the authors have written books or articles that would not pass a review process but want the legitimacy of a printed book that looks like one that has passed the review process. They may need publications as a credential for a job or may wish to circulate a book or article that expounds their opinions or theories. These days, authors can also self-publish on the web.

Wikipedia has a list of vanity presses, companies that print on demand, and those that aid self-publishing.[42] Another list of vanity presses is Beall's list.[43] You also can check the submission requirements for the publisher to see whether the authors need to pay for publication and what kind of review process is involved. Generally, material that is published by vanity or subsidy presses or journals is less reliable than that published by traditional publishing houses.

Tutorials for Fact-checking

If a fact-checker has looked into the issue you are examining, that may be all the information you need. But you may encounter some story or advertisement that fact-checkers have not dealt with. And you may encounter stories whose origins or authors are unclear. If you want to hone your own skills and pick up some professional tips, you can take some of the tutorials at firstdraftnews.com. This website is aimed primarily at professional journalists to protect news sites from picking up and repeating false news. It lists ways to find out who posted a story or video, or where and when the contents of a video were shot. It lists many useful apps and makes recommendations about the order in which to check out a story. You may not need anything so detailed, but it is good to know that if you do, First Draft is there to help, with easy-to-follow instructions and helpful suggestions.

Conclusion

Advocacy for one point of view or another is not evidence of misleading material, but the case for skepticism is strengthened if a website or an author has a reputation for biased or false material. Fact-checkers can be useful when it comes to an individual story or claim or evaluating a site or an author. Sometimes the problem will be obvious, as when a website is imitating a more reliable site and doing a sloppy job of it, but even if the site is real, you can do a number of checks yourself to test for bias and for false or distorted information. The following chapters give you some ideas of how to do it.

Notes

1. Dan Macguill, "Did Trump Vow to 'Terminate' Social Security?," *Snopes*, August 10, 2020, www.snopes.com/fact-check/trump-terminate-social-security/.
2. Carole Fader, "Fact Check: So Who's Checking the Fact-Finders? We Are," *The Florida Times Union*, September 28, 2012, www.jacksonville.com/article/20120928/NEWS/801246493.
3. Jon Greenberg, "Kamala Harris' Flawed Social Security, Medicare Attack on Donald Trump," *Politifact*, August 13, 2020, www.politifact.com/factchecks/2020/aug/13/kamala-harris/kamala-harris-flawed-social-security-medicare-atta/#sources.
4. Sophie Austin, "Donald Trump Falsely Says Democrats Don't Want to Protect People from Evictions," *Politifact*, August 13, 2020, www.politifact.com/factchecks/2020/aug/13/donald-trump/donald-trump-falsely-says-democrats-dont-want-prot/#sources.
5. Talk of the Nation, "Political Fact-Checking under Fire," *NPR*, January 10, 2012, www.npr.org/2012/01/10/144974110/political-fact-checking-under-fire.
6. Glenn Kessler, "Joe Biden's Worst-Ever Campaign Moment, Revisited," July 27, 2020, www.washingtonpost.com/politics/2020/07/27/joe-bidens-worst-campaign-moment-revisited/.
7. Kalev Leetaru, "FactCheck Review, Fact-Checkers Rely Heavily on Media Reports for 'Truth,'" *RealClearPolitics*, September 12, 2019, www.realclearpolitics.com/articles/2019/09/12/fact-checkers_rely_heavily_on_media_reports_for_truth_141239.html.
8. Media Bias/Fact Check, https://mediabiasfactcheck.com/zebra-fact-check/.
9. https://leadstories.com/hoax-alert/2020/09/fact-check-military-ballots-not-found-in-pennsylvania-ditch.html.
10. D'Angelo Gore, "The Viral Spiral of 2018," *Factcheck.org*, December 20, 2018, www.factcheck.org/2018/12/the-viral-spiral-of-2018/.
11. Ibid.
12. Glenn Kessler, "Not Enough Pinocchios for Trump's CrowdStrike Obsession," *The Washington Post*, December 2, 2019, www.washingtonpost.com/politics/2019/12/02/not-enough-pinocchios-trumps-crowdstrike/obsession/?utm_campaign=post_most&utm_medium=Email&utm_source=Newsletter&wpisrc=nl_most&wpmm=1.
13. Salvador Rizzo, "Schiff's Claim That the Whistleblower Has a 'Statutory Right' to Anonymity, Washington Post Fact Checker," *The Washington Post*, November 20, 2019.
14. Glenn Kessler, "Warren's Misleading Pitch for Her Tax on Billionaires, Washington Post Fact Checker," *The Washington Post*, November 15, 2019.
15. Elyse Samuels, "President Trump's Misleading Spin on the Border Crisis, Washington Post Fact Checker," *The Washington Post*, November 13, 2019.
16. Meg Kelly, "Anti-Impeachment Ad Twists Ocasio-Cortez's Words, Washington Post Fact Checker," *The Washington Post*, November 22, 2019.
17. Beatrice Dupuy and Arijeta Lajka, "NOT REAL NEWS: A Look at What Didn't Happen This Week," *AP*, November 22, 2019, https://apnews.com/a648719297cc4028be72c16e6a375dcb.
18. Daniel Funke, "No Evidence Israel Hit Beirut with a Nuclear Missile," *Politifact*, August 5, 2020.

19 Bill McCarthy, "Steve Scalise Says Ady Barkan Asked Joe Biden, Do We Agree That We Can Redirect Some of the Funding for Police?," *Politifact*, August 31, 2020, www.politifact.com/factchecks/2020/aug/31/steve-scalise/house-republicans-video-manipulates-activists-comp/.
20 All Things Considered, "Why a Company in the Netherlands Has Stopped Helping Facebook Fact-Check Content," *NPR Fact Check*, November 29, 2019, www.npr.org/2019/11/29/783762453/why-a-company-in-the-netherlands-has-stopped-helping-facebook-fact-check-content.
21 Kim LaCapria, "Are Private Prisons Suing States for Millions of Contract Quotas?," *TruthorFiction*, December 2, 2019, www.truthorfiction.com/are-private-prisons-suing-states-for-millions-of-contract-quotas/.
22 www.ifcncodeofprinciples.poynter.org/signatories.
23 www.animalpolitico.com/elsabueso/onu-no-entrego-dos-medallas-a-lopez-obrador/.
24 www.aap.com.au/category/factcheck/.
25 https://theconversation.com/us/topics/factcheck-6544.
26 https://demagog.cz/.
27 Fullfact.org.
28 https://en.wikipedia.org/wiki/List_of_fake_news_websites.
29 mediabiasfactcheck.com.
30 Julie Mastrine, "Media Bias Alert: Coverage of Don Cherry's Firing Differs on Left and Right," November 13, 2019, www.allsides.com/blog/media-bias-alert-don-cherry-fired-over-comments-about-honoring-military-veterans.
31 Elisha Fieldstadt, "Don't Get Fooled by These Fake News Sites," *CBS News*, December 2, 2016, www.cbsnews.com/pictures/dont-get-fooled-by-these-fake-news-sites/.
32 http://d279m997dpfwgl.cloudfront.net/wp/2016/11/Resource-False-Misleading-Clickbait-y-and-Satirical-%E2%80%9CNews%E2%80%9D-Sources-1.pdf.
33 https://docs.google.com/document/d/10eA5-mCZLSS4MQY5QGb5ewC3VAL6pLkT53V_81ZyitM/preview.
34 Gabby Deutch, "A Website Wanted to Restore Trust in the Media. It's Actually a Political Operation," *The Washington Post*, February 6, 2020, www.washingtonpost.com/opinions/2020/02/06/is-it-local-journalism-or-just-local-propaganda/.
35 www.truthorfiction.com/identifying-fake-news-series-contact-us/.
36 Daniel Funke, "Fact-Checkers Have Debunked This Fake News Site 80 Times. It's Still Publishing on Facebook," *Poynter*, July 20, 2018, www.poynter.org/fact-checking/2018/fact-checkers-have-debunked-this-fake-news-site-80-times-its-still-publishing-on-facebook/.
37 Josh Kalven, "In Follow-Up Article on Reid, AP's Solomon Continued Pattern of Distortion," *Media Matters for America*, June 2, 2006, www.mediamatters.org/john-solomon/follow-article-reid-aps-solomon-continued-pattern-distortion.
38 Ted Dabrowski and John Klingner, "Why Chicago's Lightfoot Should Push for a Pension Amendment, Not Tax Hikes," *Wirepoints Special Report*, August 29, 2019, https://wirepoints.org/why-chicagos-lightfoot-should-push-for-a-pension-amendment-not-tax-hikes-wirepoints-special-report/.
39 Elizabeth Bauer, "Is Your City Safe from Pension Debt?," *Forbes*, January 29, 2019, www.forbes.com/sites/ebauer/2019/01/29/is-your-city-safe-from-pension-debt/#d6b5a5629a27.
40 Anisa Subedar, "The Godfather of Fake News," *BBC*, www.bbc.co.uk/news/resources/idt-sh/the_godfather_of_fake_news.
41 Joshua Gillin, "If You Are Fooled by Fake News, This Man Probably Wrote it," *PolitiFact*, May 31, 2019, www.politifact.com/punditfact/article/2017/may/31/If-youre-fooled-by-fake-news-this-man-probably-wro/.
42 List of self-publishing companies, https://en.wikipedia.org/wiki/List_of_self-publishing_companies.
43 https://beallslist.weebly.com/vanity-press.html.

4
ANALYSIS
Logic and Completeness

If you have looked at the fact-checkers and checked out the source and still do not know whether to accept an argument, the next step is to do your own analysis. In this chapter we concentrate on the logic and completeness of the argument. Different approaches to analysis are treated in later chapters.

Looking for Patterns of Illogic

Some forms of illogic are common and easy to detect.

It Could Be True, Therefore It Is True

If you can fit the argument into the form of "it could be true, therefore it is true" you should probably not trust it. Many things *can* happen that *don't* actually happen.

For example, if you became curious about the argument put forth by 9/11 deniers claiming that the Twin Towers were taken down in an explosion planted by a group inside the intelligence community, not by militant Muslims, you could examine the logic these deniers used. They argue it could have happened the way they claim and insist therefore it did happen that way.

It Sounds Reasonable, It Must Be True

A related form of illogic is that an argument sounds reasonable, therefore it must be true. The *Chicago Sun Times* summarized a story: "Just how many criminals are taking advantage of the pandemic to commit crimes is impossible to estimate, but law enforcement officials have no doubt that the numbers are climbing." The law enforcement officials with whom journalists spoke had no doubt about the numbers because it seemed reasonable to them that criminals wearing masks like everyone else would take advantage of the pandemic. Their argument fit the form: it seemed reasonable, so it must be true.[1]

This kind of illogic should make you curious about what we know about crime trends during the pandemic. A report updated August 14, 2020 found that crime rates overall were declining in major U.S. cities. Residential burglaries declined, while commercial burglaries increased, but most relevant to the story, aggravated assaults and robberies declined. It looks like criminals increased the frequency of going into now unoccupied commercial buildings to take something or other, but less often wore masks and entered occupied buildings using force or a threat of force to demand money or valuables from those present. The predicted increase in masked robberies did not happen.[2] According to FBI data, bank robberies decreased dramatically from 2019 to 2020, while burglaries, which are break-ins without confronting individuals with threats of violence, increased over the same time period.[3] Later, as the pandemic continued, car thefts increased, which presumably has nothing to do with masks.[4]

The Conclusion Doesn't Follow from the Evidence

Another common form of illogic is building a case and drawing a conclusion from it that doesn't follow from the case.

Attorney General William Barr wrote a summary of the Mueller report on the president's Russian involvement, a summary that was considered by many, including Special Counsel Robert Mueller, as biased in the president's favor. Commentator Rich Lowry defended the attorney general: "Let's be clear. If Barr wanted to cover for Trump, he could have crimped the Mueller probe, sat on the report, or redacted it into meaninglessness. He did none of the above." Therefore, we were to conclude, Barr did nothing wrong. Wait a minute. The charge was that Barr chose to defend the president by issuing a biased summary of the Mueller report, a charge which Lowry didn't address. That Barr did not choose tactic A or tactic B does not mean that he didn't choose tactic C to defend Trump. Lowry's argument was illogical; his conclusion didn't follow from the evidence he provided.[5]

Another illustration of jumping to conclusions occurred recently when political opponents of Governor Pritzker of Illinois sought to blame him for benefiting financially from his policies with regard to the coronavirus. These opponents discovered that in 2016 an investment company owned by the Pritzker family invested in a medical testing company. In March 2020, that testing company added covid-19 testing, so opponents of the governor concluded that the governor was benefiting financially from his policies concerning the virus.

The evidence did not support that conclusion. The governor did not benefit financially from his policies concerning the virus. The state did not grant the testing company any contracts. In fact, the company, Pathgroup, did no business in Illinois at all; whatever the governor's policies toward the virus in the state, they could not affect the profits of Pathgroup. The governor's detractors didn't check; they jumped to a conclusion not justified by the evidence.[6]

It Worked Well in the Past, So It Must Be Good Now

A different form of argument that you may encounter is that something worked well or was good in the past, so it must be good now or will be good in the future. Alex Epstein is a defender of fossil fuels. He has argued that fossil fuels have made our lives better over generations, so we should stop blaming them for global warming, and instead praise them for all the good they have done. The illogic here is that they were good in the past, therefore they must be good now. As one reviewer of his book pointed out, it is as if one justified a marriage gone bad because the first few months were wonderful.[7]

After This, Therefore Because of This

A common form of illogic has a Latin name, suggesting it has been around for a very long time—post hoc ergo propter hoc, which means after this, therefore because of this. But if one thing happens and then something else happens afterward, it doesn't mean that the first thing necessarily caused the second thing. Many things could have preceded and caused the outcome.

One of the early objectors to vaccines had lost a child after an inoculation. She was sure that the inoculation was the cause of her child's death—the death occurred after the inoculation, so the inoculation must have been the cause. There are many things which can cause a child to die, and an inoculation is an unlikely cause. If I got a toothache after I drove home, it doesn't mean that driving home caused the toothache.

Trump uses this pattern of argumentation frequently when he takes credit. Credit taking in general should make you curious about the truth value of the claim. One of Trump's arguments is of the form, "I was elected, the economy improved, therefore I improved the economy." In reality, the economy had been improving before he was elected and continued to grow during his administration until the coronavirus pandemic hit.

When you encounter an argument that says this occurred before that, so it must have caused that, you should look for evidence of a causal link before you accept the argument. How did the first event cause the second event, what is the mechanism?

False Equivalence Arguments

As you become alert to illogical arguments, you will probably find many examples of false equivalence. False equivalence means that you treat two arguments as having similar weight although one has much stronger evidence than the other.⁸

Isaac Asimov in his essay "The Relativity of Wrong," wrote,

> When people thought the earth was flat, they were wrong. When people thought the Earth was spherical they were wrong. But if you think that thinking the Earth is spherical is just as wrong as thinking the Earth is flat, then your view is wronger than both of them put together.⁹

In other words, the two errors are not equivalent to each other, one is much more wrong than the other. The earth is much closer to being spherical than to being flat. There are degrees of right and wrong, and conflating little wrongs with big ones is a problem that signals that the argument might not be credible.

Giving equal weight to arguments pro- and anti-global warming is an illustration of pretending that two arguments are of equal weight, have equal force, logic, and evidence behind them, when one perspective is supported by few people based on distorted evidence, and the other is mainstream, supported by the vast majority of scientists and lots of convincing evidence.

In another illustration of false equivalence, Trump threatened to designate the anti-fascist group, Antifa, as a terrorist organization. He described the group's members on Twitter as "gutless Radical Left Wack Jobs" and compared them to the international criminal gang MS-13.¹⁰

The name calling should alert you to a potentially problematic argument. If you look for information about MS-13 and Antifa, you will find that MS-13 is a ruthless, murdering gang, while Antifa attacks have primarily been with milk shakes, eggs, and silly string. Through July 2020, the *Guardian* reported that Antifa had been linked to zero murders in 25 years in the U.S.¹¹ In September of 2020 one self-identified Antifa supporter was suspected of killing a right-wing counterdemonstrator and was shot dead by federal officers within days. Trump created a false equivalence, treating as similar a relatively moderate protest group and a group of violent murderers.

Returning briefly to a topic covered in Chapter 3, the credibility and bias of fact-checkers, Democrats have charged the *Washington Post* fact-checkers with false equivalence. The *Washington Post* fact-checkers gave three Pinocchios to Trump's claim that he had already built a large section of wall along the Mexican border, a false claim he made many times. The *Post* fact-checker also gave three Pinocchios to Bernie Sander's claim that 500,000 people would declare bankruptcy that year because of medical bills.

Those two cases were not equivalent, though each earned three Pinocchios. Sander's claim was slightly overstated; the medical bills in some cases might be only a contributing cause of bankruptcy, not the major cause. Trump's repeated claim that he had already built large sections of the border wall was untrue, because most of what he claimed as new wall was only a limited amount of replacement fencing. Both claims were flawed, but not equally so.[12]

Not all incorrect statements are equally untrue. When they are treated as if they were, you should be on your guard and look further into the claims.

Looking for What Is Missing

It can take some creative thinking to figure out what may have been left out of an argument. You don't need to have all the answers to begin with; you only need to think about what could be missing that might disprove or weaken the case being made. Once you have the questions in mind, you can do the fact-checking yourself; much of the material is online, but it is easier to look first to the professional fact-checkers.

Whose Policy Was It?

During the debates among democratic candidates for president in 2019, Tulsi Gabbard attacked Kamala Harris on her record as the attorney general in California. Gabbard blamed Harris for keeping prisoners incarcerated too long in order to be able to use them to fight fires.[13]

The argument was that Harris's office sought to keep the inmates locked up rather than free them early because they were needed to fight fires. But did the state actually hold prisoners too long in order to use them as firefighters, and if so, whose policy was it? Did Harris know about it at the time, and did she agree with it, either then, or later?

A court had mandated early releases for minimum security prisoners to reduce overcrowding. In 2014, lawyers under Harris's supervision opposed early release in a petition to the court because the prisoners who volunteered for firefighting were needed for that work. The court denied the request.[14]

Harris told Buzzfeed news in 2014 that she was shocked by the argument her staff had put forward. She later elaborated that she had looked into it and instructed her staff not to make that argument again. So, the requested permission to deny early release was never granted, the policy that Gabbard was criticizing was never implemented, and it was not clear that Harris had ever approved the argument against early release.[15]

The Trend

Tulsi Gabbard also complained that there were thousands of people jailed for marijuana on Harris's watch. The complaint was true but misleading, because the data showed the numbers dropping over time to a very low level. What was missing in this case was the trend. Had that been included, the critics would have concluded that Harris was not trying to arrest lots of people for marijuana offenses.[16]

Evidence

What is often missing is evidence to back up a claim. A common meme says that immigrants are swarming into the country and will overwhelm us culturally, financially, and economically. They are all from Mexico or Central America, with few skills and low education, and are often criminals. The negative stereotypes should alert you to an argument that needs further investigation. What is the evidence for such charges against immigrants?

Finding the evidence, once you have the question, is easy in this case. The AP news service looked into some of the issues in 2019.

They looked at the number of immigrants as a percent of the U.S. population over time and found it very small—around .3 of one percent. They found that the numbers coming into the country were about average over time, not particularly high or particularly low. Immigrants are a larger proportion of the population now than in 1970, but the reason is that native-born people are having fewer children, not that there are more immigrants.

The second claim is an economic one, that immigrants take jobs away from the native born, and because they work for less money, they bring down wages. The threat of competition for jobs and displacement of the native born is more likely at the bottom of the economic ladder, where the low-skilled jobs are taken by those with little education and one person can easily substitute for another. However, immigrants with little education tend to have different skills and take different low-skill jobs than non-immigrants. Further, the number of jobs for people with low levels of education is increasing as our population ages. Research cited by the AP fact-checkers notes little if any drop in wages for the native born during and after an influx of immigrants.

The AP fact-checker questioned whether immigrants created a financial burden on government services. First-generation immigrants may cost the government more than they pay in taxes, but for second- and third-generation immigrants—that is the children and grandchildren of immigrants—the ratio is reversed; they pay more in taxes than they draw in services.

Critically, the AP cites research on immigrants and crime that indicates a drop in violent crime with immigration rather than an increase.[17]

Other sources confirm a lack of correlation between undocumented immigrants and crime. At least until the pandemic, violent crime remained relatively flat since 2007, regardless of whether the number of undocumented immigrants rose or fell. A majority of areas actually experienced a decline in violent and property crimes between 2007 and 2016. Areas with more undocumented people experienced a slightly larger decline than those with fewer. A rise in crime beginning before and increasing during the pandemic occurred during a decline in immigration, both documented and undocumented.[18] Much of the violent crime was committed with legally purchased guns; undocumented immigrants are not allowed to purchase guns legally.

One could argue that undocumented residents would be less likely to report crimes against themselves, but if they were the perpetrators against native-born residents, the native born and their families would have no such constraints. Crimes against the native born are not increasing because of increases in undocumented residents.

So, what was missing in this case was evidence to back up the variety of claims.

Other Cases

A common problem in essays intended to persuade is that they select cases to make their point, (cherry picking) rather than to discover some truth. What is often missing is a selection of other appropriate cases.

The omission of relevant cases is apparent in efforts to provide evidence for the shibboleth that lower taxes stimulate economic growth. The right-wing website, wirepoints.org, published an article contrasting the job growth of low-tax Michigan with that of high-tax Illinois. The author concluded that Michigan was doing much better than Illinois in terms of job growth and recovery from the great recession of 2008–2010 because of its lower taxes.

The argument looks reasonable, and the sources of data are standard. The conclusion drawn from the data presented also seems sound. One thing that was missing was an explanation of why these two states were chosen for comparison, suggesting that the authors may have cherry picked these two states because they seemed to make the authors' case.

If you pick different nearby states to make the comparison, sometimes the state with a higher corporate tax rate has a *higher* rate of growth. Wisconsin has a higher corporate rate than Michigan, 7.9 percent compared to Michigan's 6.0 percent, but the number of jobs grew in Wisconsin at 1.6 percent between 2018 and 2019, while in Michigan the rate of year-to-year growth was 1.38.

Advocates on the left chose a different state to compare to Wisconsin. Minnesota has higher corporate tax rates than Wisconsin (9.8 percent vs 7.9 percent) and has outgrown the lower tax state since the great recession that began in 2008. Minnesota has had faster population growth, the rate of increase in number of non-farm jobs has outstripped Wisconsin, and median family income has grown more rapidly in Minnesota. Minnesota and Wisconsin are comparable in many ways but differ in politics.[19]

Depending on what states you select for comparisons the results are likely to be different, even opposite, so that conclusions are less clear than the WIREPOINTS essay suggests.[20]

What was omitted in WIREPOINTS's study was not only a rationale for choosing the particular two states for comparison and not others, but also other factors that might influence economic growth. The variety of outcomes when making other state comparisons suggests that factors other than or in addition to tax rates are influencing the rate of economic growth.

A Test Case

In an unbiased study, one where the researchers want to know what is true rather than want to find evidence to support a particular point of view, the design often concludes with a test case. If what the authors think is going on is actually happening, it should definitely occur in this test case. Representative Todd Akin, in his argument for including victims of rape and incest in a prohibition of abortion, omitted this crucial step.

Representative Akin, while running for Senate, replied to the question whether he believed that abortion is justified in cases of rape. "It seems to be, first of all, from what I understand from doctors, it's really rare. If it's a legitimate rape, the female body has ways to try to shut the whole thing down."[21]

What might alert you to the possibility that his argument might not be true? The first clue is that Akin is arguing from authority, and a very vague one at that. "Doctors." Which doctors are those? What did they say, what evidence did they present? When did they say it? In what context? This argument from authority is so vague it cannot be examined or evaluated. Vague arguments from authority should raise suspicion.

The second problematic element of the argument is that it attacks the credibility of women who reveal that they conceived during a rape. By using the term "legitimate rape" (a color word), Akin implies that women who conceive often falsely claim to have been raped to cover up for a voluntary consensual sexual liaison. Legitimate rape, that is, real, forcible rape, seldom produces offspring, he argues. Denying the legitimacy of the claimant (ad hominem or in this case ad feminam argument) does not deal with the argument, doesn't require evidence, or counterevidence, it just says, I don't believe you, you are not credible. If you had a baby, then it wasn't real rape.

The fact-checking sites didn't pay much attention to Akin's claim. There was one major exception, though. Politifact checked out U.S. Representative Phil Gingrey's statement that he half agreed with Akin's original claim. Politifact came down on the side of disagreeing that women can shut down reproduction during a rape. There was no evidence that Akin's claim was true.[22]

Lack of evidence to support a position is suspicious, one might stop there, and say, hey, if there is no evidence for this argument, I am not going to accept it. But you can go further and look for a test case. If there are documented cases of forcible rape resulting in pregnancy, that would prove

Akin wrong. One way of checking whether "genuine" or violent rape can produce offspring is to examine the cases of women sexually abused during years of war where such terror tactics were used.

Colombia

Rape was often used in Colombia during the long years of warfare between the Revolutionary Armed Forces of Colombia and the Colombian government.[23] Official Colombian records after the war list 28,096 victims of sexual violence due to the war, of whom 1481 have received court judgments under the agreements ending the war. Many more women have not applied for either symbolic acknowledgment or actual financial settlements, some out of shame or because they have not revealed to their children who their father was and fear the consequences of doing so, or because the memory of what happened remains so painful. In some cases, fear of retribution renders them helpless. Advocates estimate the number of women who bore children from war-related rape number in the thousands. Some of the women who bore children as a result of these rapes have come forward to advocate for themselves and their children.

Rwanda

Jonathan Torgovnik has documented the lives of the children born of rape in Rwanda, 12 years and then 25 years later. The children have been stigmatized; their mothers would have no motive to acknowledge rape in that social setting, and yet have told their children that they were conceived in rape by the enemy. Many individual women and their children told their stories, as reported in the *New York Times*.[24]

During Rwanda's genocide, many women were raped, some were murdered, some survived and contracted AIDS, and of the survivors, a number conceived and had children who are now adults, talking to the journalist. Estimates of the number of children born of those rapes are in the thousands—some estimates have been as high as 20,000. The U.N. estimated 250,000 women were raped.[25]

Bosnia

In Bosnia, the results of rape in war also produced offspring. Some women and their children later identified the fathers, who confessed in court after DNA tests proved their paternity. There was rape, the women conceived, and a child was born.[26]

So, can women conceive from rape? Yes, they can. What was missing from Akin's argument besides credible evidence of a mechanism that would prevent conception during rape was a search for cases of non-consensual rape that might disprove his argument. The logic, or illogic, of his argument prevented such a search, but a sensitive reader could see what was missing and go looking for it.

The Rest of the Costs

The Defense Department boasted to the public that it had gotten the costs of the now notoriously expensive F-35 aircraft down to below $80 million per plane. The DoD was engaged in credit claiming, as well as deflecting attention from the really expensive F-35s. But if you look at the Defense Department's budget, the below $80 million figure represents only a fraction of the actual costs of each aircraft. It includes only the airframe and the engine. It omits replacement parts, development costs, training simulators, and maintenance costs. Of several different models, the price applies only to the least expensive one. Moreover, the price does not include the future development of some features not yet included in the plane. The Pentagon's own figures, which are still not inclusive, list $101 million per aircraft for the initial purchases in 2020. A similar aircraft for the Navy is listed at $123 million per aircraft, and a more expensive model is listed at $166 million per aircraft.[27]

The Next (Follow-up) Question

What is often missing from a story is a follow-up question that gets deeper into the material. For example, President Donald Trump claimed that "58,000 non-citizens voted in Texas, with 95,000 non-citizens registered to vote." Factcheck.org called this claim "misinformation." Out of all the investigations of voter fraud being used to limit the electorate and prevent people from voting, none of them has turned up evidence of substantial voter fraud, so, on its face, this charge is unlikely to be true.

When a story charges that a given number of non-citizens have voted illegally, you might ask, what is the evidence for that. The next logical question should be, is that number big or small? Out of how many total voters, over what period of time? Then you might want to ask, why were these non-citizens not turned down when they tried to register to vote?

For example, "In an audit of the 2016 elections, North Carolina investigators caught 41 voters—out of 4.8 million—who cast a ballot despite being a citizen of another country."[28]

In the Texas case that Trump tweeted about, 58,000 possible cases of non-citizens voting should be compared to 15.8 million registered voters in Texas. Also, 58,000 was the cumulative number over 22 years. Thus, the potentially illegal voters represented a really tiny fraction of one percent of registered voters each year.[29]

Without such follow-up questions, though the initial charge is intended to tell the whole story and tell you how to feel about it, the charge is distorted.[30]

Context

If you follow sports, you might have run across the argument that NFL teams located in high-tax states risk losing their star players to lower tax states.

> Mr. Petutschnig's research into team performance over more than two decades shows that National Football League franchises based in high-tax states lost more games on average during the regular season compared to teams in low or no-tax states. That's because of the NFL's salary cap for teams, according to Mr. Petutschnig; if they have to give certain players more money to compensate for higher taxes, it reduces how much they pay other players and lowers the talent level for the whole team.[31]

You don't have to know much about taxes to be suspicious of an argument for low taxes that would mobilize every NFL football fan to your side. It would be too convenient (too good to be true?). If your curiosity was roused, you might then look for the missing context.

On FiveThirtyEight (a website that uses statistics to explain and analyze political polling, sports, science, and economics), Ty Schalter found no correlation between state income tax rates and NFL team *championship* wins. His argument? Context matters. Many players declare residence in locations different from where their team is located; they can live in a low-tax state and play for a high-tax state. A second issue clouding the analysis is that many cities and states tax high-paid athletes who come into their territory to play, and these NFL players play in a variety of locations. So, an athlete could live in a low-tax state and still have to pay taxes in the high-tax state where the team played. Add to that complexity the differences in property taxes by location within and between states for the expensive homes of some of the NFL players, and it becomes difficult to figure out in which state a tax burden would actually be lower.

Equally revealing, not all players are trying to maximize their regular incomes—as opposed to their bonuses for championship play. Winning a championship depends on the excellence of the whole team, not just an individual player. Famous quarterback Tom Brady took less salary than he could have gotten so that the team could afford to pay other excellent players. If he added in bonuses for championship play, he could end up better off than if he chose a lower tax state that won fewer championships.[32]

Petutschnig's initial analysis assumed that choosing the state with the lowest income tax rate was straightforward and would result in the most compensation for a player, but that assumption ignored the complexity of state and local taxation, and the fact that players don't always live in the states where their teams are located. It also ignored championship bonuses. There was a lot of context missing.

The Outcome

President Trump, in a dramatic turn, insisted that he had the power to order the states to end stay-at-home and social distancing orders aimed at curtailing the covid-19 pandemic. He thought he could just order them to resume economic activities. If they refused, he implied they were mutineers, and he was the captain of the ship, and they were dependent on him, so they had better comply. If they persisted against his order, he could shut them down. It is not clear exactly what the threat entailed, but his claims of broad power were very clear.

The use of labels like "mutineers" making state officials sound like criminals should alert you that President Trump might have been exaggerating his powers. Given the federal structure of the constitution which clearly gives limited powers to the central government and the residual powers to the states, his claim seems unlikely to be true.

What is missing in this story is what happened next. The states not only resisted, they formed coalitions of neighboring states to determine when and how they would lift restrictions. President Trump backed off his threatening posture, announcing a policy of allowing the states to determine for themselves when and how to reopen their economies, offering only guidelines for consideration.

If you never asked the follow-up question, what happened next, you might conclude that the president had arrogated the states' constitutional powers to himself.

How Could Anyone Know That?

Those who are trying to persuade you of something often attribute motives to others or tell you what someone else is thinking or plotting. Such arguments are not meaningful unless it is clear how the speaker or writer could possibly know what is going on in someone else's head. Maybe the subject wrote or spoke about his or her intentions; if not, the speaker or writer may be only guessing. Similarly, sometimes an argument is based on statistics that in fact no one collects.

Senator Chris Murphy tweeted that President Trump is deliberately killing people: "his plan is to kill people. Let's just say it." While Murphy had good evidence that President Trump did things like hold rallies without masks and without social distancing, the consequence of which were that people got infected with covid-19, he had no evidence that Trump was deliberately killing people, or that that was Trump's plan.[33] How could he have possibly known what Trump's plan was unless Trump told him, or told someone else who then informed him?

When police "know" that there will be an increase in robberies because everyone wears masks during a pandemic and criminals will take advantage of that, you should ask yourself, how could they know that? It turns out that they didn't know that, they only assumed it.

Speculation about what caused a trip for the president to the hospital focused on a series of ministrokes. The president's former physician, Ronny Jackson, claimed that that could not be true. He tweeted "Here's the truth: As the President's doctor, I knew about this trip WEEKS in advance & it had NOTHING to do with his brain or heart."[34] But the hospital trip took place in November 2019, and Jackson had left the White House in March 2018. He was not the president's physician for many months before the president's hospital trip, so how could he have known about it?

Conclusion

Analyzing logic requires the reader or listener to summarize an argument, to look at the initial claim, the evidence presented, and see if the conclusion follows from that evidence. Arguments such as it used to be good therefore it is good now ignore changing circumstances; arguments of the form it could be true, therefore it is true jump over the evidence. And sometimes the evidence presented doesn't address the initial charge.

In many arguments intended to persuade you, something important is left out, such as evidence or context. Don't be discouraged by the difficulty of finding the answers; what is most important is being able to see what is missing and what would make a stronger case. Finding the missing pieces is often easy and highly satisfying.

Notes

1 Associated Press, "Coronavirus Masks a Boon for Crooks Who Hide Their Faces," *Chicago Sun Times*, May 16, 2020, https://chicago.suntimes.com/crime/2020/5/16/21261008/coronavirus-masks-a-boon-for-crooks-who-hide-their-faces.
2 David S. Abrams, "COVID and Crime: An Early Empirical Look," *Penn Law Legal Scholarship Repository*, November 2, 2020, https://scholarship.law.upenn.edu/faculty_scholarship/2204/.
3 FBI Bank Crime Statistics, https://www.fbi.gov/investigate/violent-crime/bank-robbery/bank-crime-reports
4 Nicole Sganga, "Homicides in major American cities increased in 2021, new study finds", CBS News, January 26, 2022, https://www.cbsnews.com/news/homicides-2021-increase-council-on-criminal-justice/
5 Rich Lowry, "The Absurd Barr Scandal," *Politico Magazine*, May 1, 2019, www.politico.com/magazine/story/2019/05/01/the-absurd-barr-scandal-226788.
6 Matthew Rago, "Pritzker Family Owns Stake in Company Providing COVID-19 Tests," *Northeastern University's Independent*, May 18, 2020, https://neiuindependent.org/16852/news/pritzker-family-owns-stake-in-company-providing-covid-19-tests/.

7. Rob Hopkins, "Review: 'The Moral Case for Fossil Fuels'—Really?," *Our World*, February 5, 2015, https://ourworld.unu.edu/en/review-the-moral-case-for-fossil-fuels-really.
8. Stephanie Sarkis, "This Is Not Equal To That: How False Equivalence Clouds Our Judgment," *Forbes*, May 19, 2019, www.forbes.com/sites/stephaniesarkis/2019/05/19/this-is-not-equal-to-that-how-false-equivalence-clouds-our-judgment/#31c06f785c0f.
9. Isaac Asimov, "The Relativity of Wrong", *The Skeptical Inquirer*, Fall 1989, Vol. 14, No. 1, p. 36.
10. Trump's Twitter posts have been removed, but the linking of Antifa and MS-13 also appears here: Orion Rummler, "Trump Threatens to Classify Antifa as Terrorists," *Axios*, July 27, 2019.
11. Lois Beckett, "Anti-Fascists Linked to Zero Murders in the US in 25 Years," *The Guardian*, July 27, 2020, www.theguardian.com/world/2020/jul/27/us-rightwing-extremists-attacks-deaths-database-leftwing-antifa.
12. Michael Calderone, "Democrats Decry Double Standard in Fact Checking," *Politico*, September 11, 2019, www.politico.com/story/2019/09/11/democrats-fact-checking-1489135.
13. Posted by Ian Schwartz, "Locked Up for Labor, Blocked Evidence That Would Free Man on Death Row," *Real Clear Politics*, July 31, 2019, www.realclearpolitics.com/video/2019/07/31/gabbard_vs_harris_you_kept_prisoners_locked_up_for_labor_blocked_evidence_that_would_free_man_on_death_row.html.
14. David Fathi, "Prisoners Are Getting Paid $1.45 a Day to Fight the California Wildfires," American Civil Liberties Union, Northern California, November 15, 2018, www.aclunc.org/blog/prisoners-are-getting-paid-145-day-fight-california-wildfires.
15. Adam Serwer, "California AG 'Shocked' to Learn Her Office Wanted to Keep Eligible Parolees in Jail to Work," *Buzzfeed*, November 18, 2014, www.buzzfeednews.com/article/adamserwer/some-lawyers-just-want-to-see-the-world-burn.
16. Chris Nichols, "Were Tulsi Gabbard's Attacks on Kamala Harris' Record as a California Prosecutor on Target?," *Politifact*, August 1, 2019, www.politifact.com/california/article/2019/aug/01/were-tulsi-gabbards-attacks-kamala-harris-record-c/.
17. Josh Boak, "AP Fact Check: Trump Taps False Stereotypes about Immigrants," *AP*, February 8, 2019, https://apnews.com/7eb07814117f46a098bed1f3466f4775.
18. Anna Flagg, "Is There a Connection Between Undocumented Immigrants and Crime?," *NYT*, May 13, 2019, www.nytimes.com/2019/05/13/upshot/illegal-immigration-crime-rates-research.html; Stuart Anderson, "Illegal Immigration in America Has Continued to Decline," *Forbes*, March 10, 2021, www.forbes.com/sites/stuartanderson/2021/03/10/illegal-immigration-in-america-has-continued-to-decline/?sh=57faa6b94e14.
19. David Cooper, "As Wisconsin's and Minnesota's Lawmakers Took Divergent Paths, So Did Their Economies," *Economic Policy Institute*, May 8, 2018, www.epi.org/publication/as-wisconsins-and-minnesotas-lawmakers-took-divergent-paths-so-did-their-economies-since-2010-minnesotas-economy-has-performed-far-better-for-working-families-than-wisconsin/.
20. Ted Dabrowski and John Klingner, "A Tale of Two Manufacturing Recoveries: Illinois vs. Michigan," *WIREPOINTS*, August 9, 2019, https://wirepoints.org/a-tale-of-two-manufacturing-recoveries-illinois-vs-michigan/.
21. Lori Moore, "Rep. Todd Akin: The Statement and the Reaction," *New York Times*, August 20, 2012, www.nytimes.com/2012/08/21/us/politics/rep-todd-akin-legitimate-rape-statement-and-reaction.html.
22. Janel Davis and Eric Stirgus, "Gingrey Defense of Akin's Rape Comments Misses the Mark," *Politifact*, January 16, 2013, www.politifact.com/georgia/statements/2013/jan/16/phil-gingrey/gingrey-defense-akins-rape-comments-misses-mark/.
23. Megan Janetsky, "They Were Raped During Colombia's Civil War. Now They Want Justice for Their Children," *Public Radio International*, June 24, 2019, www.pri.org

/stories/2019-06-24/they-were-raped-during-colombia-s-civil-war-now-they-want-justice-their-children.
24. Jonathan Torgovnik, "Rwanda's Children of Rape Have Come of Age," *The New York Times*, March 31, 2019, www.nytimes.com/2019/03/30/opinion/rwandas-children-of-rape-have-come-of-age.html.
25. Kieron Monks, "Rwandan Rape Survivors and Their Children, 25 Years Later," *CNN*, 2019, www.cnn.com/interactive/2019/04/africa/rwandan-daughters-cnnphotos/.
26. PBS NewsHour, "Children of Bosnian Wartime Rape Victims Seek Justice," *PBS WTTW*, July 8, 2018, www.pbs.org/newshour/show/adults-born-from-wartime-assault-in-bosnia-search-for-paths-to-justice.
27. Dan Grazier, "Deceptive Pentagon Math Tries to Obscure $100 Million+ Price Tag for F-35s," POGO (Project On Government Oversight), November 1, 2019, www.pogo.org/analysis/2019/11/deceptive-pentagon-math-tries-to-obscure-100-million-price-tag-for-f-35/.
28. Will Doran, "Fact Check: Are Immigrants Voting Illegally in North Carolina?," *The News and Observer*, November 21, 2019, www.newsobserver.com/news/politics-government/article237507069.html.
29. Anna M. Tinsley, "58,000 Non-U.S. Citizens May Have Voted in at Least One Election Here, Election Official Says," *Fort Worth Star-telegram*, January 25, 2019, www.star-telegram.com/news/state/texas/article225094315.html.
30. Robert Farley, "More Voter Fraud Misinformation from Trump," *Factcheck.org*, January 30, 2019, www.factcheck.org/2019/01/more-voter-fraud-misinformation-from-trump/.
31. Bloomberg, "NFL Teams in High-Tax States Risk Talent Drain," *InvestmentNews*, October 19, 2018, www.investmentnews.com/nfl-teams-in-high-tax-states-risk-talent-drain-76587.
32. Ty Schalter, "Are States With Lower Income Tax Rates Better at Winning Championships?," *FiveThirtyEight*, May 28, 2020, https://fivethirtyeight.com/features/are-states-with-lower-income-tax-rates-better-at-winning-championships/.
33. Tweet, August 29, 2020, https://twitter.com/chrismurphyct/status/1299701890322706432?lang=en.
34. September 1, 2020, https://twitter.com/ronnyjacksontx/status/1300967057433997315?lang=en.

5
ANALYSIS BY COMPARISON

Why Look at Multiple Sides of an Argument?

If something is missing from an argument and you have some questions, the answers are often available on trusted websites or provided by the standard fact-checkers. But sometimes there isn't much neutral analysis. The topics are controversial and there are arguments on both (or multiple) sides. Regardless of which side of the argument you are looking at, you can look for arguments on the other side. This is an easy way to learn about a subject about which you are curious but do not know much. When you look at both sides, you can decide which side presents more convincing arguments or whether parts of each side are supported by good evidence. Sometimes by looking at another side of the argument you can see what is missing from the first side.

How to Find Arguments on the Other Side

Finding arguments on the other side of an issue is usually straightforward. One way is to look for research and summary arguments put forward by think tanks, that is, organizations whose purpose is to carry out research and publicize the findings to influence public opinion and public policy. Such think tanks are typically dedicated to one side or another of key policy issues. Some have broad missions; they are for the poor or for the rich, for Democrats or Republicans, for big or small government. Others focus on narrower issues, such as defending fossil fuel industries or advocating for renewable energy sources. Regardless of their specific focus, they put their studies and position papers up on the web and often make their arguments on mass media. They sometimes feed material to commentators on major networks and volunteer to be interviewed on television and radio.

The *New York Times* compiled a list of prominent think tanks, dividing them into groups such as conservative, liberal, centrist, and libertarian. Though some might quibble with whether one or another is labeled correctly, the *Times*' categories present a good starting point. If the argument you are examining sounds liberal, you can search the conservative think tanks for a possible reply or vice versa. The more centrist think tanks might provide responses to arguments from the left or the right. Liberal think tanks and libertarian ones should carry opposite positions too.

Among the conservative think tanks are the Heritage Foundation, the Manhattan Institute, the Hoover Institute, and the Center for Immigration Studies; among the liberal are the Center on Budget and Policy Priorities, the Economic Policy Institute (EPI), and the Center for American Progress. The centrist list includes Brookings, the Constitution Project, and the Aspen Institute. The best known of the libertarians (libertarians argue for individual freedom and against government regulation) are Cato, Ayn Rand, and the Mercatus Center.[1]

In addition to the think tanks, some academics and a variety of nonprofit advocacy groups also get into the act. There are groups against gun violence, groups that advocate for legalization of drugs, groups that oppose vaccinations, and groups that try to drum up support for the environment. Chances are good that whatever issue you are examining, you will find some group advocating for or against it. These advocates want you to see their arguments; they do not make it difficult for you to find them using an internet search engine. You can put in a term like "arguments about electric cars" or "wage gap between men and women" to locate different sides of the argument.

The websites Allsides and Media Bias/Fact Check, mentioned in Chapter 3, also can be useful in finding multiple sides of an argument. Allsides's section on dialogue and debate focuses on current issues and presents different points of view. They don't weigh the evidence but call attention to the arguments pro and con. Allsides offers current news stories from left-biased sources, right-biased sources, and those in between. In one example, they describe the *New York Times* as left-biased, the *Washington Examiner* as right-biased, and the AP news service as representing the center. As a second example, Allsides lists Town Hall on the right, BBC in the center, and Politico on the left. Media Bias/Fact Check offers an extensive list of news sources, telling whether they are biased left or right, or whether they are not very biased in either direction.

Examples of Looking at Both Sides

This chapter offers some examples of an argument and rebuttal, looking at two sides of an issue, exploring and weighing the evidence for each side.

Example 1. Marijuana Legalization Results in High Crime; No, It Doesn't

Marijuana legalization is one of those highly controversial issues where objective information is hard to come by. Supporters and opponents often seize on a report that says marijuana is dangerous (causes car accidents or harms teenagers' brains) or marijuana is relatively safe and use that single report as if it represented truth—cherry picking. Sometimes those studies are flawed, but to see those flaws, you may have to look to the research of those with the opposite or at least a different point of view.

San Diego's former police chief, Shelley Zimmerman, testified against the expansion of legal marijuana before the city council, arguing that medical marijuana shops in the city had increased crime. She cited data on police calls. On the other side of the issue, an investigation by the *Voice of San Diego*'s Jesse Marx claimed that the former police chief of San Diego had misrepresented the evidence.[2]

Chief Zimmerman had cited data on 272 calls for service for burglaries, robberies, thefts, assaults, and shootings relating to the city's marijuana dispensaries. The *Voice of San Diego* looked at the actual calls. (*Voice of San Diego* is rated by Media Bias/Fact Check as least biased, neither left nor right ideologically.)

More than a quarter of the calls were near dispensaries but had little to do with them. One, for example, was of a woman with a possible stroke who fell in a parking lot, and the address given on the report was of a nearby pain clinic. One was a call about a fuel truck being driven recklessly on the freeway. The caller was near the marijuana dispensary, but the call had nothing to do with the dispensary. Crank calls to 911, false alarms, and even calls for a tow truck were included on the former chief's list. Only about a fifth of the 272 radio calls were even traceable to a dispensary. Among those were complaints about graffiti and vandalism, water leaks, and men being refused service because they couldn't bring a dog inside the shop.

There were only three incidents that involved a report of a gun. One was mistaken, a rock not a bullet had caused some damage. A second report involved a security guard who accidentally shot a gun while cleaning it. In the third, a security guard fired a gun at a group of burglars.

The reader should conclude that the original statistics were greatly exaggerated. In this case, a relatively unbiased source—the *Voice of San Diego*—provided the other side of the argument.

Example 2. Poverty Programs Didn't Work; Poverty Programs Did Too Work

A common conservative argument is that more money should not be spent to alleviate poverty because poverty programs have not worked. Liberals have argued the opposite, that the programs have reduced poverty, and by inference should be continued.

The conservative position was summarized by Michael Tanner, at Fox News (ranked as right-biased by Media Bias/Fact Check).[3] Tanner added up spending for all the federal, state, and local anti-poverty programs for 2012, coming up with a total of almost a trillion dollars. He then compared government statistics of the percent of Americans living under the poverty line in 2015 to the percent living under the poverty line when the program was founded 50 years earlier. He claimed that 19 percent of Americans were under the poverty line in the early period, 15 percent at the time of his writing in 2015. His conclusion was that there was little to show for all those trillions of dollars spent, so the program was a failure.

A counterargument was presented by a member of a centrist think tank, The Brookings Institution.[4] Gary Burtless at Brookings noted that after the passage of the anti-poverty program, poverty rates fell dramatically. The census statistics reported a poverty rate of 22 percent in 1960, dropping to 12 percent in 1980, and rising slowly thereafter to 15 percent by 2015. But, if poverty was measured by consumption rather than income, the poverty rate continued to drop to a remarkably low 3 percent.

You might wonder, why would anyone want to measure poverty by consumption rather than income? It turns out that when the anti-poverty program began, it consisted primarily of cash transfers, which were included in income estimates. If you boost the income of poor people, fewer will fall under the official poverty line. As time went on, an increasingly larger proportion of the anti-poverty program was in non-cash transfers, such as for housing subsidies, food stamps, and health insurance benefits. Those were not counted in the official figures as income. This exclusion would make people look poorer than they were. Estimates of spending capture those non-cash benefits and show a very different trend line, which argues for a very successful program.

When looking at the conservative argument with the Brookings response in mind, it becomes clear that Tanner included all federal, state, and local spending on poverty programs in his estimate of the money spent on anti-poverty programs, but when it came time to look at poverty rates, he examined only cash transfers as income, ignoring non-cash transfers. He thus biased his results. Unless you knew the programs well, you would not see this bias without looking at the counterargument.

Looking at the Brookings argument from the perspective of the Fox News analysis brings up the question, why did Burtless choose 1960 as his starting point when the program didn't begin until 1965? In 1960 the poverty rate was 22 percent, but by 1965 it had already dropped to 19 percent. So Burtless was attributing a substantial part of the drop in the poverty rate to anti-poverty programs that had not yet begun. He too was exaggerating, but in the opposite direction from the Fox News version.

Looking at both sides, one might conclude that even though the Brookings argument was somewhat exaggerated, the argument that anti-poverty programs have been successful seems stronger.

Example 3. The Wage Gap between Men and Women Isn't Real; Yes, It Is

Women earn substantially less than men for comparable or the same work. Much debate surrounds this idea of a wage gap: How big is it and what causes it? Libertarians, especially those who generally oppose government regulations and want the market to determine all outcomes, argue that the gap is small and doesn't represent discrimination, only women's choices or market forces. Liberals, especially those who support women's issues, argue that the gap is significant, especially when comparing minority women with white men, and that it does represent discrimination based on sex. So, who is right, is there discrimination, as the women's advocates suggest, or is the gap due to women's choices, as the libertarians argue, or are they both right or both wrong in some key way? Examining both sides of the argument helps to explain the issues and points out where the analyses are faulty.

Gary Galles presented the libertarian position.[5] He challenged the narrative that women doing the same work as men experienced discrimination in pay, arguing that if you control for all the relevant variables, such as hours worked, marital status, number of children, education, occupation, number of years of continuous uninterrupted job experience, working conditions, work safety, workplace flexibility, family friendliness of the workplace, job security, and time spent commuting, much of the difference in pay disappears. He further claimed that those who argue for the existence of a pay gap intentionally omit these variables from their analyses. Moreover, men *should* be paid more because they work more and less often require flexible hours.

Galles noted that discrimination in hiring is illegal. He reasoned that if there were a lot of discrimination, there would be a huge number of lawsuits. He claimed, without evidence, that there weren't many lawsuits, and concluded that therefore there was not much discrimination. One place to look for a counterargument is the Equal Employment Opportunity Commission (EEOC), the federal agency that deals with such complaints. The EEOC reported that it receives well over 20,000 complaints per year of sex discrimination. While most of those cases are dismissed with a judgment of not justified, the agency reports monetary settlements of over $100 million a year.[6] One case, brought by female employees at Uber, resulted in a settlement of $4.4 million. Those numbers suggest that there is at least some illegal sex discrimination in the workplace.

A quick web search on the key words "lawsuits about sex discrimination" reveals several major class action lawsuits, including charges against Nike and Google. Nike, in response to the lawsuit, announced that they were going to raise the salaries of 7000 employees, about ten percent of its global workforce so those with the same jobs would get the same pay. They also changed the standards for awarding bonuses.[7] The Google suit alleged that Google paid women $16,794 less than men in similar positions and offered women smaller bonuses and less stock in the company than their male coworkers. In July of 2020, the plaintiffs asked that the case be considered a class action suit, meaning that it would benefit 10,800 women besides the four bringing the case.[8] Such cases provide evidence against Galles's argument that there was no discrimination because it was against the law.

A blog post from the liberal think tank the Economic Policy Institute deals with the pay gap between black women and white men.[9] The authors claim that on average, "in 2017, black women workers were paid only 66 cents on the dollar relative to non-Hispanic white men, even after controlling for education, years of experience, and geographic location."

The authors argue that getting a higher education or shifting to higher paying jobs would not eliminate the gap: "black women earn less than white men at every level of education and even when they work in the same occupation." For those with high school or less, black women earn 57.5 percent of what white men earn; for those with an advanced degree, women earn 59.6 percent of what white men earn. The authors note that if black women chose different careers that were higher paying, the gap would not disappear because "In almost every occupation—both female-dominated and male-dominated—black women earn less than white men." This gap holds both in fields dominated by black women and those dominated by white men. The gap exists among primary and middle school teachers, doctors and nurses, lawyers and accountants, social workers, and software developers. The evidence for a wage gap between black females and white males is strong.

As Galles points out, one of the key issues in examining a wage gap between men and women is the number of working hours. In many, if not all, occupations, women on average work fewer hours than men do, which could explain away much of the gap.

An article from Towardsdatascience.com documents this difference in work hours, arguing that it accounts for almost all the wage gap in unmarried men and women, but not for married men and women, and especially not for married men and women with children. It turns out that women who work fewer hours earn less *per hour* than men do. This effect is magnified as people age, though the burden on women of raising children declines with age.[10] The author concludes, "the time spent at work does not explain all of the gender pay gap ... for each hour spent at their jobs, male married managers without kids earn about 34 percent more than women." The author attributes this difference in hourly earnings to market trends. That is an argument that diffuses (or confuses) blame, but it doesn't explain the source. Market trends may be what we are seeing, but they do not explain themselves.

Some libertarians argue that a wage gap exists but doesn't reflect discrimination, just women's choice of jobs. The solution to the wage gap is for women to get more education and choose higher paid fields, that is, those dominated by men, but that argument isn't supported by the data. For example, an academic study, "Women Can't Win," from Georgetown University claims that discrimination is responsible for some of the wage gap.[11]

Claiming that women tend to work in low paid fields like childcare doesn't answer the question of why the fields that women work in are low paid, why women are concentrated in such low paying fields, or what happens when they work in higher paid, male-dominated fields. When women work in high paid men's jobs, they still earn less than men, and the more women enter the field, the less pay everyone gets, including the men.[12]

When men work in traditionally female fields, they generally earn more than the women in those same fields. The left leaning Fastcompany reported

> A recent study published in the Journal of the American Medical Association that focused on pay data from nearly 300,000 registered nurses found that male nurses earn $5,100 more on average than their female counterparts who hold similar positions. The same study found that this wage gap had remained unchanged since 1988.[13]

Galles's argued that advocates for women's equality intentionally ignore a range of variables that if controlled would eliminate most if not all of the gap, but in fact advocates for women have run models with a variety of variables controlled. These models reduce but do not eliminate the gap.

For example, Gould, Schieder, and Geier from EPI on the left of the political spectrum describe that they ran a model with more of the controls. They found that without controls, the wage gap was 17.9 percent; with a variety of controls, the gap shrunk to 13.5 percent but was still noticeable. Blau and Kahn (2016) found an unadjusted gap of 20.7 percent, a partially adjusted gap of 17.9 percent, and a fully adjusted gap of 8.4 percent.[14]

Models that control for more of the variables that wage gap deniers insist shrink the wage gap don't make it disappear. And if you control for occupation, that is, you argue that any gap is due to women choosing low paying fields, you ignore the discrimination that influences a woman's occupational choice.

From the arguments pro and con, one might conclude that there is a wage gap, but it is probably not as wide as the proponents of the wage gap claim, except when comparing black women and white men. It is greater in some fields than in others. That the gap doesn't narrow much when education and experience are controlled is suggestive of discrimination. Moreover, when men and women are in the same profession, men still make more than women, and when women join men's professions, the status and pay for both shrinks. On balance, it looks like discrimination plays some role in the wage gap.

ANALYSIS BY COMPARISON

Example 4. Electric Cars Are Not Good for the Environment; They Are Pretty Good and Getting Better

The web and news media offer a wide variety of articles that claim that electric vehicles are overhyped and will not actually help reduce greenhouse gases that contribute to climate change. One of those articles on the website called *City Journal*, published by the right-wing think tank the Manhattan Institute, is titled "Battery Derangement: Electric Vehicles Won't Save the Planet and Won't Survive without Subsidies" by Mark P. Mills.[15]

Mills's basic argument is that the production of the batteries for electric cars requires a lot of energy. Many of those batteries are produced in Asia, where the energy is produced by coal, and hence electric cars and their batteries produce more, not less climate-warming carbon dioxide. Critically, he argues that "There's no prospect of creating a domestic EV [electric vehicle] supply chain anytime soon, regardless of incentives." Moreover, when the cars are plugged in, they require electricity which is generally (70 percent) produced by carbon dioxide emitting power plants.

Mills also considers the raw materials that go into batteries, lithium, cobalt, manganese, and carbon, and the electricity and pollution that goes into the mining of these minerals. And, since most of the U.S. consumers' vehicles are gas fueled, even a dramatic increase in electric vehicles would not displace ten percent of the world's oil. This is the argument that says even if electric vehicles were greener, they could not be scaled up sufficiently to make a dent in the problem of greenhouse emissions. This part of the argument sounds like "it won't solve the whole problem" so let's take it off the table.

Carbon Brief's Zeke Hausfather examined Mills's attack. Carbon Brief is a website that focuses on the science of climate change, a good location to look for a counterargument. Hausfather accepted parts of Mills's argument, that is, that electric cars run on electricity that is often produced by power-generating stations using fossil fuels; he also accepted that energy is required to make the cars, especially the batteries. As a result, in countries with coal-intensive electricity production, the benefits of electric vehicles are less, and are similar to the most efficient conventional vehicles.

Parting ways with Mills, Hausfather argues that since countries are producing more of their energy in less carbon dioxide producing ways, the advantages of the electric vehicles are increasing. "Producing batteries in regions with relatively low-carbon electricity or in factories powered by renewable energy, as will be the case for the batteries used in the best-selling Tesla Model 3, can substantially reduce battery emissions."[16]

Moreover, the energy used by the plug-in cars once they are on the road depends on the mix of renewable and traditional power sources. So, the degree of improvement in CO_2 emissions depends on where cars and batteries are manufactured and where they are driven. Hausfather directly contradicts Mills's assumption that the supply chain for electric batteries is unlikely to change as it is already changing.

Going beyond Mills, Hausfather examined the many studies that come up with different conclusions about how helpful electric cars will be in reducing CO_2 emissions, noting that the different studies rely on different assumptions about the electricity grid mix (how much coal, how much wind, how much solar power, how much nuclear), whether the authors assume that electric cars will use additional electricity requiring expansion of polluting plants, and which specific vehicles are being compared. Even estimates of miles per gallon of gas are based on varying assumptions. From Hausfather's description of the literature, it looks like researchers could make their study come to the conclusions they want by varying these assumptions.

Given this variation, Hausfather did his own analysis. In his study, under a range of assumptions from the least favorable to the most favorable to electric cars, electric vehicles were better for the environment than all but the most efficient gas burning cars. His conclusion was nuanced. How much improvement one gets with electric vehicles compared to gasoline powered ones depends on where the batteries are made and the mix of resources used to create electricity, such as coal, gas, wind, or solar. In parts of the U.S. where coal is the major resource for electricity production, an electric vehicle would provide little gain over conventional engines. As the mix of energy sources for electricity production improves, the benefits from electric cars will also improve.

Comparing the arguments pro and con, Mills's conservative argument makes some important points, especially that CO_2 emissions should be compared over the life cycle of the vehicle, from mining the minerals, to battery and auto manufacture, to actual use on the road. However, he probably overemphasizes production of batteries in China where coal is the dominant source for electricity production; there are U.S. factories (Tesla batteries are produced in Nevada) and they produce much less CO_2. Moreover, Mills misses the trajectory, that is, that energy production has been and will likely continue to rely more on renewable resources that emit less CO_2.

Conclusion? Electric cars are not a silver bullet, they won't solve all the problems of CO_2 emission and global warming but should be in the mix going forward. They are generally better for the environment than most of the gasoline burning cars and are likely to be better in the future.

Example 5. The Death of Immigrant Children: Not Our Fault; Yes, It Is

Between September 2018 and May 2019, six immigrant children in U.S. custody died. Between 2010 and September 2018 no children had been reported as dying in U.S. custody, which prompted questions about why this was happening, and generated many efforts to avoid blame and assign it elsewhere.

Among the government's claims are that the surge of would-be immigrants had overcrowded facilities and that medical personnel were inadequate to meet the demand. Crowding at detention facilities and inadequate screening of immigrants contributed to the spread of contagious illness, such as flu. The official response from the government was that the children were sick when they came into the country and the border was understaffed medically and could not deal with the overwhelming number of sick people coming across the border. Officials blamed parents who brought their children on this arduous trip, and blamed the Mexican camps for migrants hoping to enter the U.S. Officials also blamed smugglers (human traffickers) for encouraging families to try to cross the border.[17] You might recognize these arguments as the diffusion-of-blame strategy.

In another effort to shift blame, President Trump blamed his opponents, the Democrats:

> Any deaths of children or others at the border are strictly the fault of the Democrats and their pathetic immigration policies that allow people to make the long trek thinking they can enter our country illegally ... . If we had a wall, they wouldn't even try!

Trump lamented that the border patrol worked so hard and got so little credit. He not only refused to accept any blame, he wanted his administration to get credit, if not for doing a good job, then at least for working hard.[18]

An examination of individual cases of children's death in custody confirms that some of the children were sick at the time of crossing the border and may have contracted illness in the camps in Mexico. The government's explanation for the children's death is thus at least partly true, but ignores the fact that people are piled up in the Mexican shelters because the U.S. has refused them entry by any other means than the legal ports of entry, which are understaffed and slow. The Trump administration demanded that migrants remain in Mexico until their requests for asylum could be processed, under a policy called Migrant Protection Protocols.[19] Thus, the squalid camps on the Mexican side of the border were a direct result of the Trump administration policy.

As for the charge that the Democrats were responsible for the deaths because they passed the laws governing refugees, that law was passed in 1980 (The United States Refugee Act of 1980, Public Law 96-212). Its main sponsor was Ted Kennedy, a Democrat, and the law was signed by a democratic president, that much is true. But the law has remained in effect for 40 years, through both democratic and republican administrations. Moreover, it grants a large amount of discretion to the president and the attorney general in terms of how many refugees to admit and how to determine whether they are genuine refugees and whether there is some humanitarian crisis that requires an increase in the ceiling. The Trump administration increased the security vetting process for asylum claimants, increasing the backlog and the length of stay for those hoping to enter the country. Blaming Democrats exclusively for allowing or encouraging immigrants who claim refugee status is not supported by history or law, even though the law initially was passed by a democratic administration.

One clue to unraveling the government's justification of the children's death is that an article in the conservative *Washington Times* refers to a surge of sick migrants, without providing evidence about how many migrants were actually sick or what illnesses they had. The article quotes unnamed Homeland Security officials as saying that "dozens of people a day" in Border Patrol facilities need medical treatment.[20] Note the weasel words, a surge (how many?), dozens of people a day (how many?), and unnamed sources.

After a critical report from the Centers for Disease Control, the Border Patrol increased the number of doctors and the amount of volunteer screening. Of almost 150 children examined under the new procedures, four were sent to regional hospitals. This number does not equal dozens per day, nor is it an overwhelming surge of sick kids.[21]

Those who blame the government for the death of children crossing the border point to the poor health conditions in the detention facilities, where temperatures are kept very cold and where inoculations are not given for flu or other contagious diseases like chicken pox. A group of doctors showed up at one of the detention camps, volunteering to give flu shots to the detainees in an effort to prevent flu deaths in children. They were turned down by the Border Patrol, which argued that most of the detainees were only in the facility a short time, and when they left for more long-term detention, they would get immunizations. The protesters responded that thousands were sent back across the border to Mexico, to wait "in teeming, unhealthy border camps."[22] Whether or not the children were sent back to Mexico or held in detention camps in the U.S., the Centers for Disease Control had advised inoculations on initial entry, not later.

The Inspector General of the Department of Homeland Security, the watchdog in charge of overseeing the Department of Homeland Security, wrote a report claiming that there was dangerous crowding at detention facilities. He found 900 people in a space designed for 125.[23]

An article in *Time Magazine* (ranked as having a slight liberal bias) summarized one critic's description of conditions at one of the detention facilities:

> Babies have to drink from unwashed bottles and there are not enough diapers. They are subjected to "extreme cold temperatures" with "lights on 24 hours a day," a pediatrician who has treated migrant children told CNN. There have been outbreaks of flu, lice, chicken pox and scabies.[24]

Conclusion? The extensive blame shifting of the Trump administration might have caught your attention and led you to look further into the case. The exaggeration, vagueness, and lack of evidence for surging cases of sick children should have further put you on your guard. On checking, you would have found that at least some of the blame was correctly placed on the administration. The idea that all the blame should be on Democrats was not supported.

Example 6. There Is a Bee Apocalypse; No, There Isn't

Bee apocalypse refers to what is called colony collapse. Bee colonies, used for pollinating many commercial crops, have been declining in the U.S. The reason has been a subject of speculation, some arguing it is the result of a mite (a tiny insect), and others saying that it is the result of the use of commercial insecticides that kill bees, which probably isn't good for people either. Some postulate the decline in bee population is a result of both factors combined. Although the demise of many bee colonies has been observed, there are many who deny that there is a problem. The denialists claim there are more bee colonies than ever, so there is no problem. From their perspective, it is all hype.

If particular insecticides kill domestic bees, they could be taken off the market, as they have been in Europe. So, manufacturers of insecticides have a vested interest in denying the problem. That suggests that readers should be at least a little skeptical and look at the evidence on both sides.

The website beeinformed.org, which does annual sample surveys of beekeepers, reported that during the winter of 2020–2021, 32.2 percent of the managed beehives in the U.S. were lost. This was a 9.6 percent greater loss than the previous year, and a 3.9 percent increase over a 14-year average winter colony loss.

Total losses, winter and summer added, were 45.5 percent over the year 2020–2021. While the losses vary somewhat from year to year, in recent years the figure has run close to 40 percent losses a year. Something is going on that is harming bees.[25]

Beeinformed doesn't attribute the loss of colonies to any one cause, but Greenpeace, an environmental group, has been blaming pesticides for the decline in the number of pollinators.[26]

On the other side of the argument are the denialists. The federal Environmental Protection Agency (EPA) focused on the few years when the decline in bee colonies shrank to suggest that colony collapse, where worker bees disappear, is not a serious problem.[27] From the perspective of today, it looks like the agency engaged in cherry picking, that is, selecting specific years to make a predetermined argument rather than looking at the trends over time. Further, the agency argued that there is a difference between colony collapse, a very specific diagnosis, and loss of bees over the winter to other causes and argues that "the number of those losses attributed to CCD has dropped from roughly 60 percent of total hives lost in 2008 to 31.1 percent in 2013; in initial reports for 2014–2015 losses, CCD is not mentioned." The agency acknowledges that pesticides can harm bees but claims that is why there are warnings and instructions on the insecticides in terms of how to use them to minimize damage to bees. Pesticide poisoning is avoidable, a result of error, nothing more, according to the Environmental Protection Agency.

Maryann Frazier, a retired senior extension associate for the College of Agricultural Sciences at Pennsylvania State University, worried that not enough was being done to curb the use or misuse of pesticides, declaring "The EPA has been incredibly ineffective." She noted that the pesticide industry has tried to shift the focus solely on the varroa mites.[28]

The denialists argue that there is a difference between colony collapse, a specific syndrome in which worker bees disappear without leaving corpses, leaving a queen behind, and loss of bees over the winter. They find a *decrease* in colony collapse technically defined. On the other side, those who worry about the decline in bees measure die-offs over winter as a loss of colonies, whether or not the die-off fits the formal pattern of colony collapse. Thus, pro and anti-groups are counting different things.

Second, denialists shift the focus away from pesticides toward mites, dismissing the impact of pesticides as merely poor agricultural practice, blaming the farmer rather than the pesticide. More neutral analysts argue that both mites and pesticides are involved, and there are other factors as well.

While one set of arguments acknowledges that there has been a decline in bees but claims that the cause is not pesticides but mites, and defines colony collapse narrowly, a second set of denialists claims that there has been no loss of bees. One article on the right-biased American Council on Science and Health looks not at the losses of colonies reported each year by beekeepers, but the total number of bee colonies in the U.S. each year from 1995 to 2017 and finds the numbers reasonably stable. There were 2.6 million colonies in 1995, and 2.6 million colonies in 2017. The author, Jon Entine, also notes there was a 13.1 percent increase between 2007 and 2012. Conclusion? No problem.[29]

Entine set out to debunk the environmentalist claim of a dangerous loss of bees due to a specific pesticide. He argues that the demise of beekeeping is greatly exaggerated, but at the same time, he uses rhetorical devices that make one question his logic. For example, he notes that our honeybee is not a native species. And further, that bees aren't cute, they are a managed species, like livestock. These arguments presumably are supposed to make you less sympathetic to bees. Moreover, he focuses on the mites and the miticides that are used in an effort to control them and deemphasizes the importance of pesticides. He also follows the pattern of differentiating colony collapse and winter losses due to other sources. Beekeepers rebound from winter losses by dividing hives; others import hives from abroad. Thus, there is no loss of bees, no danger of bee apocalypse.

As far as this argument goes, it is correct, there are still bees out there pollinating our crops, but it doesn't address the costs of continual replacement or ways of reducing the winter losses. Nor does it deal effectively with the time series numbers provided by surveys posted on beeinformed.com. Entine draws a trend line from 2007 to 2017, through increases and decreases of winter bee losses, showing a decline from about 33 percent losses in 2007 to a mere 22 percent in 2017. His numbers for these years match the survey results posted on beeinformed.com, but if you were to continue the trend line, from 22 percent in 2017, to 32 percent in 2018, and 37 percent in 2019, you might be less optimistic about increasing survival rates. The recent trend is increased losses.

Entine is probably right that there is no apocalypse, bees are not going extinct, and they are still pollinating crops. The environmentalists may be exaggerating in an effort to curb the use of pesticides and chemical seed treatments. It may be that bees are not essentially cute, but that argument seems more aimed at opposing environmentalists' campaigns against insecticides than proving that there is no problem with bee numbers. The losses are real, they are made up by hive divisions and imports, but Entine is focusing on the total after more bees have been added to make up for the losses. This selective use of data reinforces the idea that the denialists are engaging in a persuasive argument to diminish the pressure against insecticides.

In this debate there is some persuasive rhetoric on both sides, but by examining both we learn about the pressures on both sides, to attack and to protect commercial insecticides. One can see how much it matters what exactly one is counting, when one wants to make a case for or against a loss of honeybees. Is one counting formally defined colony collapses, or winter losses of beehives? Or the total number of bees? And if one is counting the latter, when is one doing the counting, at the end of winter, when the numbers are low, or later, when the beekeepers have added more bees? If one is looking at a time series, is one focusing only on the years of increase, the years of decrease, or picking beginning years and ending years that make a case for more losses or fewer?

Dividing hives and buying bees abroad to replace losses are expensive. In order to continue in business, beekeepers have to raise their prices, which in turn raises the prices of the crops they pollinate and the honey they sell. Honey production has dropped per hive. As a result of the decline in production, and in the face of rising demand, prices have risen. The *Wall Street Journal* reported that since 2013, the retail price of honey has increased 25 percent.[30]

We may not be seeing bee Armageddon, but something is happening to the bees. When you see an argument that relies mainly on mites or mainly on insecticides, now you have an idea why. Blaming mites is an effort to avert blame from the chemical industry and blaming insecticides is an effort to cast blame on the chemical industry.

Example 7. Carbon Capture Is a Viable Technology to Slow Down Global Warming; No, It's Not

An excess of carbon dioxide in the air, created by burning fossil fuels, is considered by many as the driving force behind global warming. Some people have been arguing for capturing and sequestering carbon dioxide as a feasible approach to slowing down climate change, while others have argued against it. If carbon capture could work at sufficient scale, it might allow continued burning of fossil fuels, which suggests a possible motive for supporting it. But there are clearly at least two sides to this issue and looking at the supporters and detractors helps clarify the issues involved.

The authors of an article in the *Washington Post*, Jan Christoph Minx and Gregory Nemet, two professors who work in the area of climate change, argue that it takes too long to develop, test, and implement the technology required to sequester enough carbon dioxide to reach targets for reducing global warming. They urge public policies to work at speeding up that process, but add that there is no magic bullet, and that carbon dioxide emissions must also be reduced.[31]

Pushing a somewhat different theme, the Center for Climate and Energy Solutions has argued in favor of carbon capture, stating "Carbon capture, use, and storage technologies can capture more than 90 percent of carbon dioxide (CO_2) emissions from power plants and industrial facilities." The non-profit advocacy organization reports that there are 26 commercial scale carbon capture projects up and running, with 21 more in development, and that carbon capture could achieve a 14 percent reduction of greenhouse gas emissions worldwide to meet targets by 2050.[32]

So, one argument is that the technology is not ready and won't be implemented in time, and hence more reduction is needed in the production of greenhouse gases, fossil fuels need to be curtailed, while the opposition argues that large-scale commercial projects already exist, more are on the way, and this is a technique for capturing most if not all of the greenhouse gases emitted from power plants and industries.

Whether carbon capture could be scaled up in a timely fashion to achieve global goals for CO_2 reduction is a technical question, not resolved here, as the two sides disagree on basic facts. But further, it looks like one side is saying we need to curb the use of fossil fuels, in addition to whatever carbon capture we can achieve, and the other side is saying industry can go along using fossil fuels pretty much as it has, we can just capture the carbon dioxide that the plants produce, either directly from the air or at the source where it was emitted.

In this comparison, both sides offer reasonable arguments but not sufficient evidence to be definitive. The technology and public subsidies are changing One would have to continue to watch what was happening to get an idea of which side was more likely to be correct. The environmental community itself is split on this topic.

Conclusion

Comparing arguments pro and con is a good way to learn about a topic you may not know much about. Such comparisons can point out where arguments are missing key elements, where the context is not included, and who might be engaging in cherry picking the data. Sometimes one side or the other will be more convincing, but often you will end up accepting parts of each, having a richer and more nuanced understanding of a highly controversial topic. You will also have a better idea of whose interests are being protected or attacked.

Notes

1 "The Idea of the Day: Think Tanks," *New York Times*, August 10, 2008, https://ideas.blogs.nytimes.com/2008/08/10/think-tanks/.
2 Jesse Marx, "Ex-Police Chief Cited Misleading Stats When Lobbying Against Pot Facilities," *Voice of San Diego*, June 28, 2018, https://www.voiceofsandiego.org/topics/public-safety/ex-police-chief-cited-misleading-stats-when-lobbying-against-pot-facilities/.
3 Michael Tanner, "War on Poverty at 50—Despite Trillions Spent, Poverty Won," *Fox News*, May 7, 2015, www.foxnews.com/opinion/war-on-poverty-at-50-despite-trillions-spent-poverty-won.
4 Gary Burtless, "Throwing Money at a Problem Can Work, But We Have to Count the Money We Spend," *Brookings*, July 25, 2018, www.brookings.edu/opinions/throwing-money-at-a-problem-can-work-but-we-have-to-count-the-money-we-spend/.
5 Gary Galles, "Equal Pay Day? More Like Unequal Comparison Day: The Data Used to Compare Men and Women Fails to Adjust for Differences in Several Critical Areas," *Foundation for Economic Education*, April 2, 2019, https://fee.org/articles/equal-pay-day-more-like-unequal-comparison-day/.
6 U.S. Equal Opportunity Commission, "Sex-Based Charges (Charges filed with EEOC) FY 1997–FY 2020," www.eeoc.gov/statistics/sex-based-charges-charges-filed-eeoc-fy-1997-fy-2019.
7 Stacy Cowley, "Nike Will Raise Wages for Thousands after Outcry over Inequality," *The New York Times*, July 23, 2018.
8 Aaron Holmes, "The Women Suing Google over Gender Discrimination Want to Expand the Lawsuit to a Class Action," *Business Insider*, July 22, 2020, www.businessinsider.com/google-lawsuit-pay-discrimination-plaintiffs-women-seek-class-action-status-2020-7.
9 Madison Matthews and Valerie Wilson, "Separate Is Still Unequal: How Patterns of Occupational Segregation Impact Pay for Black Women," *Economic Policy Institute*, August 6, 2018, www.epi.org/blog/separate-is-still-unequal-how-patterns-of-occupational-segregation-impact-pay-for-black-women/.
10 Payman Taei, "Is the Difference in Work Hours the Real Reason for the Gender Wage Gap?," *Towards Data Science*, January 22, 2019, https://towardsdatascience.com/is-the-difference-in-work-hours-the-real-reason-for-the-gender-wage-gap-interactive-infographic-6051dff3a041.
11 Anthony P. Carnevale, Nicole Smith, and Artem Gulish, "Women Can't Win," Georgetown University Center on Education and the Workplace, 2018, https://cew.georgetown.edu/wp-content/uploads/Women_FR_Web.pdf.
12 Claire Cain Miller, "As Women Take Over a Male-Dominated Field, the Pay Drops," *The New York Times*, March 18, 2016, www.nytimes.com/2016/03/20/upshot/as-women-take-over-a-male-dominated-field-the-pay-drops.html.
13 Lydia Dishman, "The Other Wage Gap: Why Men in Female-Dominated Industries Still Earn More," *FASTCOMPANY*, April 8, 2015, www.fastcompany.com/3044753/the-other-wage-gap-why-men-in-women-dominated-industries-still-earn-more; Ulrike Muench, Jody Sindelar, Susan H. Busch, et al., Research Letter, "Salary Differences between Male and Female Registered Nurses in the United States," *JAMA* 313(12), March 24/31, 2015, pp. 1265–1267, https://jamanetwork.com/journals/jama/fullarticle/2208795.
14 Elise Gould, Jessica Schieder, and Kathleen Geier, "What Is the Gender Pay Gap and Is It Real?," *Economic Policy Institute*, October 20, 2016, www.epi.org/publication/what-is-the-gender-pay-gap-and-is-it-real/.

15 October 10, 2019, www.city-journal.org/electric-vehicle-batteries.
16 Zeke Hausfather, "Factcheck, How Electric Vehicles Help to Tackle Climate Change," *CarbonBrief*, May 13, 2019, www.carbonbrief.org/factcheck-how-electric-vehicles-help-to-tackle-climate-change.
17 Carol Morello, "More Children Arriving Very Sick at the U.S. Border," *The Washington Post*, December 31, 2018, www.washingtonpost.com/world/national-security/more-children-arriving-very-sick-at-the-us-border/2018/12/31/d42da3c8-0d44-11e9-84fc-d58c33d6c8c7_story.html.
18 Maggie Haberman, "Trump Blames Democrats over Deaths of Migrant Children in U.S. Custody," *New York Times*, December 29, 2018, www.nytimes.com/2018/12/29/us/politics/trump-immigrant-children-deaths.html.
19 Frank Miles, "DHS Defends Policy Keeping Asylum-Seeking Migrants at Mexico Border," *Fox News*, November 18, 2019, www.foxnews.com/media/today-on-fox-news-nov-18-2019
20 Stephen Dinan, "DHS Begs for Help, Orders Full Review after Second Migrant Child's Death," *The Washington Times*, December 26, 2018, www.washingtontimes.com/news/2018/dec/26/dhs-begs-help-orders-full-review-after-second-migr/.
21 Ian Stewart, "Trump Blames Democrats for Deaths of Migrant Kids as DHS Secretary Visits Border," *NPR*, December 29, 2018, www.npr.org/2018/12/29/680932809/trump-blames-democrats-for-deaths-of-migrant-kids-as-dhs-secretary-visits-border.
22 Miriam Jordan, "Why Border Patrol Refuses to Offer Flu Shots to Migrants," *New York Times*, December 11, 2019, www.nytimes.com/2019/12/11/us/migrants-flu-vaccines-border-patrol.html.
23 Department of Homeland Security, Office of the Inspector General, "Management Alert—DHS Needs to Address Dangerous Overcrowding and Prolonged Detention of Children and Adults in the Rio Grande Valley, (Redacted)," July 2, 2019, www.oig.dhs.gov/sites/default/files/assets/2019-07/OIG-19-51-Jul19_.pdf.
24 Madeleine Joung, "What Is Happening at Migrant Detention Centers? Here's What to Know," *Time Magazine*, July 12, 2019, https://time.com/5623148/migrant-detention-centers-conditions/.
25 Nathalie Steinhauer, Dan Aurell, Selina Bruckner, Mikayla Wilson, Karen Rennich, Dennis vanEngelsdorp, and Geoffrey Williams, "United States Honey Bee Colony Losses 2020–2021: Preliminary Results," *beeinformed*, June 23, 2021, https://beeinformed.org/wp-content/uploads/2021/06/BIP_2020_21_Losses_Abstract_2021.06.14_FINAL_R1.pdf
26 Guest Blogger, "EU Bans Three Bee-Killer Pesticides: A Light of Hope for Bees and Agriculture," *Greenpeace*, May 6, 2013, www.greenpeace.org/usa/eu-bans-three-bee-killer-pesticides-a-light-of-hope-for-bees-and-agriculture/.
27 www.epa.gov/pollinator-protection/colony-collapse-disorder.
28 Frazier was quoted on NPR, Susie Neilson, "More Bad Buzz for Bees: Record Number of Honeybee Colonies Died Last Winter," *NPR*, June 19, 2019, www.npr.org/sections/thesalt/2019/06/19/733761393/more-bad-buzz-for-bees-record-numbers-of-honey-bee-colonies-died-last-winter.
29 Jon Entine, "The Bee Apocalypse Was Never Real; Here's Why," *American Council on Science and Health*, April 17, 2018, www.acsh.org/news/2018/04/17/bee-apocalypse-was-never-real-heres-why-12851.
30 Lucy Craymer, "You'll Need a Lot More Money to Buy That Jar of Honey," *Wall Street Journal*, May 22, 2019, www.wsj.com/articles/youll-need-a-lot-more-money-to-buy-that-jar-of-honey-11558526402.
31 Jan Christoph Minx and Gregory Nemet, "The Inconvenient Truth about Carbon Capture," *The Washington Post*, May 31, 2018, www.washingtonpost.com/news/theworldpost/wp/2018/05/31/carbon-capture/.
32 Center for Climate and Energy Solutions, "Carbon Capture," www.c2es.org/content/carbon-capture/.

6
WHAT DOES A CITED SOURCE ACTUALLY SAY?

What Does a Cited Source Actually Say?

Advocates often cite interviews, reports, articles, or raw data and draw their own, possibly incorrect, conclusions from them. People who favor one candidate or policy position sometimes charge opponents with misuse of sources in order to delegitimize them. If something in an argument has triggered your curiosity about whether it is accurate, it is a good idea to check the source that speakers or writers cite as evidence. The people who cite a source may be misrepresenting what it says or the evidence itself might be weak. If you find a quotation or original study that is cited as evidence in an argument, how should you check it out and what should you look for?

Misrepresenting a Source

There are a number of ways to misrepresent a source. People can misquote someone or attribute a conclusion to a report that was not included in the report. They can intentionally misinterpret the data, claiming a number is bigger or smaller than the source reported. Or they can just make a mistake, and you may never know if it was intentional or not.

Misinterpreting the Evidence

A prominent member of the Liberal Party in Australia made a statement delegitimizing the rival Labor Party, claiming that it could not reflect society because 90 percent of its members were chosen from the Trade Unions and bring that background to the table. As evidence, a spokesman for Simon Birmingham presented an application for membership for the year 2015–16 for the South Australian branch of the Australian Labor Party, with the claim that the applicant had to be a member of a union. The fact-checker, the Conversation, examined the evidence, that is, went to the source, and found that it didn't say what the spokesman said it said. The form offered a discount for membership if the applicant was a union member but it did not require union membership to join. The fact-checker went on to count the number and proportion of Labor members who had been union members or worked in unions and roughly a third of the Labor members of Parliament had union backgrounds.

You might have been suspicious initially because of the effort to delegitimize a rival; if you checked out the evidence cited, you would have found it didn't say what the spokesman claimed it said.[1]

Misquoting People

For President Trump, misquoting is one way of deflecting blame. When Trump was criticized for withholding military aid to Ukraine unless the Ukrainian president investigated presidential rival Joe Biden, Trump responded that the president of Ukraine had cleared him, saying he had done nothing wrong. What President Zelensky actually said was that he (Zelensky) didn't deal in quid quo pros, but he was critical of Trump for withholding badly needed military aid, saying it was unfair. He was also critical of Trump for claiming that Ukraine was very corrupt. Zelensky said he felt no pressure from Trump, but his complaints suggest the opposite.[2]

Trump also sometimes misquotes people in an effort to claim credit. He approvingly repeated a list of his accomplishments offered by an adviser to his campaign, "He's devastated ISIS & killed AlBaghdadi, building Wall." But the adviser had never mentioned the wall. Trump put the praise of his accomplishment for building the wall in his adviser's mouth.[3]

Misquoting may run in families. Ivanka Trump seriously misquoted Albert Einstein, "If the facts don't fit the theory, change the facts." (posted on Twitter on June 23, 2013). In this misquote, Ivanka was arguing from authority, claiming one of the world's most famous geniuses agreed with her that facts could be shaped or reshaped to fit whatever narrative one chose. Einstein never said what Ivanka claimed he said. As a mathematician and theoretical physicist, Einstein didn't hold onto a theory when facts disproved it.[4]

What is especially significant about this misquote is that it supports the attack on truth described in Chapter 1—if you don't like the facts, just change them.

Attributing a Biased Conclusion to a Neutral Study

Sometimes writers describe the result of a study putting their own slant on the material, while stating or implying that the slant was in the original source.

In one example, an opinion writer in the conservative *Washington Examiner* argued that the Congressional Budget Office had detailed the

Democrats' plan to depress the economy until the 2020 election in order to reduce the president's chance of winning.[5]

If you had never heard of the Congressional Budget Office and looked it up, you would see that the CBO is non-partisan. It gets its clout from being utterly neutral between political parties in Washington where neutral analysis is rare. Since the CBO depends on its reputation for unbiased studies, it seems unlikely that the CBO took such a partisan stance. If your curiosity was roused, you might want to compare the *Washington Examiner* opinion piece with the original CBO report it cites. Did it really say what Tiana Lowe of the *Washington Examiner* claimed it said?

Lowe was arguing against the democratic proposal to extend from July to December the pandemic-related increase in unemployment benefits. She noted that the extension would continue the increased payments past the election, creating an incentive for those laid off because of covid-19 not to return to work because they would be getting more from unemployment benefits than from working. The consequence would be to maintain a high unemployment rate until after the election, boosting the Democrats' chance of winning. Lowe was certain that electoral victory was the intent of the proposal and hence urged Republicans to oppose it.

What the CBO report actually said was that extending the increased unemployment benefit would have several impacts that go in opposite directions. On the one hand, it would increase people's ability to spend for basics like food and rent, and generally increase demand, which would stimulate business and increase the gross domestic product. On the other hand, it would create an incentive for those receiving the extra payment to stay home and reduce their job hunting, because they could earn more by staying on unemployment than going back to work for less money. The CBO report concluded that such a policy would keep the unemployment rate higher than it would otherwise be. This much of the argument was consistent with the *Washington Examiner* article.

But the CBO report also noted that its analysts had not estimated the strength of the impact on unemployment. There was no discussion of how people would treat the temporary benefit of more money for a few months compared with a long-term job offer at less money. Without knowing how many people would go back to work and give up a few months of extra unemployment pay, one has no idea how much higher the unemployment rate would be with the extension of increased unemployment benefits. Second, and equally important, the CBO made no reference to democratic plans to derail the economy for the purpose of aiding Democrats in the election. In fact, the CBO report did not discuss how any of its projections might impact the 2020 election.

Lowe's claim that the CBO accepted and provided evidence for the existence of a democratic conspiracy to steal the election goes well beyond the actual CBO report, which was just a quick effort to imagine how various and contradictory effects of the extension of benefits might balance out over time.⁶

In a second example, a global lukewarmer—someone who accepts that warming is occurring but thinks it is not important and nothing should be done about it—misstated the conclusion of a study he cited as evidence for his position. Part of Bjorn Lomberg's argument was that reducing fossil fuel emissions to curtail global warming would increase food insecurity for the poor; thus, for him, the solution was worse than the problem. He concluded that one should do nothing to prevent global warming, just cope with its limited consequences. He presented a false dichotomy: either do nothing or choose the option of reducing emissions by using biofuels and thereby impoverish many millions of people and increase food insecurity. This alternative to doing nothing is clearly unacceptable. False dichotomies should put you on your guard.

Your next step could be to go to the source and see whether Lomborg quoted it or used it appropriately. Dr. Lomborg's source for his conclusion that reducing emissions would hurt the poor more than doing nothing did *not* come up with the conclusion that Lomborg drew. The source, "Risk of Increased Food Insecurity under Stringent Global Climate Change Mitigation Policy,"⁷ compared the impact of doing nothing with the impact of a carbon tax to reduce emissions. If this strategy alone were used, it would have negative impacts on the poor, so the authors recommended *that emissions reduction should continue*, but that emissions mitigation should be carefully designed and policy should include encouraging more productive and resilient agricultural production and efforts to counteract the negative consequences of climate change mitigation strategies. The authors did not conclude that nothing should be done.

Lomborg mostly publishes for a general audience rather than a scientific one that can check his claims. His arguments sound reasonable if you don't check his sources, but when scientists do check his sources, they find that some of his sources didn't say what he said they said.

Intentional Misinterpretation of Data

Another story in the *Washington Examiner* claimed that an increasing number of undocumented immigrants were applying for gun permits and being denied.⁸ An earlier version of the story falsely claimed that every undocumented person in the FBI database was applying for gun permits. The original, uncorrected version was picked up and repeated on other websites. For example, the website Townhall claimed that "The FBI is reporting that a record number of illegals tried to purchase firearms this year. Over seven million illegals tried to purchase guns," citing the flawed *Washington Examiner* article. Those seven million people did not try to buy guns or apply for permits; they were merely on a list maintained by the FBI of those who were not permitted to buy a gun.[9]

Even when corrected, the story sounds frightening, suggesting that the undocumented pose an immediate threat. If they are trying to get guns, they must be dangerous criminals. This argument is unlikely to be true. Why would undocumented people, who generally try to avoid contact with police, reveal themselves to law enforcement by applying for a legal gun permit? In my neighborhood, undocumented people don't dare ask a police officer to help them get into their own cars if they have locked the keys inside. If your suspicion has been aroused, you might want to look at the FBI data that is the basis of the article.[10] What do the data actually say compared to the anti-immigrant claims in the *Washington Examiner*?

The corrected story claims there was a large increase in the number of undocumented immigrants on the FBI list of those not permitted to own a gun and notes that 3300 of these immigrants had applied for and been denied a gun permit in 2017.

What do the data actually say? As for those applying for gun permits and being rejected (because the applicants' names appear in the database of ineligibles), the actual numbers and percent of the total have been minuscule. In 2017, there were 3337 reported rejections of gun applications from undocumented immigrants. Estimates of the number of undocumented immigrants in the country (a larger number than the FBI list of undocumented) range from 10 to 20 million; using the smaller estimates of total undocumented people living in the U.S., the percent of undocumented people who were rejected for gun permits in 2017 was *three one hundredths of one percent*. If the larger number of undocumented is near correct, the percent is even smaller. So, the data indicate that, in general, the undocumented in this country are not applying for gun permits and being rejected.

There was an increase in the number of rejected applications from undocumented aliens from 2016 to 2017 but the amount was trivial, from 3076 in 2016 to 3337 in 2017, or 261 rejections, out of over seven million undocumented people in the FBI database.[11]

There were thus several problems with the original story that should lead the reader to reject the inference that the undocumented are particularly dangerous, as seen in the numbers applying for gun permits. First, the uncorrected story vastly overestimated the numbers who applied for gun permits. Second, only a really small percentage of undocumented in the country applied for gun permits. And third, the story focused on a single year of an increase of gun applicants among the undocumented (cherry picking). Even that one year turned out to experience only a very small increase. Looking at the actual data on which the story was based provided context, so the reader could tell if the numbers were in fact big or small.

Simple Mistakes

Leprosy, now called Hansen's disease, is a long-feared disease. Thus, when Lou Dobbs, a popular, populist commentator on CNN claimed that the number of cases in the U.S. was going up dramatically because of immigration, he was making an emotional argument against immigration. This effort to scare the audience into taking an anti-immigration stance should put you on alert.

Is it true? Are cases of Hansen's disease going up dramatically? What do the numbers actually say? There is not much tracking of cases in the U.S. because there are so few cases and because of recent budget cuts in the program that used to monitor Hansen's. At the time that Dobbs made that claim, the data were still routinely collected and published in a government registry. David Leonhardt, a columnist for the *New York Times*, questioned Dobb's claim.[12]

Dobbs had claimed in 2005 that there were 7000 cases of Hansen's disease over the prior three years, way more than in the past. The 7000 figure turned out to be the number of cases over a 30-year period, not a three-year period.

Estimates vary about how many new cases there are each year in the U.S, but most agree that there are between 200 and 250 cases per year, which is to say, not many. Moreover, despite the obvious attempt to frighten people with a scourge of biblical proportions, 95 percent of people cannot contract the disease as their immune systems would fight it off; in addition, the disease is curable. After only a short period on antibiotics, it is no longer contagious to anyone.

Looking at the data revealed clearly where the mistake had come from—30 years became three years—and then the narrative fit with an anti-immigrant stance.

In a second example of a mistake, The Hill Morning Report of April 17, 2020, included the following:

> the astonishing number of jobs shed in the last month, estimated by some analysts to be pushing April unemployment north of 15 percent—a situation that would be worse than the Great Depression—means the economic struggles across the country have raced ahead of Congress. (The New York Times).[13]

The quotation implies that the unemployment rate during the Great Depression was less than somewhere "north of 15%." A quick check reveals that the actual unemployment rate during the Great Depression was almost 25 percent in 1933, and between 15 and 20 percent for much of the time, so this comparison sounds exaggerated. This news summary cites a story in the *New York Times*; you might want to check what the *New York Times* article actually said.

If quarterly unemployment hits 30 percent—as the president of one Federal Reserve Bank predicted—15.4 percent of Americans will fall into poverty for the year, researchers found, even in the unlikely event that the economy immediately recovers. That level of poverty would exceed the peak of the Great Recession and add nearly 10 million people to the ranks of the poor.[14]

The *Times* briefing talks not about the current rate of unemployment but speculates about what could occur if unemployment reaches roughly twice what the current estimates are, and if that higher rate does occur, the article suggests what the effect would be on poverty rates, and how those speculative poverty rates would compare to the actual poverty rates during the Great Recession, which occurred from December 2007 to June 2009, not the Great Depression of the 1930s. Oops. The Hill made a mistake.

Citing a Flawed Study

Sometimes a study is quoted or described accurately but the study itself is not credible. You won't know that unless you look at the original study.

Misuse of Percentages, Lack of Before and After Comparison

Both Ilhan Omar, democratic representative from Minnesota, and Bernie Sanders, democratic senator from Vermont, both on the left wing of the Democratic Party, claimed that counties that hosted a Trump election rally in 2016 experienced a 226 percent increase in hate crimes. The implication was that Trump's heated, hate- and fear-filled rhetoric against immigrants, Muslims, Jews, gays, and blacks was either causing or unleashing violent hate crimes. The claim was based on an academic study called "The Trump Effect: How 2016 Campaign Rallies Explain Spikes in Hate."[15]

As described in Chapter 5, one way of analyzing this partisan claim is to look at the arguments on the other side and see if they give us some clues. And if we look at the actual data on which the original study was based, we should be able to tell how accurate the leftist Democrats' claims are.

By now the reader knows that the *Washington Examiner* is a good place to look for arguments on the right of the political spectrum. Robby Soave, writing in the *Washington Examiner*, objected to the claim that Trump rallies increased hate crimes, arguing that the study on which it was based was absurdly flawed.[16] He noted that the figure of 226 percent relied on the count of hate incidents done by the Anti-Defamation League (ADL), which he rejected because many were anti-Semitic incidents which did not rise to the level of hate crimes.

Soave also argued that a small increase in the number of incidents looks like a very large percentage increase if the base is small. Many of the cities reported no hate crimes or only one or two. With such small numbers, any increase looks huge in percentage terms. An increase from one to two is an increase of a hundred percent. Soave was on firm ground with this argument.

As for the design of the study, which Soave called absurdly flawed, it looked only at the few months after the Trump rallies, comparing the counties that did and did not hold rallies, controlling for geographic location, crime rates, size of minority population, percentage of college educated, and number of active hate groups. The idea was to compare similar counties that did and did not have Trump rallies. Soave argued that the comparison counties were not comparable, that rallies were held in cities with big populations, big cities have more hate crimes, and that if population were controlled, the differences would disappear. Without denying the increase in white supremacy activity and anti-Semitic incidents in cities where Trump held a rally, Soave argued such increases were the result of population size, not heated rhetoric. Big cities have more incidents. When he controlled for city size, the difference between Trump rally cities (or more correctly counties) and similar non-rally counties virtually disappeared.

One of Soave's complaints was that the study didn't actually compare before and after in the same cities or counties. That was definitely a weakness in design, but one relatively easily corrected. Since the Anti-Defamation League reports the FBI data on hate crimes in addition to its own data, one can look at the before and after of recorded hate crimes in the cities where Trump's rallies occurred, and the before and after in cities where rallies did not occur. Since Soave was focused on the large cities, I chose a few big cities that did and a few that did not have Trump rallies and looked at the before and after numbers. Using this data, I concluded Soave made some good points: the big cities did experience an increase in hate crimes, regardless of whether or not they had a rally. The number of hate crimes generally rose from 2014 to 2017 or 2018. And some cities reported very few hate crimes, regardless of whether there was a Trump rally.

Thus, a quick look at the data, without fully replicating the academic study, suggests that there were generally increases in cities where Trump held rallies *and* in cities where he did not hold rallies. Much of the increase was in the activity level of white supremacist groups and in anti-Semitic incidents, with a scattering of extremist murders and police shootouts.

On the one hand, the conservative critique holds, there was not a huge increase in cities that held Trump rallies compared to similar cities that did not; on the other hand, there was a general increase in most large cities in the level of white supremacist activity and anti-Semitic acts. The FBI hate crimes data confirms a similar rise in a broad range of hate crimes across cities.

One need not conclude that Trump's divisive rhetoric had no effect; the opposite conclusion is possible, that it had a broader geographic reach through the news media and social media platforms. Trump's rhetoric may have added to an existing upward trend in hate crimes. Alternatively, as the critics on the right argue, the increase in reported hate crimes may not be real, but only an artifact of increased reporting, making more apparent the level of hate crimes that had been occurring for some time.

The claim that Trump rallies vastly increased the level of hate crimes in cities where he held rallies compared to other similar cities was exaggerated and misleading. However, the conclusion of the study's critics that Trump's rhetoric had no effect on increasing hate crimes was not demonstrated. That conclusion goes beyond the data.

False Assumption

Another illustration of relying on a flawed analysis occurred when President Trump repeated the charge that undocumented immigrants committed 63,000 murders since 2001. Since Trump does sometimes repeat false information, and this number seems exaggerated for political purposes, it is worth tracking down the source to see if he quoted it or summarized it accurately. In this case, he did; he was drawing on a blog post by Representative Steven King in 2006. King got his figures from a 2005 Government Accountability Office report that stated that about 27 percent of federal prisoners were criminal aliens. King made mistakes when he used the GAO report.[17]

The GAO report discussed only federal prisons. Federal prisons hold people for criminal violation of immigration laws, such as returning to the U.S. after having been kicked out for illegal entry. Many immigrants held in federal prisons are there for such reasons, not for violent crimes like rape or murder. King concluded that if 28 percent of prisoners were immigrants, then they committed 28 percent of the murders, rapes, and all sorts of other crimes in the U.S., an illogical and incorrect conclusion.[18]

Measuring the Wrong Thing

Sometimes a flawed study is cited over and over, such as the study in California that concluded that a tax increase on the rich increased the out-migration of wealthy people and resulted in a decrease in revenue for the state. That study out of Stanford was flawed: it omitted a key variable and focused on the wrong thing.

When the Governor of Illinois proposed a constitutional amendment to change the state's flat-rate income tax to a graduated tax that would fall more heavily on the rich, opponents immediately charged that the result would be a flight of the rich to lower tax states. They cited the experience of California to make their case, relying on that study out of Stanford University that claimed that after a big hike on top earners in California, there was an increase in millionaires leaving the state, and that they took their income with them, denying the state much revenue. But did this really happen in California? And what about other states that have raised taxes on millionaires; is their experience similar to California's? If the conclusion were true in California, it should also be true in other states, so a test case or two would help in judging the truth value of the claim.

The study cited by the opponents of the millionaire's tax is "Behavioral Responses to State Income Taxation of High Earners: Evidence from California," by Joshua Rauh and Ryan J. Shyu.[19] The study reported that there was an increase over normal migration of .8 percent among those hit by the tax increase, that is, those whose adjusted gross income was over one million dollars a year. The paper did not mention how many people that was, or how many people earning a million dollars or more moved *into* California, or how many millionaires there were after each tax increase that affected the high earners. Critically, the paper did not mention that the number of in-migrants who earned more than one million dollars a year exceeded the numbers of out-migrants.

A pair of academic researchers looked at the number of millionaires after a so-called millionaire's tax was imposed in New Jersey and the one that was imposed in California. In both cases, these researchers found that there were more millionaires after the increase than before.[20]

Young and Varner attribute the increase in millionaires less to in-migration of millionaires and more to native residents becoming millionaires, new people in the ranks. During a period of growth, the rich got richer. In- and out-migration of millionaires, they concluded, was a minor issue compared to the creation of new millionaires and the length of time they remain millionaires.

> For example, in New Jersey in 2005, the out-migration of millionaires increased by 37 individuals—a loss that could be attributed to the new tax. In the same year, however, the millionaire population increased by over 3,000 individuals. Similarly, in California the net migration of millionaires fluctuates each year by about 120 people, while the millionaire population as a whole fluctuates by about 10,000 individuals. Shifts in migration account for only 1 to 3 percent of year-to-year changes in the millionaire population.

Based on the Young and Varner study, one can conclude that out-migration of millionaires, while it does occur, is a very minor event, affecting few people. Those who opposed the so-called millionaire's tax were measuring the wrong thing; they should have been looking at the total number of millionaires, not just the number who left the state of California. Also, the claim was missing context; was the number of rich people leaving the state big or small?

Selective Use of Data (Cherry Picking)

Sometimes when you look at actual data that underlies an argument, you can see that an author relied only on a relatively small portion of the results and ignored the rest. A look at what is missing sometimes reveals a different conclusion.

Black Lives Matter has charged that police kill blacks disproportionately. That charge has been backed up by many researchers. An article in the conservative *National Review* claimed that what accounts for the police shootings is not bias on the part of police, but the level of violent crime in the locations where the shooting takes place. Black neighborhoods are more violent than white neighborhoods, so that is why police kill more blacks than whites. The author goes on to argue that anyone who supports Black Lives Matter protests is inviting and legitimating crime against police officers and destroying the trust relation between police and community.[21]

Several clues in this argument warrant your attention. First, there is a kind of blame-the-victim content; police shoot more blacks because blacks are more violent. It is not the fault of the police; it is the fault of the black community that police shoot them more than they shoot whites. Further, this argument is an example of denialism: the author claims there is no epidemic of racist police shootings. Finally, what might rouse your suspicion is the argument that anyone who protests is hurting police and inviting violence. This is the "shut-up" defense, silencing the opposition. If you protest, you are doing harm.

If you look at the data, the correlation between violent crime rates and police shootings is only about 30 percent, which means that there is a lot of variation still unexplained. (I calculated the correlation using the data spreadsheets from the Mapping Police Violence webpage https://mappingpoliceviolence.org/). MacDonald presented a modest correlation of 30 percent as if it indicated a strong causal relationship that applied to all cities. But it doesn't.

For example, Las Vegas has about half the rate of violent crime as San Bernardino, California, but their rate of police killings is nearly identical. Miami has a rate of violent crime less than half that of Kansas City, Missouri, but has a higher rate of police killings. New York City, with a moderate level of violent crime, has almost no police killings. So, something else is involved besides the level of violent crime in a city.

There is variation in the rate of police killings, not only between cities with similar crime rates, but within cities over time, and this is critical. Oakland, California, when successfully sued by victims of police violence, was put under a court-appointed monitor who oversaw police department reforms, and the city went from one of the highest police shootings in California to one of the lowest.[22]

Some cities that had both high crime rates and high rates of police killings have instituted policies to curb police violence, which have had the effect of reducing *both* the danger to police and the police violence. So, a high violent crime rate does not inevitably turn into (or justify) a high level of police violence. There is a powerful intervening variable of internal police department policies for dealing with threatening or violent situations.

The idea that community violence somehow justifies and explains police violence, and that trying to curb that violence will lead to more police dead or wounded, is not accurate. A more nuanced conclusion was presented by The Use of Force project. "These results indicate that while the chances of killing a civilian increases the more arrests a police department makes, that likelihood is shaped by the department's policies governing how and when police can use force during those encounters." Further, the project report noted, "Officers in police departments with more restrictive policies in place are actually less likely to be killed in the line of duty, less likely to be assaulted, and have similar likelihood of sustaining an injury during an assault."[23]

To summarize, the argument rests initially on the premise that a high rate of violent crime causes the police killings. In recent years, several databases of police killings have been compiled, and federal data lists crime by type, including violent crime, by city, so you can (and I did) look first at the data to see if that assumption is questionable. A close look at the data indicates that there is a modest correlation, but not sufficient to explain the variation between cities in rates of police killings. Moreover, some cities that have had high rates of police killings have been able to bring the numbers down. There is nothing inevitable about the relationship between high crime rates and police killings.

One variable that helps explain that variation is the difference between police departments in their policies regarding use of force. Cities that have more and better policies, such as using alternative means to defuse violence before resorting to force, have fewer police killings, and also have fewer police killed. The argument that police need to be violent in violent cities to stay alive and unharmed turns out to be a shibboleth.

The key to analysis in this case is finding the raw data, checking the degree of correlation between violent crime rates and police killings (easy with spreadsheets), and seeing that the correlation is modest, which brings the initial premise into question. One can then examine the variation between cities that have high rates of violent crime. Some of them have high rates of police violence while others do not. Police department policies concerning the use of deadly force have an effect on police killings of civilians. Further, departments with well-designed policies on the use of force have fewer injuries and fewer killings of police officers.

The author assumed that a correlation observed in some cities applied to all cities, a form of cherry picking, or selective use of data. Second, the author left something important out of the analysis. What else besides the violent crime rate might influence the number of police killings? In this case, the variable that was missing was the nature of the departmental policy on the use of deadly force.

A second example of selective use of data involves estimates of the number of deaths from covid-19. A Fox News host, Laura Ingraham, claimed that the number of deaths from covid-19 had been grossly exaggerated, implying that the virus was much less dangerous than the media and the government claimed. Ingraham cited as evidence the CDC data on deaths, which was much lower than any other source. But if you go to the CDC page for the estimated number of deaths from covid-19, in a highlighted box, the CDC warns that their numbers will not match other sources because the CDC numbers are based on death certificates that are sent to them. Their numbers are not based on state public health reports or governors' tallies. Even if all death certificates were sent to the CDC, there would be a considerable time lag between the deaths and the CDC reports of death. At the very least, the CDC numbers would be out of date.[24]

The *Washington Post* analysis indicates that if anything, the number of officially reported deaths has been underestimated, because many of the "excess" deaths, that is, deaths over the normal rates of death, have been attributed to other causes but are actually the result of covid-19.

No Real Data

To this point, the chapter has dealt with misuse or misinterpretation of data, but sometimes there is no data underlying the claim.

For example, the idea that 80 percent of America's medicine comes from China has been circulating widely. If you are of a curious turn of mind, the first question that should occur to you is how anyone could know what proportion of medicine in the U.S. is imported from China. The Food and Drug Administration doesn't track the quantity of drugs imported from any foreign country. There is no data. That should give you pause and lead you deeper into the story.

Following the advice in the previous chapter, a good place to start to look for answers is in the opposition view. Eric Boehm challenged the conclusion that most of America's medicine comes from China. He was writing in *Reason Magazine*, which promotes a libertarian, free market ideology. He worried that the overestimate of dependence on China would lead to a policy of manufacturing all drugs in the U.S. in order to prevent the possibility of the Chinese cutting off our medical supplies during a pandemic.[25]

Boehm traced the source of the 80 percent figure to a single government report and claimed that that study did not say what the China mistrusters say it says. He demonstrated that those who claim the 80 percent figure could not possibly know that.

He found that Politico published the figure, citing a press release from Senator Chuck Grassley. Boehm quoted from the press release: "80 percent of Active Pharmaceutical Ingredients are produced abroad, the majority in China and India." The press release was vague, using weasel words like "the majority." How big a majority? 51 percent? 80 percent? It was unspecified. Second, India and China were classed together, with no indication how their shares might be divided up. Was most of it produced in India? Or most in China? Or half and half? It was unclear. The source of the information did not say what opponents of U.S. imports of medicine from China said that it said.

Boehm then continued to track backward. Grassley had relied on a Government Accountability Office study drawing on FDA data that actually said "Nearly 40 percent of finished drugs and approximately 80 percent of active pharmaceutical ingredients (API) are manufactured in registered establishments in more than 150 countries."[26] From this, we do not have any idea what proportion of those finished drugs or components were made in China. Moreover, as Boehm points out, FDA tracks only manufacturing facilities, not supply chains for any particular drug. Only 13 percent of the manufacturing facilities tracked by the FDA are in China, but no one has tracked how much each factory produces, where it gets its raw materials, or how much of its product is exported to the U.S. It was impossible for anyone using such data to know what proportion of our medicines are being produced in China.

To get started with this analysis, you would have to look for an opponent to the argument you are looking at. To do that, you need to look at who is promoting the argument you are looking at and what they hope to achieve. In this case, anti-China hawks hoped to curtail trade with China and perhaps stimulate a domestic pharmaceutical industry through regulation that prohibited companies from locating abroad where costs were cheaper. This goal would have been apparent if you looked for congressional testimony or read the articles and books that claimed the 80 percent figure was correct. Once you had one side, you could then look for the other side, the free trade side, which might lead you to *Reason Magazine*, one of the outstanding publications with this point of view. Boehm does a lot of the work for you, but if you didn't find an opposition piece, you could do the tracking yourself. Who is cited as the source of the figure, and who did that person cite? And what did those sources actually say? By the time you get that far, you may not be a free trade advocate, but you will probably accept that the 80 percent figure used as a justification for policy is simply wrong. Boehm makes a good case.

Weaponizing the Misuse of Sources

Bryce Hill of Illinois Policy, an anti-tax website, was trying to undermine the credibility of his opponent, accusing Ralph Martire of bias and misuse of data. He claimed that Martire, a supporter of a progressive income tax for Illinois, had misquoted or misinterpreted the sources he cited that demonstrated that progressive taxes had little effect on economic growth.[27] Efforts to undermine the credibility of opponents instead of dealing directly with their arguments should put you on your guard. It is worth checking out the charges. Did Martire misrepresent his sources?

Martire cited as evidence an article by Donald Bruce and John Deskins.[28] Martire quoted from the study, "We find no evidence of an economically significant effect of state tax portfolios on entrepreneurial activity." Hill charged that this quote "is particularly misleading because 'state tax portfolios' refer to the share of revenue generated by certain taxes in a given state—not the level of taxation." But what the source Martire cited actually said is that "state tax policies generally do not appear to have quantitatively important effects on entrepreneurial activity." It appears that Hill, rather than Martire, was misinterpreting the source, which included both the level of the income tax and its progressivity.

A second citation that Hill critiqued was a reference to a Congressional Budget Office testimony. Hill claimed "Martire suggests the CBO research finds no correlation between tax policy and job creation, but this is simply not what the testimony says." Hill argued that what the testimony actually said is that if tax breaks that were slated to be terminated were extended, it would increase economic growth in 2013. What did the testimony actually say?

> Policies that would primarily affect businesses' cash flow but would have little impact on their marginal incentives to hire or invest would have only small effects. Such policies include reducing business income taxes and reducing tax rates on repatriated foreign earnings.[29]

Thus, what the CBO testimony actually said was that reducing income taxes on businesses, by itself, was unlikely to have much positive effect on speeding up an economic recovery.

What Martire actually said, in context, was

> In fact, after an exhaustive study, the nonpartisan Congressional Budget Office found no statistically meaningful relationship between federal tax policy—which is far more material than any state tax policy—and job growth. What the CBO did find, however, was that the real reason businesses hire more workers—drum roll please—is to meet growing demand for the products or services they produce.[30]

In this latter example, Martire overstated the CBO conclusion, but he did get at the essence of it, that tax reduction by itself is unlikely to produce growth, because businesses expand, creating new jobs to meet market demand, not because they have more cash on hand. Martire can be appropriately charged with oversimplification of CBO's results, but not of distorting the meaning.

Conclusion

Checking out sources is a useful way of evaluating opinion pieces. Did some expert, political opponent, or report actually say what a writer or speaker claims he, she, or it said or did the speaker or writer misrepresent the source? Was the source itself correct or misleading? Was there actually credible evidence provided in the source? When the sources are included in the story, checking them out is usually straightforward. Political opponents sometimes charge each other with misrepresentation of sources in an effort to deny their opponents legitimacy. Those charges are also worth checking out.

Notes

1. Raymond Markey, "FactCheck Q&A: Have 90% of Labor MPs Worked in Trade Unions?," *The Conversation*, November 12, 2018, https://theconversation.com/factcheck-qanda-have-90-of-labor-mps-worked-in-trade-unions-104226.
2. Linda Qiu, "Trump Misquotes Ukrainian President in Latest Impeachment Defense," *New York Times*, December 2, 2019, www.nytimes.com/2019/12/02/us/politics/trump-zelensky-fact-check.html?action=click&module=RelatedLinks&pgtype=Article.
3. Annie Karni and Maggie Haberman, "Trump Has a Habit of Quoting His Allies on Twitter Saying Things They Never Said," *NYT*, December 20, 2019, www.nytimes.com/2019/12/20/us/politics/trump-twitter-quotes.html.
4. Jessica Estepa, "Albert Einstein Estate Corrects Old Ivanka Trump Tweet: No, He Didn't Say That," *USA Today*, July 24, 2017, www.usatoday.com/story/news/politics/onpolitics/2017/07/24/albert-einstein-estate-corrects-ivanka-trump-tweet-no-he-didnt-say/504692001/.
5. Tiana Lowe, "CBO Details the Democrats' Plan to Depress the Economy until the 2020 Election," *The Washington Examiner*, June 5, 2020, www.washingtonexaminer.com/opinion/cbo-details-the-democrats-plan-to-rig-the-2020-election-using-the-coronavirus.
6. Letter from Phillip Swagel, Director of the Congressional Budget Office, to Senator Charles Grassley, June 4, 2020, Subject: Economic Effects of Additional Unemployment Benefits of $600 per Week, www.cbo.gov/system/files/2020-06/56387-CBO-Grassley-Letter.pdf.
7. Tomoko Hasegawa, Shinichiro Fujimori, S. Petr Havlík, et al., "Risk of Increased Food Insecurity under Stringent Global Climate Change Mitigation Policy," *Nature Climate Change* 8, 2018, pp. 699–703, https://doi.org/10.1038/s41558-018-0230-x.
8. Paul Bedard, "FBI: Record Number of Illegal Immigrants Barred from Buying Guns," *The Washington Examiner*, December 27, 2018, www.washingtonexaminer.com/washington-secrets/fbi-record-number-of-illegal-immigrants-tried-to-buy-guns.
9. Matt Vespa, "Oh Goodie: FBI Says a Record Number of Illegal Tried to Purchase Guns This Year," *Townhall*, December 29, 2018. https://townhall.com/tipsheet/mattvespa/2018/12/29/oh-goodie-fbi-says-a-record-number-of-illegal-tried-to-purchase-guns-this-year-n2538234.
10. FBI National Instant Criminal Background Check System, www.fbi.gov/services/cjis/nics.

11 The data come from the FBI National Instant Criminal Background Check System (NICS), various years, www.fbi.gov/services/cjis/nics.
12 David Leonhardt, "Truth, Fiction and Lou Dobbs," *NYT*, May 30, 2007, www.nytimes.com/2007/05/30/business/30leonhardt.html.
13 https://thehill.com/homenews/morning-report/493281-the-hills-morning-report.
14 Corona Virus Briefing, "22 Million Americans Have Filed for Unemployment in the Past Four Weeks," *NYT*, April 16, 2020, www.nytimes.com/2020/04/16/us/coronavirus-cases-live-updates.html?utm_source=&utm_medium=email&utm_campaign=29097#link-15da1e43.
15 Ayal Feinberg, Regina Branton, and Valerie Martinez-Ebers, "The Trump Effect: How 2016 Campaign Rallies Explain Spikes in Hate," https://lmas.unt.edu/sites/lmas.unt.edu/files/lmas/Hate%20Incidents%20Spike_0.pdf.
16 Robby Soave, "Hate Crimes Hogwash," *The Washington Examiner*, September 19, 2019, www.washingtonexaminer.com/opinion/hate-crimes-hogwash.
17 Philip Bump, "The Original Source for Trump's Claim of 63,000 Immigrant Murders? Bad Data from Steve King in 2006," *The Washington Post*, June 22, 2018.
18 Arturo Garcia and Bethania Palma, "Have Undocumented Immigrants Killed 63,000 American Citizens Since 9/11?," *Snopes*, June 22, 2018, www.snopes.com/fact-check/have-undocumented-killed-63000-us-9-11/.
19 NBER Working Paper No. 26349, October 2019.
20 Cristobal Young and Charles Varner, "Do Millionaires Migrate When Tax Rates Are Raised?," *Pathways*, Summer 2014, https://inequality.stanford.edu/sites/default/files/Pathways_Summer_2014_millionaire_tax_rates.pdf.
21 Heather MacDonald, "There Is No Epidemic of Racist Police Shootings," *The National Review*, July 31, 2019, www.nationalreview.com/2019/07/white-cops-dont-commit-more-shootings/.
22 Darwin BondGraham, "'Out of Control Police Department': Vallejo Faces New Claims of Racial Profiling and Brutality," *The Guardian*, September 20, 2019, www.theguardian.com/us-news/2019/sep/20/vallejo-police-department-racial-profiling-brutality-claims.
23 Samuel Sinyangwe, "Examining the Role of Use of Force Policies in Ending Police Violence," *Use of Force Study*, September 20, 2016, https://static1.squarespace.com/static/56996151cbced68b170389f4/t/57e17531725e25ec2e648650/1474393399581/Use+of+Force+Study.pdf.
24 Aaron Blake, "Fox News and Trump Allies Keep Floating Debunked Theories about an Inflated Coronavirus Death Toll," *The Washington Post*, May 4, 2020, www.washingtonpost.com/politics/2020/05/04/fox-news-trump-allies-keep-searching-evidence-an-inflated-coronavirus-death-toll-all-wrong-places/.
25 Eric Boehm, "Why You Shouldn't Trust Anyone Who Claims 80 Percent of America's Drugs Come From China," *Reason Magazine*, April 6, 2020, https://reason.com/2020/04/06/why-you-shouldnt-trust-anyone-who-claims-80-percent-of-americas-drugs-come-from-china/.
26 GAO-17-143.
27 Bryce Hill, "'Fair Tax' Backer Spreading Falsehoods, Misinformation," *Illinois Policy*, May 6, 2019, www.illinoispolicy.org/fair-tax-backer-spreading-falsehoods-misinformation/.
28 "Can State Tax Policies Be Used to Promote Entrepreneurial Activity?," *Small Business Economics*, 38(4), 2012, pp. 375–397, https://doi.org/10.1007/s11187-010-9262-y.
29 Statement of Douglas W. Elmendorf, Director, Congressional Budget Office, Policies for Increasing Economic Growth and Employment in 2012 and 2013 before the Committee on the Budget United States Senate, November 15, 2011, p. 2.
30 SJR, Ralph Martire, "Progressive Tax Will Help Illinois Address Its Problems," April 16, 2019, www.sj-r.com/opinion/20190416/ralph-martire-progressive-tax-will-help-illinois-address-its-problems.

7

CONSPIRACY THEORIES

Recognizing Conspiracy Theories

A conspiracy theory is an unlikely story or claim about an event or set of events. The story often involves at least several people engaged in a secret plot that the author has found out about. Conspiracy theories may contradict an official or widely accepted version of an event. They usually provide little or no evidence, although they often contain a kernel of truth. They often target opponents and can be wildly illogical.

Little or No Evidence

Typically, conspiracy theories present no evidence, faked evidence, or only creative, plausible-sounding guesswork. Some conspiracy promoters claim that rock-solid evidence exists and will be made public in the future, but that future never comes. Alternatively, there is evidence, but the promoters of the conspiracy cannot get it because suppressing the evidence is part of the plot they have identified.

A classic illustration of a conspiracy theory that provided no evidence was the claim that Obama was not born in the U.S., and hence was ineligible to be president. In order to keep this fact secret, many people had to be in on the plot, including the officials who produced Obama's birth certificate and the newspapers that reported the birth at the time. According to this conspiracy theory, the real documents that would have shown Obama's ineligibility to be president were kept hidden. Thus, the so-called "birthers" were unable to present any evidence supporting their claims about Obama's birthplace.[1] Trump, who supported the conspiracy, questioned in 2013 why the state health director who verified Obama's birth certificate was killed in an airplane crash while others on the plane survived.

Contains a Kernel of Truth

Another common feature of conspiracy theories is that they contain a kernel of truth, which makes them more convincing. For example, anti-vaxxers circulated a conspiracy theory that vaccinations contained microchips intended to track people. This argument probably was based on a real event. Researchers had engaged in a science project in which quantum dots, tiny semiconductors, were injected into animals (with the goal of eventually injecting them into people) that would allow researchers to know who had received what vaccinations. The dots are not microchips, they just emit a bit of light, but the real story was close enough to be misinterpreted.[2]

Conspiracists build on the factual core, often adding some outrageous or illogical conclusions. For example, there is a right-wing group in Germany that, building on a court decision that actually occurred, denies the existence of the German Republic. Members of this group argue that the Third Reich of the Hitler era still exists. They appoint themselves as officials, rejecting the authority of German government. They don't pay taxes. They claim territory that was once German. And some members shoot police. The members promote a conspiracy theory that the German Federal Republic is controlled by Jews or a Zionist-Freemason combination.

Since there is an internationally recognized modern German state with all the institutions to run a country, including courts, a parliament, and a civil bureaucracy, you should be skeptical about claims that it doesn't exist or that it is controlled by a small group of Jews and Freemasons. Nevertheless, there is some basis, some kernel of truth in this theory.

After Germany surrendered after World War II, the allies occupied Germany for four years, after which a determination had to be made as to whether the government in West Germany was a successor to the Reich, or if it was the same as the Reich that was in power before 1945. In 1973, the Federal Constitutional Court concluded that despite the German surrender, the Reich continued in existence, but lacked the institutions that would allow it to govern.[3] Building on this court case, the Reichsburgers decided to recreate the institutions of the Reich, claiming that old boundaries and the Weimar constitution of 1919 are currently in effect.[4]

Since conspiracy theories may be partly true, it is important to be able to identify and examine the logic (or lack of logic) separating the true part from the imagined part.

Targets Opponents and Enemies

You cannot always recognize conspiracy theories by their targets, but they are usually aimed at traditional enemies. Sometimes they target minorities, as in the German case, at other times they target candidates for office. They also target rich and famous people outside of government who are thought to endorse or fund causes with which the conspiracy theorists disagree. There might be some loose association linking such people with the issue. Billionaire Bill Gates supports health issues around the world, so linking him with dangerous vaccinations has a kind of (perverse?) logic to it. Billionaire George Soros gave some one-time contributions to organizations funding gun control, so in conspiracy theories, he became the controlling hand behind survivors of a mass school shooting who made demands for gun control.

Illogical

Conspiracy theories often begin with a core of something that did happen, and then come to some utterly illogical conclusion. Germany took in many Muslim immigrants, so conspiracists conclude that Germany is now under sharia law. Former president Obama had spent a little time in Indonesia as a child, thus according to conspiracy theories he wasn't born in the U.S. and was not eligible to be president.

Analyzing Conspiracy Theories

Because conspiracy theories often lack evidence, examining the evidence is not the main tactic for checking them out. Conspiracy theories are often fact-checked, so looking at the fact-checkers is a useful approach. If the fact-checkers have not addressed the charges of conspiracy, you can examine who was promoting the conspiracy, its goal, and the site where the story appeared. If the goal of the conspiracy theory is to undermine someone, derail some policy, or deflect blame, you might want to withhold your approval until you can check out the claims. You can also check the logic of the narrative. If you find a major gap in logic, you should mistrust it. A different approach that works sometimes is to ask yourself, what happened next. Did what happened next disprove the conspiracy theory?

Look for the Purpose

Sometimes conspiracy theories are created by people trying to prevent gun control, limit women's access to legal abortions, or derail climate change policies. Sometimes those who create or pass along conspiracy theories cast blame on and attribute evil motives to their enemies. For such folks, the covid-19 pandemic has proved a useful foil. Blaming China for the virus, and hence all Chinese regardless of whether they live in China or elsewhere, has been common.

A commentator on Turkish state television claimed that Jews engineered this virus, building on their earlier work with avian flu. The motive of the Jews was global domination. In a related conspiracy theory in Turkey, the head of a small Islamist party assumed Zionism was responsible. He stated as fact that Jews wanted to decrease the number of people in the world. A columnist from East Jerusalem, a member of the Popular Front for the

Liberation of Palestine, claimed the virus was part of a joint U.S.-Israeli effort to attack China and Iran.[5]

Sometimes conspiracy theories are the work of campaign staffers or political supporters trying to take down a political opponent. Pizzagate is a good example of such an effort, since the clear purpose of this conspiracy theory was to delegitimize Hillary Clinton and make sure she would lose her race for president. If that goal made you suspicious, there are several ways you can take the story apart.

Delegitimizing Opponents

According to a conspiracy theory that has been called Pizzagate, Hillary Clinton and other top Democrats were running a human trafficking and child sex ring at a pizza restaurant. What possible motivation could Hillary Clinton have for running a child sex ring, or running it out of a pizza parlor? It sounded crazy, and the perpetrators of this conspiracy never addressed the question of motivation. If a story sounds unlikely to be true, you should probably try to check it out before accepting it or passing it along.

A man with an AR 15 style automatic weapon showed up at a pizza parlor because he believed the conspiracy theory circulating on the web that Hillary Clinton and other top Democrats were running a human trafficking and child sex ring there. He fired one or more shots, determined to wipe out the child sex ring. There was nothing there but a pizza parlor. *What happened next?* The man, Edgar Maddison Welch, was arrested and charged with assault with a deadly weapon.

In the Pizzagate case, *the goal* was to prevent Hillary Clinton from being elected president. One should be skeptical of outrageous claims about political opponents that are made just before an election, and hence cannot be examined carefully before the vote takes place. A Reddit user had posted this anti-Clinton conspiracy theory on November 4, 2016, four days before the presidential election.[6]

As for *evidence*, those promoting the sex conspiracy at the pizza parlor claimed that there were secret, coded words in the filched email of Democrat John Podesta that suggested a sex ring. A plot depending on a secret code that only the narrator(s) can decipher gets away from documentable narrative and into imagination. Or paranoia.

Why did Podesta get so many emails about eating pizza, the conspiracists wondered. Pizza, they thought, was a code word for illegal sex trafficking. This conclusion was reinforced by an email in which the restaurant owner, Alefantis, "thanked Podesta for attending a fundraiser at the restaurant but regretted not making him a pizza."[7]

Most likely, pizza had nothing to do with sex trafficking, but rather with lunch or dinner. The unlabeled doors to the restaurant's restrooms were to indicate that they were not restricted to one sex. They didn't lead to some secret back room. The actual back rooms were for ping-pong players, which relates to the restaurant's name, Comet Ping-Pong Pizzeria. Some of the photographs which were presented as evidence were taken from random websites; some pictures of children were taken from Facebook pages of the restaurant's customers and from family and friends.[8]

Preventing a Policy

Looking into the intention of a conspiracy theory can be helpful in examining it. For a large group of conspiracy theories, the goal is to prevent the political or policy consequences of something that happened. The strategy in such cases is to deny that the events actually took place. Since many people were involved in the events and know that they happened, it can be difficult to make a convincing argument that they did not occur. Consequently, one technique commonly used by denialists is to try to undermine the credibility of those who say that the event happened.

One conspiracy theory stated that the survivors of the Parkland school shooting who were advocating gun control were paid actors. There was no real shooting, there were no real deaths. If the legitimacy of the survivors could be questioned, if they were not actual survivors, their arguments would have little or no power. Note that the argument here works to delegitimize the opposition, so that nothing they say will be taken seriously. This kind of argument should encourage further examination.

Those putting forth this conspiracy theory tried to offer proof that David Hogg, a survivor who publicly advocated gun control, was a "crisis actor" and not a student at Parkland. A crisis actor is someone who plays a role in a simulation to train first responders to deal with a crisis. Those who denied that the Parkland shooting was real maintained that Hogg went to school in California, not Florida, so he was not a survivor of a mass shooting.

What did the fact-checkers say about this conspiracy theory? Fact-checkers are good at looking into evidence when such is provided. Snopes rated the accusation false, calling attention to a clumsily cut-and-pasted photo from the Parkland yearbook into that of a California school.[9] Politifact rated the claim "pants on fire," its designation for a flagrant lie.[10]

One of the people promoting this conspiracy was well-known conspiracist Alex Jones on the right-wing site Infowars. Media Bias/Fact Check describes the site: "Overall, InfoWars/Alex Jones is a crackpot, tin foil hat level conspiracy website that also strongly promotes pseudoscience. The amount of fake news and debunked conspiracy claims, as well as extreme right-wing bias, renders InfoWars a non-credible source on any level."

The conspiracy spewing site, gatewaypundit.com, pushed a related conspiracy story. Wikipedia describes the Gateway Pundit site as an American far-right news and opinion website created to "speak the truth" and to "expose the wickedness of the left." Any website or individual who claims publicly to have "The Truth" should make you suspicious; use of color words like "wickedness" should further make you wonder about the reliability of stories posted on the site.

The Gateway Pundit version of the events emphasized that operatives linked to liberal billionaire George Soros had "selected anti-Trump kids to be the face" of the Parkland tragedy and maintained that the students were paid actors.[11]

The site provided no evidence, claiming only that it had received a tip from the father of one of the students who said the young folks were all in the same drama club. Elaborating their claims, the site argued "BEHIND THE TEENAGERS, WORKING AS THE STRING-PULLERS, ARE THE SAME PEOPLE BEHIND THE WOMEN'S MARCH. THEY ARE VEHEMENTLY ANTI-GUN, ANTI-AMERICAN, AND ANTI-TRUMP – THIS IS PART OF THEIR SALES PITCH." Note the capital letters in the original, signifying shouting.

The Gateway Pundit site further claimed that brainwashing was the goal of the adults behind the student protests. The students were brainwashed into thinking that taking guns from people would keep them safe. No proof was offered that the students were paid actors and not survivors of the violence; further, no proof was given of the connection between founders of the Women's March and the students, and additionally, no evidence was provided supporting the claim that the students were brainwashed.

Whenever you see the claim that an event was carried out by crisis actors, you should be skeptical. Similar conspiracy theories were woven about the Sandy Hook elementary school massacre in 2012, stating that the shooting was fake, carried out by actors. Parents whose children were killed were stunned, adding to their grief.

David Clarke, former sheriff of Milwaukee County, passed along the charge that democratic billionaire George Soros had organized the students to demand gun control. Clarke claimed to have "two missions right now, the re-election of President Donald Trump and the total destruction of the progressive movement, a parasite that is destroying America." The use of color words like "parasite" and exaggerations such as the progressive movement is destroying America should alert you to what might be a baseless conspiracy theory. Clarke later continued his attacks on Soros, claiming that Soros was behind the pandemic of covid-19 that swept the world in 2020. He called for bars and restaurants to stay open, ignoring the threat of contagion.

Clarke's claim was that there had been a conspiracy, a secret plot, between the students and Soros, to push for policies favoring gun control. By bringing Soros into his theory, Clarke picked on a favorite target of the right wing, since Soros was Jewish, rich, and supported liberal causes such as popular movements for justice, education, public health, and independent media. Was there any evidence for Clark's conspiracy theory? Soros's foundation had made some grants to organizations that favored background checks for gun purchases and bans on assault weapons.[12]

The Trace, a pro-gun control newsletter, reported that Soros's foundation made only limited, one-time contributions to organizations working toward reducing gun violence after the Parkland massacre, and that gun control had not been a serious focus of Soros's foundation. Thus, there was a kernel of truth to the conspiracy theory, but the rest was made up.[13]

The former sheriff provided no actual evidence to support his accusation that Soros was the mastermind behind the plot to take guns away from people. "The well ORGANIZED effort by Florida school students demanding gun control has GEORGE SOROS' FINGERPRINTS all over it," Clark had written [capitalization is in the original]. It was obvious to him that the students could not have organized themselves so it must have been Soros. This argument is not logical. The students may well have organized themselves, contrary to his assertion, but even if they didn't, there is no reason to conclude that they had been organized by Soros. This is a common form of argumentation in conspiracy theories, "it cannot be X so it must be Y." They may present some slight evidence of why it cannot be X, (though in this case there was none), but generally do not present evidence why it must therefore be Y.

In the Parkland mass shooting case, the opponents of gun control chose to deny the legitimacy of the students who were advocating for fewer guns. Other strategies include directly denying that an event took place or agreeing that it happened but arguing for its unimportance.

Opposing a Mandate

In the face of a pandemic, with over a million cases of covid-19 worldwide and over 60,000 deaths by early April 2020, before the epidemic had reached a peak, deniers were busy saying it was all exaggerated, a hoax. The purpose of the hoax, they claimed, was to expand government control over everyday lives, telling people what to do and what not to do. Those spreading this conspiracy theory deny the severity of the virus and the need for shelter-at-home orders. Citizens should just ignore the virus and go back to school and back to work.

On the one hand, the purpose of the denial of the pandemic was to reopen the economy, allowing people to go back to work, to socialize, and to go to restaurants and shows. On the other hand, a flourishing economy supports the election of the incumbent, in this case President Trump.

What kind of evidence was provided to back up the theory? Advocates went around to hospital parking lots, saw them empty, and hence challenged the narrative that hospitals were overcrowded with covid-19 patients. They talked to nurses who said their hospitals were not full. They jumped from these observations to the conclusion that the virus was a sham, without considering other possibilities. This is a problem in logic, jumping to conclusions not warranted by the evidence presented.

In this case, hospitals were delaying nearly all discretionary surgery; visitors were prohibited from entering the hospital; and staffing was getting thinner due to illness among the medical service providers. Some hospitals were getting ready for a deluge, emptying beds in anticipation of a flood of patients. Parking lots were emptier than usual because of the presence of the pandemic, not because of its absence. Politifact (the fact-checker) declared as false the claim that the "Pictures and reports of empty hospitals" prove COVID-19 spread is a "fake crisis for real government planned agendas."[14]

Virus deniers don't wear masks, don't obey stay in place orders, and don't get vaccinated. They are more likely to catch the disease and spread it to others. Being able to see through a conspiracy theory like this one can be a matter of health and even life. If you needed more motivation to finish this chapter, you now have it.

Blame Shifting

After the homicide of an unarmed black man in police custody in Minneapolis, demonstrations against police brutality broke out all over the country and in many other countries as well. President Trump advocated responding to such demonstrations and any associated looting with strong repression by police and the national guard. In Buffalo, police, trying to clear an area for an 8 pm curfew, pushed an old man, who fell backwards and hit his head on the ground, knocking him out and causing bleeding from one ear. The police then walked by his inert body without stopping to help. The video went viral.

President Trump responded by retweeting a claim that the elderly man, a frequent attendee at peace marches, was really an Antifa provocateur who only pretended to fall. Trump often criticized Antifa, short for anti-fascist, because the group opposed his supporters and policies. If he maintained an enemies list, Antifa would have been on it. The president's retweet was an effort to divert blame from the police to Antifa and to the victim, which should make you question the claim. According to Trump, the police were innocent, they didn't push the man down. Moreover, the protester had been carrying something in his hand which the conspiracy theory called a device to track and disable police communications.

No evidence was provided that the protester had anything to do with Antifa, and none has surfaced since the event. No evidence was provided that the protester was waving some handheld device for scanning and blocking police communications. And no evidence was provided that the protester only pretended to hit his head on the concrete.

The video shows a cell phone; it took a bit of imagination to claim that it was a secret device to locate and black out police communications. BBC reality check noted that a cell phone cannot jam police communications, that a much more sophisticated bit of equipment would be needed, that most emergency communications can block such devices, and that a person would not need to be close to an officer to make it work.[15]

Where did this conspiracy theory appear? The idea that the protester was a member of Antifa was posted first on a conservative blog ConservativeTreehouse, and then appeared on the conservative One America News Network (OANN), where President Trump picked it up.

ConservativeTreehouse is a known site for originating conspiracy theories, such as that Puerto Rican truck drivers were withholding hurricane relief and that a top official at the Centers for Disease Control and Prevention was weaponizing the coronavirus to hurt Trump. The site also promoted the conspiracy theory that the Russia investigation was put forward by members of the deep-state to undermine Trump. In the Buffalo case of the old man pushed down by police, the site claimed that the old man was using a police tracker.[16]

One America News picked up the conspiracy theory, citing ConservativeTreehouse as a source. One America News often promotes conspiracy theories. Media Bias/Fact Check describes OAN as follows: "Overall, we rate One America News Questionable based on far-right bias, lack of sourcing, promotion of conspiracy theories, and propaganda as well as numerous failed fact checks. OAN is not a credible news source."

The reporter on OAN who elaborated the theory was Kristian Rouz. Besides OAN, he also worked for a Kremlin news service, Sputnik, that had been implicated by the FBI as trying to interfere in the 2016 presidential elections. Rouz was not a trustworthy source either.

In this case, it was not difficult tracking down the origin of this conspiracy theory. Trump's tweet acknowledged the One America News; the reporter on the One America News identified the ConservativeTreehouse as a source.

Looking at the sources of this conspiracy theory, the lack of evidence presented for it, and its purpose—blaming the victim, diverting blame from the police—this conspiracy theory looks fake. The fact-checkers agreed. For example, the *Washington Post* fact-checker gave it four Pinocchio's, its strongest rating for a no-good, very bad, utterly untruthful, made-up story.

In another example of a blame-shifting conspiracy theory, Trump and his followers tried to divert blame for Russian intervention in the 2016 election on Trump's behalf. According to this conspiracy theory, Hillary Clinton contracted with Ukrainian agents to pretend to be Russian hackers. These fake Russians broke into the computers of the Democratic National Committee and took emails, which were then made public. The Ukrainian-owned security company CrowdStrike was called to cover the tracks of the Ukrainians.

The hacked server was then hidden, presumably in Ukraine, to make sure no one ever detected the scheme.

What actually happened was that the Democratic National Committee, suspecting it had been hacked, called in the experts—CrowdStrike—to investigate. Crowdstrike took digital images of all the DNC mail servers, a normal procedure, and turned over the evidence to the FBI.

There is no indication that anything was missing or not turned over. Both CrowdStrike and the intelligence services agreed that the Russians had done the hacking. Working around this evidence, the conspiracists imagined another secret server that was not turned over. Note that this charge cannot be proved or disproved. The server's location was so secret no one can find it. That a key piece of evidence cannot be found is typical of conspiracy theories.[17]

If you had been confronted with the CrowdStrike conspiracy, that Hillary had schemed to steal the Democratic National Committee's email and publish it in order to blame the Russians, how would you go about examining it?

First, did it sound reasonable? Would Hillary Clinton and the Democratic National Committee hack and release their own emails in order to discredit Trump, knowing the damage that those emails might do to their own election chances? That sounds unlikely on the face of it, and hence invites further investigation.

You might then ask yourself, what is the purpose of this conspiracy theory? If it was true that Russia stole and published the damaging email, then Russia was helping Trump win the election. If Russia helped Trump win the election, then Trump's legitimacy as president was questionable, and Trump would be under an obligation to Russia's president. The purpose of this conspiracy theory was to shift blame for the hacking from Russia to Ukraine. Blame shifting should make you skeptical about this conspiracy theory.

If you looked up CrowdStrike online, you would find out that it is an American information technology company based in Sunnyvale, California with no ties to Ukraine. It specializes in helping companies and governments prevent intrusions into their cyberdata. One of its three founders, Dmitri Alperovitch, was born in Russia, not Ukraine.

The fact-checkers have repeatedly debunked the claim that Hillary and the DNC stole their own email. All the basic elements of the story that could be checked were incorrect. The CrowdStrike company was not owned by a wealthy Ukrainian. There was no connection between CrowdStrike and Ukraine. There was no evidence anywhere of a Ukrainian connection.

A common claim of conspiracy theorists is that one group of actors has secretly carried out a destructive action in order to put the blame on selected others. This tactic is called "a false flag." The origin of the term comes from a time when pirate ships hoisted a flag from another country, casting blame on the country whose flag they were flying while they sailed off with stolen goods.

Along these lines, some Republicans claimed that Democrats were behind explosive devices sent to the Obamas, the Clintons, and former CIA director John Brennan. The Republicans argued that Democrats did this to fellow Democrats in order to blame Republicans.[18]

False flags are a way of deflecting blame, and so should make you suspicious enough to look into the claim. A useful technique in this case is to ask, what happened next? The bomb maker, Cesar Sayoc, a registered Republican and avid Trump supporter, was arrested, convicted, and sentenced to 20 years in prison.[19] Apparently, the judicial system did not believe that Democrats sent the explosive devices in order to blame Republicans.

One of the most important and long-lived conspiracy theories claims that the collapse of the Twin Towers and building 7 in New York City in 2001 did not occur in the way that the U.S. government claimed. What really happened, according to these conspiracy theorists, is that a secret cohort in the U.S. government was responsible for the buildings' collapse, not airplanes flown by militant Muslims crashing into the World Trade towers. They argued that the buildings were taken down by explosives planted in the buildings.

One effect of this conspiracy theory is to shift blame from militant Muslims to actors in the U.S. government. The idea that the buildings were brought down by a faction within the U.S. government contradicted widely accepted versions of what occurred, another clue that the story deserves a deeper look.

The conspiracy theorists argued that airplane fuel could not have created a fire hot enough to melt steel beams and bring down the buildings so it must have been the work of a secret cabal inside the U.S. government. Note the pattern of illogic; it could not have been X so it must have been Y.

Experts refuting the conspiracy theory responded that the fire need not have been hot enough to melt steel beams in order to weaken them and make them unable to bear the load of the upper stories. So, it certainly was possible that the airplanes which flew into the building caused its collapse.

What about the second portion of the argument? A cohort of conservatives inside the government presumably brought down the Twin Towers in a massive false-flag action blaming the militant Muslims.

One place to begin analyzing this claim is to look at who was circulating the conspiracy version of 9/11. What were they trying to accomplish? Why would they try to divert blame in this manner?

A central promoter of this theory is an architect named Richard Gage, who founded an organization called the Architects and Engineers for 9/11 Truth. It is wise to be at least a bit skeptical about any claim of having *the truth*, which has been withheld from the public by the conspirators.

The organization, founded in 2006, consists of over 3200 architects and engineers and thousands of members of the general public. Many of the members are people who should know something about building design and strength. The group was active in trying to refute the official explanation put forth by the National Institute of Standards and Technology (NIST), a federal agency located in the Commerce Department.

Some of the credibility of the 9/11 Truthers eroded when they claimed the evidence for their conclusions was reported in a peer-reviewed and highly respected science journal. Peer reviewing is a way of checking the facts and logic of an academic article. Checking out the source they cited, fact-checkers discovered that that prestigious journal had not published the article and had nothing to do with their conspiracy theory or the evidence they claimed.[20]

It is easy to check if an article has or has not appeared in a particular journal, especially if you know the approximate date of publication. Many journals, especially the mainstream ones, have an online website that shares the list of articles they publish, issue by issue. In reality, the article was published in a journal that was not peer reviewed, one that was willing to air the article for discussion without checking its accuracy because of the importance of the topic.

As noted in a previous chapter, when a source for evidence is cited, it is a good idea to check it out. When the strong reputation of a source is intended to be an argument from authority, it is even more important to check it out. In this case, it didn't check out.

A second blow to the credibility of the Architects and Engineers for 9/11 Truth was that the professional organization of architects, The Institute of Architects, was careful to disassociate itself from the group, suggesting its board doubted the claims of the 9/11 truthers.[21]

What was the purpose of this conspiracy theory? To find out, you have to trace Gage's arguments to their source. He was reportedly influenced by David Roy Griffin, a retired professor of philosophy of religion and theology.

> Mr. Gage became interested in researching the destruction of the WTC [World Trade Center] high-rises after hearing on the radio the startling conclusions of reluctant 9/11 researcher David Ray Griffin in 2006, which launched his own unyielding quest for the truth about 9/11.[22]

Griffin's main political thrust was against neo-conservatives and the wars that they engaged in and bungled. He argued that the Twin Towers collapsed due to controlled demolitions, probably engineered by Bush and Cheney (note the weasel word, "probably"). Griffin's book was published in 2004.[23] Griffin cited and relied heavily on Thierry Meyssan's 2002 book, *9/11: The Big Lie*.[24]

Meyssan claimed the 9/11 attacks were false-flag operations, directed by right-wingers and the military industrial complex looking for an excuse for war in Afghanistan and Iraq as they fought to extend U.S. imperialism and promote conspirators' oil interests. These right-wingers reportedly brought down the Twin Towers themselves in order to cast blame on Muslims.

Meyssan was living in Damascus, Syria, writing for the main Syrian newspaper, and was supportive of the Syrian regime. He claimed that no Muslim took part in the attacks because the Koran forbids suicide. According to Meyssan, right-wing elements inside the U.S. government were planning a coup unless Bush went to war in Afghanistan and Iraq to protect U.S. oil interests.[25]

Since President Bush did go to war against Afghanistan and Iraq, Meyssan's argument had a kernel of truth that made it sound plausible, but Meyssan's goal was to protect Syria from U.S. military action by deflecting blame away from Muslims. His conspiracy theory was later picked up and echoed by others, such as Gage, who may or may not have seen its purpose.

In addition to looking for a purpose or goal of a conspiracy theory, you should examine whatever evidence is offered and the logic of the argument. Meyssan argued that the Koran prohibits suicide so Muslims could not have been involved. Islam does prohibit suicides (the factual kernel), but not every Muslim follows the rules. We have seen Muslim suicide bombers and know they exist, which does terminal damage to Meyssan's logic that Muslims could not have been involved. The form of argument is that something should not happen, therefore it didn't happen, which is not logical. Lots of things shouldn't happen but happen anyway.

From this analysis, it looks like the Architects and Engineers for 9/11 Truth probably didn't actually have *the truth*. Their case has some logical flaws; it assumes rather than proves that Bush went to war against Afghanistan and Iraq to protect oil interests, and it presents no evidence at all for a cabal of right-wingers inside the U.S. government who plotted to collapse the buildings and to blame militant Muslims for it.

There could have been a group inside the U.S. government that wanted to go to war to protect U.S. oil interests, but it doesn't follow that there was one, that it threatened a coup if the president didn't go to war, and that the president complied.

The lack of evidence, the illogic of the argument, and the blame-shifting purpose of the original conspiracy theory all speak to the probability that this claim is not true. That the original publisher had previously published other conspiracy theories strengthens the case against the 9/11 "truthers."

Making Money

If a child is autistic, parents need some way of understanding what has happened. Some parents latch on to vaccines as the cause because autism was noticed after vaccination, so they conclude the vaccination must have caused the autism. Other parents, fearful of having children with autism if they allow vaccinations, join the movement. The villain they blame, the target, is the entire medical industry, which keeps from the public the truth about side effects of vaccinations.

While the willingness of some parents to buy into the anti-vaccine model is understandable and of long duration, the recent strength of the movement is traceable to an article by Dr. Andrew Wakefield, published in the prestigious medical journal *The Lancet* in 1998.[26] In that article, Wakefield linked the triple vaccination called MMR (measles, mumps, and rubella) to autism. As a result of his article, many parents refused to have their children vaccinated, resulting in several major outbreaks of diseases that had been under control.

The consequences were so serious that researchers looked in more detail at the original article (examining the source). What they found led the journal to retract the article (what happened next). There were only 12 children in the study, and it turned out that they had been carefully selected to make Wakefield's point (very small sample, cherry picking); his evidence was based on reports of what the parents thought had happened to cause the autism, which is a weak form of evidence; moreover, his study was funded by a lawyer of parents who were suing the vaccine manufacturers claiming that the vaccines had caused their child's autism. The lawyer had paid Wakefield to assist with the lawsuit, a potential conflict of interest that had not been revealed to the journal.[27]

The anti-vaxxer conspiracy story reinforces the idea that it is useful to go to the source, to find out what the original article said, and to see how strong or how weak the evidence is that was presented. It was also useful to figure out what the purpose of this conspiracy was, what Wakefield hoped to achieve. After you have looked at that material, you would not need to be a doctor or a medical researcher to realize Wakefield had taken advantage of parents' inability to understand the causes of their children's developmental difficulties to enrich himself. They were willing to accept the conspiracy theory that blamed the medical profession for their unwillingness to warn them about the dangers of vaccinations.

Undermining an Existing Policy

At times, the goal of those who promote a conspiracy theory is to cast aspersions on the motivations of their opponents in order to undermine a policy. Claiming opponents are acting out of malevolent motives undermines their legitimacy. Conspiracy theories about abortion sometimes take this tack.

Anti-abortion conspiracists start off with the fact that abortions are much more common among the poor and among people of color than they are among whites and people of middle income or higher. Much of this is true, but conspiracy theorists take off from there with more questionable analysis.

They argue that abortion providers prey on the poor and people of color. They also maintain that abortions are paid for by government, so doctors get paid and poor people get free abortions.[28]

Anti-abortion activists, including some black clergy, have accused abortion clinics, especially Planned Parenthood, of aggressively marketing to minority communities. Their proposed solution is for government to restrict access to abortion.

How can one analyze this conspiracy argument? It blames government funding of abortions, which encourages abortions among those who otherwise could not afford them, and it assumes that because abortion providers are getting paid by government, the providers encourage abortions among the poor and minorities. Let's look at those arguments.

The Hyde Amendment, passed by Congress in 1976, prohibits federal funding of abortions for the poor through the Medicaid program, except in instances of rape, incest, or when the mother's life is in danger. Most states have followed the federal government's example. The majority of states do not, in fact, pay for abortions, though some do.

The states that do pay for abortions do have higher abortion rates overall, as the conspiracy theory notes. But in both the states that pay for abortions and in those that don't, abortion rates are decreasing. Moreover, in states that do not cover abortions for poor women, poor women needing abortions rely on charities that pay for abortions, sometimes including travel costs to the few remaining clinics after abortion opponents have had others shut down. Money does matter for poor women, but maybe not as much as the conspiracists think.

Part of the reason that ministers in the black community accepted the idea that doctors were plotting against blacks by performing abortions disproportionately on black women is that Planned Parenthood, a major provider of birth control including abortions, had a bad reputation in the black community. That reputation was based on what appeared to be the political prejudices of its founder, Margaret Sanger, a birth control advocate. Fact-checker Politifact delved into the charges that Margaret Sanger had tried to prevent the birth of blacks in this country and found the charges false.

Sanger did believe in eugenics, the idea that selective breeding could make the world better. That much was true. Politifact observed that the idea was widespread before World War II and acknowledged that some people who held such beliefs were racists, but not many, and not Margaret Sanger. Sanger wanted "to improve the human race by having people be healthier through exercise, recreation in parks, marriage to someone free from sexually transmitted diseases, well-baby clinics, immunizations, clean food and water, proper nutrition, non-smoking and drinking." She was focused on public health, not the elimination of black people. She helped women of all classes and races avoid unwanted pregnancies, primarily through birth control.[29]

Examining Conspiracy Theories for Logic

In the cases described above, there were often startling gaps in reasoning. The illogic is a clue that the story was made up. In the Pizzagate narrative, pizza was interpreted, illogically, as illicit sex. In the 9/11 conspiracy case, it was argued that Muslims are forbidden to commit suicide, therefore they didn't. Utterly illogical. A major problem with the abortion conspiracy theory was also faulty logic. There are more abortions among blacks than among whites, so abortion providers must be discriminating and trying to eliminate the black population. The conclusion doesn't follow from the premise. Discrimination was only one possible cause, others were not considered, and no evidence was provided either to support the thesis or rule out alternatives. In the anti-vaxxer case, people thought that if autism came after a vaccination, the vaccination must have caused it. That was not logical either.

Examining the Credibility of the Author, Reposter, or Publisher

A conspiracy theory against Hillary Clinton just before the 2016 election was posted by a member of Trump's transition team, General Michael Flynn. He tweeted: "U decide – NYPD Blows Whistle on New Hillary Emails: Money Laundering, Sex Crimes w Children, etc. ... MUST READ!"[30]

The rumor that Flynn was reposting was first published on the fringe right-wing website True Pundit on November 2, according to fact-checker Truthorfiction. Media Bias rated the site True Pundit as low on factual reporting and high on the frequency of posting conspiracies. So, the site was suspicious.

What about Flynn? Was he *a trustworthy source*? Flynn had previously "retweeted theories that Clinton 'waged war' on the Roman Catholic Church and that President Obama 'laundered' billions of dollars in cash to terrorists."[31] Flynn had also passed along the claim "that Clinton's campaign manager takes part in occult rituals in which bodily fluids are consumed."[32]

None of these stories that Flynn retweeted had any basis in fact.

Factcheck.org clarified that Obama did not give Iran $150 billion in cash. "The deal, approved by six countries and the European Union, gave Iran access to its own frozen assets."[33] Flynn, known to retweet conspiracy theories, was not a reliable source.

What about Wakefield, the anti-vaxxer? Was he a reliable source? "Even before publication of the study, Wakefield was working on patenting his own version of a measles vaccine, which he would sell at a great profit as a supposedly "safe" alternative to the MMR vaccine. The father of one of the children in Wakefield's study was a cofounder of the planned business that would market this product."[34] Wakefield thus had a financial interest in discouraging MMR vaccines.

Many of the conspiracy theories circulate online, but the origin of the 9/11 conspiracy theory was actually a book. What about the publisher? The publishing company that distributed Meyssan's books had a record of selling conspiracy theories. A reviewer wrote about the publisher, "More accustomed to publishing marginal books on subjects like the 'false' American moon landing in 1969 and the latest ' truth' about U.F.O.'s, Éditions Carnot can now boast of its first best seller."[35] The company was known for publishing conspiracy theories.

Look for What Happened Next

In several of the examples, if you had looked at what happened next you would have been sure that you had seen a false conspiracy theory. The outcome of Pizzagate was the arrest of the man who tried to stop the fake child sex ring; in the anti-vaxxer case, the article in which the charge was made linking vaccine to autism was retracted. In the false flag case of threatening prominent Democrats with bombs, the bomb maker was arrested. It turned out he was not a Democrat.

It is not hard to take conspiracy theories apart if you know what you are looking for.

Real Conspiracies

While our world is flooded with made-up stories, there are some real conspiracies out there. You should be able to recognize them using the techniques described in this chapter. First, is the source reputable and reliable? Second, is checkable evidence provided? Third, is the logic complete and convincing or is it just a tissue of conjecture? What do the fact-checkers say about it? Do they confirm the claims? Fourth, what happened next?

In October of 2020, the FBI discovered and interrupted a conspiracy to kidnap the governor of Michigan. The FBI had considerable evidence, including discussions on a private Facebook group, email exchanges, monitored phone calls, and sightings of anti-government militia members of a group called Wolverine Watchmen surveilling the governor's vacation home. The FBI had evidence of planning and training to attack the state capitol and kidnap officials. There was motive, the ideology of the group is individualistic and anti-government. Information about the arrests appeared across the media spectrum, including the conservative Fox News where you would not expect a negative story on right-wing militias.[36]

Because there are, occasionally, some real-world conspiracies, it is critical to be able to tell the difference between the real ones and the made-up ones.

Conclusion

Conspiracy theories are a particular kind of made-up story to achieve some goal. They are relatively easy to recognize and analyze, especially if they have been widely circulated and people have acted on them. Attacking political opponents and blame shifting are among its common goals; also common are conspiracies aimed at preventing the adoption of policies like gun control or mandatory economic shutdowns to curtail the pandemic. Lack of evidence or made-up evidence is a common characteristic and many suffer from faulty logic.

Failure to recognize and analyze conspiracy theories can be dangerous to health and safety. The owner of the Comet Ping Pong Pizzeria received hundreds of death threats. Those who deny the severity of covid-19 illness and urge early reopening of the economy while ignoring safety measures such as social distancing and wearing masks threaten the health and lives of themselves, their families, the elderly, and the immunocompromised.

It is also important to recognize that there is often some truth to conspiracy theories. Distinguishing the true bits from the made-up parts may require some very satisfying detective work.

Notes

1 Alana Abramson, "How Donald Trump Perpetuated the 'Birther' Movement for Years," *ABC News*, September 16, 2016.
2 Monika Evstatieva, "Anatomy of a COVID-19 Conspiracy Theory," *NPR*, July 10, 2020, www.npr.org/2020/07/10/889037310/anatomy-of-a-covid-19-conspiracy-theory.
3 Case: BVerfGE 36, 1 2 BvF 1/73 Grundlagenvertrag-decision East-West Basic Treaty, July 31, 1973.
4 Linda Schlegel, "'Germany Does Not Exist!': Analyzing the Reichsbürger Movement," *European Eye on Radicalization*, May 17, 2019, https://eeradicalization.com/germany-does-not-exist-analyzing-the-reichsburger-movement/.
5 Walter Russell Mead, "Amid the Pandemic, Anti-Semitism Flares Up," *The Wall Street Journal*, April 15, 2020, www.wsj.com/articles/amid-the-pandemic-anti-semitism-flares-up-11586991224.
6 Kim LaCapria, "Is Comet Ping Pong Pizzeria Home to a Child Abuse Ring Led by Hillary Clinton?," *Snopes*, November 21, 2016, www.snopes.com/fact-check/pizzagate-conspiracy/.
7 Ibid.
8 Ibid.
9 Bethania Palma, "Did David Hogg Attend a California High School?," March 26, 2018, www.snopes.com/fact-check/david-hogg-attend-california-high-school/.
10 Alison Graves, "David Hogg Not at School During Shooting? Bloggers Spread Misinformation," *Politifact*, March 27, 2018, www.politifact.com/factchecks/2018/mar/27/blog-posting/david-hogg-not-school-during-shooting-s-fake-news/.
11 Lucian Wintrich, "Exclusive: Soros-Linked Organizers of "Women's March" Selected Anti-Trump Kids to Be Face of Parkland Tragedy – And Excluded Pro-Trump Kids," *Gateway Pundit*, February 20, 2018, www.thegatewaypundit.com/2018/02/behind-various-anti-gun-movements-popping-parkland/.
12 NRA-Institute for Legislative Action, "Yes, George Soros Is a Gun Grabber," *NRA*, November 16, 2018, www.nraila.org/articles/20181116/yes-george-soros-is-a-gun-grabber.
13 Alex Yablon, "George Soros Is Not the Gun Grabber the NRA Says He Is," *The Trace*, November 6, 2018, www.thetrace.org/rounds/soros-not-the-gun-grabber-nra-says-he-is/.

14 Tom Kertscher, "Pictures and Reports of 'Empty Hospitals' Prove COVID-19 Spread Is 'Fake Crisis for Real Government Planned Agendas'," *Politifact*, April 3, 2020, www.politifact.com/factchecks/2020/apr/03/facebook-posts/hospital-beds-being-kept-empty-prepare-covid-influ/.
15 Jack Goodman, "Donald Trump's Police Scanner Tweet Fact-Checked," *BBC Reality Check*, June 9, 2020, www.bbc.com/news/52984295.
16 Adam Rawnsley and Will Sommer, via REUTERS, "The Cesspool That Spat Out Trump's New Conspiracy about Cops," *The Daily Beast*, June 9, 2020, www.thedailybeast.com/meet-the-conservative-treehouse-the-blog-thats-ground-zero-for-insane-trump-sht.
17 Frank Bajak, "Debunked Ukraine Conspiracy Theory Is Knocked Down – Again," *AP*, November 13, 2019, https://apnews.com/23c9022665dc40a1a69e613459955112.
18 Jane Coaston, "'False Flags,' Explained," *Vox*, October 26, 2018, www.vox.com/2018/10/25/18018606/false-flags-clinton-soros-alex-jones-infowars-cnn.
19 Benjamin Weiser and Ali Watkins, "Cesar Sayoc, Who Mailed Pipe Bombs to Trump Critics, Is Sentenced to 20 Years," *The New York Times*, August 5, 2019, www.nytimes.com/2019/08/05/nyregion/cesar-sayoc-sentencing-pipe-bombing.html.
20 Alex Kasprak, "Did a European Scientific Journal Conclude 9/11 Was a Controlled Demolition?," *Snopes*, October 9, 2016, www.snopes.com/fact-check/journal-endorses-911-conspiracy-theory/.
21 Jeremy Stahl, "Architects Shy from Trutherism," *Architect*, July 19, 2012, www.architectmagazine.com/design/architects-shy-from-trutherism_o.
22 Richard Gage, Great American Speakers, www.greatamericanspeakers.com/speakers/richard-gage-aia.
23 David Ray Griffin, *The New Pearl Harbor: Disturbing Questions about the Bush Administration and 9/11*, Interlink Publishing, 2004.
24 English language version by USA books; Original French version, entitled *11 Septembre: L'Effroyable Imposture*, Editions Carnot, 2002.
25 Alan Riding, "September 11 as Right-Wing U.S. Plot: Conspiracy Theory Sells in France," *The New York Times*, June 22, 2002, www.nytimes.com/2002/06/22/world/sept-11-as-right-wing-us-plot-conspiracy-theory-sells-in-france.html.
26 The article, later retracted, appeared in *Lancet*, 351[9103], 1998, pp. 637–641.
27 Laura Eggertson, "Lancet Retracts 12-Year-Old Article Linking Autism to MMR Vaccines," *Canadian Medical Association Journal*, 182(4), 2010, pp. E199–E200, www.ncbi.nlm.nih.gov/pmc/articles/PMC2831678/.
28 Sahila Dewan, "Anti-Abortion Ads Split Atlanta," *New York Times*, February 5, 2010, www.nytimes.com/2010/02/06/us/06abortion.html; Susan Cohen, "Abortion and Women of Color: The Bigger Picture," *Guttmacher Policy Review*, 11(3), 2008, www.guttmacher.org/gpr/2008/08/abortion-and-women-color-bigger-picture; Christine Dehlendorf, Lisa H. Harris, and Tracy A. Weitz, "Disparities in Abortion Rates: A Public Health Approach," *American Journal of Public Health*, 103(10), 2013, pp. 1772–1779, www.ncbi.nlm.nih.gov/pmc/articles/PMC3780732/#bib3.
29 Clay Wirestone, "Birth Control Pioneer Margaret Sanger 'Believed That People Like Me Should Be Eliminated,'" *Politifact*, October 5, 2015, www.politifact.com/factchecks/2015/oct/05/ben-carson/did-margaret-sanger-believe-african-americans-shou/.
30 Rebecca Hersher, "Webpages Linked to Pizzeria Shooting Go Dark Even As Prosecution Moves Forward," *NPR*, December 14, 2016, www.npr.org/sections/thetwo-way/2016/12/14/505577985/webpages-linked-to-pizzeria-shooting-go-dark-even-as-prosecution-moves-forward.
31 Rebecca Savransky, "Flynn Deletes Fake News Tweet about Clinton's Involvement in Sex Crimes," *The Hill*, December 14, 2016, https://thehill.com/homenews/campaign/310372-flynn-deletes-fake-news-tweet-about-clintons-involvement-in-sex-crimes.
32 Bryan Bender and Andrew Hanna, "Flynn Under Fire for Fake News," *Politico*, December 5, 2016, www.politico.com/story/2016/12/michael-flynn-conspiracy-pizzeria-trump-232227.

33 Saranac Hale Spencer, "Obama Didn't Give Iran '150 Billion in Cash,'" *FactCheck .org*, March 1, 2019, www.factcheck.org/2019/03/obama-didnt-give-iran-150-billion-in-cash/.
34 GI Society, "Andrew Wakefield's Harmful Myth of Vaccine-Induced 'Autistic Entercolitis,'" 2011, https://badgut.org/information-centre/a-z-digestive-topics/andrew-wakefield-vaccine-myth/.
35 Alan Riding, "September 11 as Right-Wing U.S. Plot: Conspiracy Theory Sells in France," *The New York Times*, June 22, 2002, www.nytimes.com/2002/06/22/world/sept-11-as-right-wing-us-plot-conspiracy-theory-sells-in-france.html.
36 Danielle Wallace, "FBI Uncovers Armed Militia Plot to Abduct Michigan Gov. Whitmer," *Fox*, October 8, 2020, www.foxnews.com/us/michigan-gretchen-whitmer-plot-abduct-kill-assassinate.

8
PROBLEMS WITH NUMBERS

What Is Wrong with the Numbers?

People who try to persuade you often engage in numerical tricks intended to mislead. With a bit of practice, you can see through them.

Counting the Wrong Thing

Starting with one of the easiest things to detect, the narrator claims to be counting one thing, while in fact counting something else. President Trump claimed that the Democrats could not impeach him because he had so much support, so many people had voted for him. The argument seems unlikely to be true since impeachment has nothing to do with the number of people who vote for you. Moreover, Trump wasn't actually counting the number of votes he had received.

President Trump presented a map with red in each county that he had won in 2016. The whole map was dominated by "his" counties, with only a few exceptions. It really looked impressive. The problem? He was counting counties he had won, not people who had voted for him. He won lots of rural counties with few people in them. In fact, he lost the popular election. His map was a misleading indicator of how many people voted for him in 2016.[1]

In another illustration of counting the wrong thing, President Trump claimed that California admitted to over 1.58 million illegal votes in 2016. But what California had "admitted to" was having a large number of inactive registrations still on the books. These were not records of people who had voted, but of people who had *not* voted. Some of them may have died or moved away, and the state needed to clean up its voter registration lists to update them.[2]

Comparing the Wrong Things

False news has dogged the covid-19 pandemic. One of the major themes has been that the new virus is no more serious than a flu, and hence does not warrant the shutting down of the economy and stay-at-home orders. One version of this argument is that by using antibody tests, many more people have had covid-19 than the official figures. Death rates for covid-19 look at the number of deaths among those who have tested positive for the virus, but many more have had the virus and not been tested, so the death rates are in fact much lower than reported, and hence more comparable to the flu. Unfortunately, something is *really* wrong with this argument.

There are two measures of the mortality rates of diseases, both of which can be useful for different purposes. One is the rate of death among those tested and confirmed to have the disease, called the *case mortality rate*. The second measure is the death rate among all those who have been infected, whether or not they were tested and confirmed to have the virus. This second measure is called the *infected mortality rate*. The number of those infected is estimated by examining a sample of people for antibodies that show evidence of having had the disease and then generalizing from that sample to the entire population.

The number of people who have died of covid-19 doesn't change no matter which measure you are using. Since there are many more people who have had the disease than have been confirmed through testing, the rate of mortality among those infected is much lower than among those tested and confirmed.

Some of those who wish to reopen the economy quickly and deny the seriousness of the covid-19 epidemic have used the lower mortality measure for covid-19 and compared it to the higher mortality measure for the flu. They declared the mortality rates comparable and concluded there was no need to take unusual steps.

Even with the distortion from pretending that different measures were the same, the mortality figures don't come close to matching. But if you make the correct comparison of like to like, covid-19's case mortality rate is 3.1 percent;[3] the flu's case mortality rate is 0.1 percent, wildly different.

Again, comparing like to like, if you compare infection mortality rates, the covid-19 figures generally range between 0.5 and 0.8 percent, compared to the infection mortality rates for the flu at 0.05 percent, again, wildly different.[4]

It would be nice if covid-19 were no more serious than the annual flu, but it just isn't so. Covid-19 is much more serious. Maybe statistics don't lie, but those who want to go back to work, get haircuts, and party at the beach, do.

Making Numbers Look Bigger or Smaller

There are many different tricks to make numbers seem bigger or smaller. If you want to make a number look bigger, add it up over a number of years or add things to it that don't belong. If you want to make a number look smaller, leave out one or more components of a total.

In Britain, the country agonized for years about whether to leave the European Union, with persuasive efforts on both sides. Those who wanted to leave the European Union created a number of advertisements, some of which exaggerated Britain's payments to the European Union by omitting the payments that Britain received from the Union. They claimed the country was paying the EU 350 million pounds a week and described all the things that that amount of money could buy if only Britain withdrew from the EU. However, they omitted the money that Britain got back from the EU. If you subtract that money, the actual amount that Britain sent to the EU per week was 150 million pounds, not 350 million pounds per week.

While those advocating leaving the EU wanted viewers to think that was a huge amount of money, it was less than one percent of government spending, 117 pounds per person per year, or 0.32 of a British pound per person, per day.[5]

In the U.S., Illinois Policy, a right-wing think tank, made one number look bigger and another look smaller in an analysis in which they argued against public pensions. The authors compared workers' contributions to their pensions with their lifetime pension benefits after retirement, exaggerating upward the benefits while minimizing the workers' contributions to their pensions.

The article says

> Since July 1, Illinois' state-run pension systems added 651 newly retired government workers who started collecting benefits. They are projected to average $1.3 million in lifetime pension benefits during their retirements. They contributed an average of just $105,000 toward their retirements while working.[6]

The author multiplied the amount of annual pension by 20 years, throwing in the cost-of-living adjustment. Retirees get over a million dollars when added up. That sounds huge. But if you look at the average *annual* retirement for new retirees, also included in the analysis, it is $40,000, not terribly high for professors, university and school administrators, teachers, doctors, lawyers, judges, scientists, legislators, librarians, social workers, prison guards, cafeteria workers, and other state employees. Many of those retirees in Illinois do not receive Social Security. For context, the lowest level income that was considered middle class in 2019 (2/3 of the median income for that year) was $46,031. Looked at that way, the average annual pension for new retirees would not even bring a retiree into the middle-income range.

While the number for pension payout was made to look large by adding up benefits over many years, the pay into the system of individual employees was made to look extra small. Teachers, state employees, and public university employees pay between eight and nine percent of their salaries to the pension fund each year. But that is only part of the story. Many school districts have picked up the teacher portion of the pension contribution.

The teachers pay less and their employers more under this arrangement, but whether the employer pays the pension or pays the teacher who pays the pension, the contribution is the same; it comes out of the same pocket, it goes into the same fund, for the same employee. By looking only at the contribution that comes out of the teacher's paycheck, Illinois Policy radically underestimated teachers' contributions to the pension fund. In 2018, the teacher contribution was 9.8 percent of the pensionable base, and the employer contribution was 30.86 percent.

In Illinois, pension revenues come from employee contributions, employer contributions, the state's contribution, *and* interest on investment of those contributions. The whole point of a pension is to put away money while one is working, and to invest it so there will be more money at retirement than there was in annual contributions.

Illinois Policy's comparison between *worker* contributions and payout is phony. Employee pension contributions are *supposed to be* less than pension payouts. If they were to match, something would be drastically wrong with the pension fund's design. Illinois Policy's portrait of pension funding was misframed in order to cause maximum resentment in the people who are not receiving pensions.

There are other techniques to exaggerate numbers. One of them is to use a percentage increase of a small number. If you increase from two to four, you have increased by 100 percent but you will have only added two cases. If a story only includes the percent increase or decrease, without the actual numbers increased or decreased, you are likely to be misled—unless you catch it.

Sometimes opponents of a tax increase intentionally tell you only the percentage increase and leave out the actual rate. This practice is particularly deceptive if the actual rate is a small number. For example, in 2011 the state of Illinois increased its income tax rate from three percent to five percent of taxable income. The percentage increase was 67 percent because it went up by about two-thirds on a *very* small base. Those who opposed the tax increase described it as a huge and unaffordable 67 percent jump. In reality, at the five percent rate, the income tax rate is moderate. Neighboring Wisconsin's top rate is 7.65 percent and neighboring Iowa's top rate is 8.98 percent. Be wary of percentage increases on small bases; since they look huge they are misleading. And you need some context or comparison to other states to tell you if the actual rate, as opposed to the percentage increase, is high or low.

Politicians naturally don't like to be blamed for anything, and the more serious the charge, the more likely to evoke defensive behavior, which can result in exaggerated or even made-up numbers.

In the following example, Secretary of Homeland Security Kirstjen Nielsen, in an effort to avoid blame, defended the Trump administration policy of separating children from their parents by claiming that the people crossing the border with children were not real families, that the kids were pawns of smugglers and traffickers. She justified the policy of family separation by arguing that there had been a 314 percent increase in these fake families and described the adults as members of the MS 13 (a murderous gang in the U.S.), criminals, and abusers.[7]

What might attract your attention, besides the attempt to deflect blame, is the mention of a percentage increase without the actual numbers, so we don't know if a more than 300 percent increase means from three to nine or from 30,000 to 90,000, or something in between. *Washington Post* reporters went looking for the actual numbers. "There were 46 cases of fraud—'individuals using minors to pose as fake family units'—from October 2016 through September 2017. In the first five months of 2018, there were 191 cases." So, was this number a large or small proportion of all those families approaching the border?

According to DHS data, there were 75,622 family units apprehended at the border in fiscal 2017, and 31,102 in the first five months of the fiscal year 2018. So, in the first five months of 2018, possible smugglers made up only 0.61 percent of the total number of family units apprehended at the border. "In other words, for every 1,000 families that approached the border in the first five months of this fiscal year, only six allegedly involved individuals pretending to be a child's parents."[8] The percentage of alleged smugglers in fiscal 2017 was smaller, at 0.1 percent. So, the Homeland Security Secretary was right, there had been a big percentage increase, but even after the increase, only a very small percentage of families crossing the border were fake families.

The other side of blame avoidance is credit claiming. Credit claiming encourages exaggeration by adding things that don't belong. For example, President Trump added something that didn't belong when taking credit for increasing the number of jobs. He claimed many more new jobs created than had actually occurred. In early November of 2019, a Bureau of Labor Statistics report indicated there were 128,000 jobs added in October. President Trump claimed that 303,000 jobs had been created, provoking a few head scratches. He got to 303,000 in several different ways. First, he included for October upward revisions of jobs estimates for two prior months—those additions reflect the jobs of those previous months, not October, so Trump took jobs attributed to earlier months and counted them again for October. He considered the return to work of striking GM workers as new jobs in October. Those were not newly created jobs. He also included 20,000 temporary census workers who completed their work in October.[9]

The clue that would encourage you to look further is the huge difference between the estimates of the staid and non-partisan federal Bureau of Labor Statistics and the *credit claiming* by President Trump.

Denialism leads to undercounting, or even pretending that something didn't occur at all. Those denying the importance or seriousness of the covid-19 pandemic sometimes claim that it has not been responsible for any deaths at all. A report on the right-wing website PJ Media was titled "Johns

Hopkins Study Saying COVID-19 Has 'Relatively No Effect on Deaths' in U.S. Spiked after Publication." The author, Matt Margolis, claimed a study demonstrating this lack of deaths was published by Johns Hopkins, a well-respected source of information on the virus, but was soon taken down.[10] The implication was that the information was being censored, a veritable conspiracy. Given the location of the story on a right-wing website that was known for misinformation, you might be skeptical enough to try to track down the story, using the tools presented in prior chapters, including looking for alternative sources of information and looking at the original study.

The claim that no deaths have been due to the pandemic in the U.S. has been roundly contradicted. An article in the modestly left of center *Washington Post*, citing data from the Centers for Disease Control, argued that the virus caused nearly 300,000 excessive deaths, compared to the average of prior years. About two-thirds of those excessive deaths above normal were attributed to the virus.[11] So, let's look at the article that was taken down. How did the author make the numbers of excessive deaths disappear?

The first thing you might notice is that the article was not an official Johns Hopkins study, instead it was from a student-run newsletter. The (denialist) author of the PJ Media article had implied that the source was a professional study from an elite research university on a topic for which the university was famous. This fake argument from authority should make you skeptical.

The article in the student newsletter quoted from a webinar created by Genevieve Briand, "COVID-19 Deaths: A Look at U.S. Data." Briand had said, "Total death numbers are not above normal death numbers. We found no evidence to the contrary." Finding no evidence to the contrary is a weasel phrase, as the reader has no idea where Briand looked for evidence, how hard she looked, or even if she knew how to find such evidence. Briand was not an epidemiologist nor even a physician, she had not done an epidemiological study, she was just comparing numbers from one year to the next. Epidemiologists do not compare raw numbers by year or month, they create models based on a variety of factors including monthly and normal variations, then they predict what is likely to occur based on past experience and compare their projection to what actually happens. Actual deaths may be fewer or greater than one would have expected based on past experience.

Briand either did not know, or if she knew, did not consider typical yearly patterns of deaths by season from various causes. To make it look like there had been no change after the coronavirus, Briand compared the low point of a virus year with the high point of a year previous to the virus.[12]

In an earlier chapter, it was suggested that the reader look to see what happened next. The student article was taken down, as the PJ Media post indicated, but then it was put back up as a PDF file for transparency purposes and to prove there was no censorship. More importantly, the article was formally retracted, with the following explanation:

Briand was quoted in the article as saying, "All of this points to no evidence that COVID-19 created any excess deaths. Total death numbers are not above normal death numbers." This claim is incorrect and does not take into account the spike in raw death count from all causes compared to previous years. According to the CDC, there have been almost 300,000 excess deaths due to COVID-19.[13]

The CDC data that Briand used shows this excess number of deaths, so if Briand could not find it, she wasn't looking very hard.

You don't have to be an epidemiologist to check out a story like this one. Your suspicion would have been roused by the site on which the story appeared, and you should have been annoyed at the claim that the article was based on a study by the Johns Hopkins University. You were supposed to believe it because it was done by an authority. It turns out that it was not an official study, it was based on a post in a student newsletter. If you looked into it, you would have seen the retraction, and could have read fact-checker reports outlining where the mistakes came from that allowed Briand to make coronavirus deaths seem to disappear.

Omitting Context

Omitting information that would indicate whether a number was big or small, a *Washington Post* article noted that there had been 5000 fatal police shootings from 2015 to 2019.[14] Are 5000 fatal police shootings over five years a lot or a little? What would a reader need to know to make that number meaningful?

While absolute numbers are sometimes important, to make sense of a raw number you may need a rate and more context. A rate is a quantity of something per unit. That unit could be time, such as minutes or hours. She types 45 words isn't very informative, but she types 45 words per minute is descriptive. Ten students were caught cheating, but you won't know if that is a lot or a little until you compare it to a given unit, say the number of students in the class at that time. You need to figure out whether some number is actually big or small, and relatedly, whether that number is a good indicator of something important. Almost every number cited in a news story or advertisement needs some base to which to compare it. The choice of base is important.

In the *Washington Post* story, one might want to know 5000 shooting deaths by police out of how many attempted arrests, or out of how many calls for service? You might want to ask, how many police shootings have there been out of how many people living in the country, what is the rate per hundred thousand people? To figure out if 5000 over five years is a lot or a little, you might want to compare the rate per thousand people to that of other countries.

To figure out if a number is big or small, get into the habit of asking yourself, out of how many? One news story proclaimed, "Dozens of educators charged with sex crimes and violent felonies lose licenses under new law, but loopholes remain." You should automatically think, how many are dozens? And dozens out of how many teachers in the state—that is, what is the rate? For comparison, what is the incidence of sex crimes, violent felonies, or certain drug offenses (the rate) in other professions or the population at large?

The number of teachers in Illinois at the time of the story was 129,178. The number cited in some versions of the story, 50, is a small fraction of one percent of that total (0.03 percent). The violent crime rate in the U.S. is considerably higher than that reported for the educators (approximately 1.19 percent in 2018). Conclusion? Teachers are a pretty harmless lot because 50 isn't a lot. Whoever created the story may have had it out for teachers.[15] Note that the basic story about the teachers is true, but it is just misleading because of the absence of the context that would explain whether this number is big or small.

An article in WTOP news on defunding the Austin, Texas police department noted that the council had approved a cut of $150 million from the police budget. But there was no indication in the article of the total size of the Austin police department budget. Did the approved reduction mean the elimination of the department, or redirecting a number of its functions to other units of government, or some combination of redirecting funds to social programs and reductions in traditional police functions?[16]

A different article provided more information; the cut was to be up to $150 million, 34 percent of the current budget of the police department, mainly through reorganizing some duties out from police enforcement. That amount is substantial but does not eliminate the police department or its traditional functions.[17]

Sometimes what you need to make sense of a figure is a rate of change, that is, a comparison with prior weeks, months, or years. Are the cases of coronavirus per day going up or down? Is the disease out of control, or is it on track to disappear? Did the number of cases of chicken pox go up after it became popular to reject vaccinations?

Let's look for a moment at the number of police killings per year, a rate which has been reasonably stable from 2016 to 2020, at a little over 1000 per year. Then look at the rate of change over time in the percentage of those cases in which charges were brought against the police. That rate declined almost every year, from 1.8 percent to 1.4 percent over the five-year period. Even more dramatically, the rate of convictions of the small number of cases in which charges were brought dropped from 0.6 percent to 0.1 percent.[18]

The number of police shooting deaths alone doesn't tell the story. The data for all three variables for a single year doesn't tell the story. But looking at all three figures over five years is revealing: The deaths by police continued unabated, but the prosecutions and punishment of police declined. Context is critical when interpreting a number.

Misusing Time Series

Many studies use time-series data. While such studies often rely on fancy statistical analysis, the basic idea is simple. The analyst lays out the quantity of something, or frequency of some event for each period of time, such as year by year, week by week, or day by day. The analyst points out at what point something of interest happened, and then looks at whether the data before the event differed substantially from the data that occurred afterward. In persuasive arguments, sometimes the analysis slides into "post hoc ergo propter hoc" illogic. As described in an earlier chapter, something that occurs before something else doesn't necessarily cause the outcome in question. My cat ran out the door when I went to get the mail; later, my computer crashed. The cat's exit occurred before the computer crash but didn't cause it.

Many anti-marijuana campaigners refer to a study of traffic accidents in Colorado after the legalization of recreational marijuana. Using time series (the before and after comparison), authors of the study show that fatal accidents increased after legalization. However, if you look at the number of fatal accidents per vehicle miles driven, the accident rates are similar before and after legalization.

The number of fatal accidents might have little to do with marijuana legalization, reflecting mainly the size of the population, the road conditions, and the number of miles driven. Increased population, more drivers, more traffic, lousy weather—the result is more accidents.[19]

Many arguments based on time series, like the one on marijuana legalization and fatal accidents, don't examine and rule out other possible causes of the outcomes. After Governor Pritzker of Illinois and the state legislature passed an increase in the minimum wage, Republican state senator Dale Righter protested that the last time the state increased the minimum wage, the state lost 50,000 jobs. This is a kind of time-series argument; there was a certain number of jobs before, then the event, raising the minimum wage took place, and afterward there were fewer jobs.

Fact-checkers jumped on Righter's claim. Politifact and the Better Government Association discovered that the state increased, rather than decreased, the number of jobs in the year after the increase went into effect. When Righter was asked where he got his numbers, his office replied that 70,000 was the increase in the number of unemployed, not a decrease in the number of jobs. So, Righter had mislabeled (measuring the wrong thing) what he was talking about.

Righter attributed the increase in unemployment to the increase in minimum wage, but he didn't control for other possible causes of the increase in unemployment claims. In this case, toward the end of 2007 the Great Recession had begun, and throughout the country the unemployment rate was increasing. Many of the states where unemployment was increasing had not increased their minimum wage.[20] It was the recession that was increasing unemployment, not the increase in minimum wage. A well-designed study would have looked at before and after data in states that increased their minimum wage and similar states that did not increase their minimum wage. Richter didn't do that. What was missing was similar data in states that did not increase the minimum wage.

Righter also committed another error that you might recognize, cherry picking his case. He ignored the cases that contradicted his claim. "Illinois upped its minimum wage by 35 cents in 2004 and by a dollar in 2005. And in the years that followed each of those increases, BLS [Bureau of Labor Statistics] data show that employment increased and unemployment declined." We can conclude that Righter's claim of a relationship between employment levels and Illinois' 2006 minimum wage increase was bogus.[21]

So, there are (at least) three ways to examine arguments based on time-series data. One is to ask what else happened besides the change in policy you are looking at that might have affected the outcome. Might a recession have caused an increase in unemployment? Second, does the change in outcome happen in other places that lacked the same event or policy you are examining? Did other states that didn't raise minimum wage also experience an increase in unemployment? And third, are there other cases of the same phenomenon that are ignored that have had a different outcome? What happened to the number of jobs after other minimum wage increases in the state? Righter's claim about the minimum wage increasing unemployment failed the test on all three counts.

Muddling the Measurement of Key Concepts

An article in the *New York Post* repeats a conservative argument that spending more public money on programs, such as on public schools or anti-poverty programs, does not produce better outcomes.[22] By implication, reducing public spending would produce as good or better results. The article compares New York and California (democratically dominated states), which spend more compared to Texas and Florida (Republican-dominated states), claiming that despite major differences in spending on anti-poverty programs, there was little difference between the four states in terms of the degree of reduction in poverty.

But wait, what anti-poverty spending is the author talking about? He briefly refers to anti-poverty spending as welfare and directs the reader to the National Association of State Budget Officers (NASBO), his source for data on expenditure. NASBO is a professional organization of state budgeters that publishes an annual report on state expenditures by category. With respect to anti-poverty spending, NASBO only reports on public assistance and Medicaid.

It is difficult to define anti-poverty spending, but it includes considerably more than public assistance (what we used to call welfare). The conservative Cato Institute counted 126 separate anti-poverty programs in 2014. Because the author is looking at only a small fraction of many anti-poverty programs, he was not actually looking at the impact of all anti-poverty spending on the levels of poverty. The author wasn't measuring what he claimed he was measuring.

But what was he measuring? NASBO data includes only TANF (Temporary Assistance to Needy Families), local supplements to TANF, and Medicaid. TANF is the joint federal-state program that replaced what we used to call welfare. TANF is a block grant, so states have considerable discretion over how the money is allocated, and they distribute those funds in very different ways. The four states in the essay spent their block grant money very differently.

The programmatic spending was so variable that to make any sense of its impact on poverty levels, one would need to examine spending for each program and track the consequences of that spending over time. The lag time between spending and expected results should vary from one program to another. For example, spending on early childhood education (Head Start) might have an impact on later educational performance, and ultimately employability and income, but over a generation, not over a few years. It is not clear over what period of time one should expect money spent on adoptions and guardianships to have an impact, or whether it should have an impact on poverty levels at all.

Adding to the confusion is the fact that not all the spending from the TANF block grants is targeted exclusively to the poor, so taking total spending on general assistance and dividing it by the number of people in deep poverty will give an exaggerated sense of spending per poor person. This problem would be particularly acute for New York State.

In an effort to address the question of whether spending on (the limited) anti-poverty programs he included did or did not reduce levels of poverty over time, the author of the *New York Post* article looked at spending in 2010 and then examined reductions in poverty rates from 2010 to 2018. The article claims that from 2010- to 2018, California, Florida, and Texas reduced their poverty rates by three percent, while New York reduced its poverty rate by only one percent. Since the states spent different amounts of money, but the percent reduction in poverty rates was similar, the author concludes that additional spending was ineffective. He included spending that was not aimed at those below the poverty level and excluded some spending programs that were aimed at the poor. Since he did not look at all poverty programs, what the money was spent on, or what period of time would make sense to look at, his argument was unconvincing.

The author measured his major concepts so poorly that the results were GIGO, a term meaning "Garbage In, Garbage Out." If measurement is so bad to start with, the conclusions are uninterpretable.

What if you didn't know much about the anti-poverty programs the author described? You might have questioned the article's conclusion because it seemed to be unlikely to be true, given the source and the strange choice of anti-poverty programs. Then you might have searched for some opposing arguments. The Center on Budget and Policy Priorities, a think tank on the opposite side of this issue, provided a more careful analysis, measuring actual anti-poverty programs and considering the different time lags for impact of different programs. They came to more positive conclusions.[23] You would need to look carefully at the Center on Budget and Policy Priorities's study because the center is a known advocate for the poor and could have biased their study in favor of poverty programs, but once you did that you would probably lean toward the side that said the anti-poverty programs have had a positive effect.

Conclusion

Authors often use numbers to back up an argument, but if they have not measured what they say they were measuring, the results are phony and should not be believed. Moreover, numbers can be deceptive for other reasons that are reasonably easy to detect. They may be exaggerated up or down to make something look more dangerous, more expensive, or to minimize some amount. A common trick is to leave out the context, to give a number without explaining whether that number is actually big or small, serious or minor. Yes, there was an increase in the number of undocumented immigrants applying for gun permits, but heck, it was so small you could barely see it with a magnifying glass.

You don't need to be a statistician to see these deceptions; you can use the same tools that this book has been using all along. For example, you can check the website or the publisher and the author's reputation. You can look at the study or data that is cited to see how a concept was actually measured, what it includes, and what it excludes. You can check out more neutral sources, look for fact-checkers, or look for stories written on the other side of controversial issues. The latter might also be biased in another direction, but still point out weaknesses in the original story you are looking at. And you can recognize some of the common tricks, such as lack of context and huge percentages on a very small base.

Notes

1 Holmes Lybrand and Daniel Dale, "Fact Checking Trump's 'Impeach This' Map," *CNN*, October 2, 2019, www.cnn.com/2019/10/01/politics/trump-impeach-this-map-fact-check/index.html.
2 Chris Nichols, "California 'Admitted' There Were 'A Million' Illegal Votes in the 2016 Presidential Election," *Politifact*, June 24, 2019, www.politifact.com/factchecks/2019/jun/24/donald-trump/pants-fire-trumps-latest-california-voter-fraud-cl/.
3 According to Johns Hopkins Corona Virus Resource Center, https://coronavirus.jhu.edu/data/mortality.
4 Joel Achenbach, "Antibody Tests Support What's Been Obvious: Covid-19 Is Much More Lethal Than the Flu," *The Washington Post*, April 28, 2020, www.washingtonpost.com/health/antibody-tests-support-whats-been-obvious-covid-19-is-much-more-lethal-than-flu/2020/04/28/2fc215d8-87f7-11ea-ac8a-fe9b8088e101_story.html.
5 "The UK Contribution to the EU Budget," Office for National Statistics, September 30, 2019, www.ons.gov.uk/economy/governmentpublicsectorandtaxes/publicsectorfinance/articles/theukcontributiontotheeubudget/2017-10-31

6 Adam Schuster, "651 New Illinois Public Pensioners Average $1.3m in Estimated Retirement Benefits," *Illinois Policy*, July 30, 2019, www.illinoispolicy.org/651-new-illinois-public-pensioners-add-26-million-in-annual-pension-costs/
7 Philip Bump, "How to Mislead with Statistics, DHS Secretary Nielsen Edition," *The Washington Post*, June 18, 2018, www.washingtonpost.com/news/politics/wp/2018/06/18/how-to-mislead-with-statistics-dhs-secretary-nielsen-edition/,
8 Ibid.
9 Victoria Guida, "Trump's 'Blowout' Jobs Number Looks Like Fuzzy Math," *Politico*, November 1, 2019, www.politico.com/news/2019/11/01/trump-october-unemployment-numbers-063870.
10 November 27, 2020.
11 Lenny Bernstein, "The Coronavirus Pandemic Has Caused Nearly 300,000 More Deaths Than Expected in a Typical Year," *The Washington Post*, October 20, 2020, www.washingtonpost.com/health/coronavirus-excess-deaths/2020/10/20/1e1d77c6-12e1-11eb-ba42-ec6a580836ed_story.html
12 Angelo Fichera, "Flawed Analysis Leads to False Claim of 'No Excess Deaths' in 2020," *Factcheck.org*, December 3, 2020, www.factcheck.org/2020/12/flawed-analysis-leads-to-false-claim-of-no-excess-deaths-in-2020/.
13 www.jhunewsletter.com/article/2020/11/a-closer-look-at-u-s-deaths-due-to-covid-19.
14 Washington Post Data Base, "Fatal Force: 1,018 People Have Been Shot and Killed by Police in the Past Year," *The Washington Post*, September 10, 2020, updated July 14, 2021, www.washingtonpost.com/graphics/investigations/police-shootings-database/
15 Zak Koeske and Sarah Freishtat, "Dozens of Educators Charged with Sex Crimes and Violent Felonies Lose Licenses Under New Law, But Loopholes Remain," *The Daily Southtown*, October 29, 2019, www.chicagotribune.com/suburbs/daily-southtown/ct-sta-educator-license-suspensions-st-1027-20191029-t3b35posqvbbjhdiqecacpzp7a-story.html.
16 CBS News, "Texas Police Group Puts Up Billboard Warning 'Enter at Your Own Risk,' Saying Austin Defunded Police," *WTOP News*, September 11, 2020, https://wtop.com/national/2020/09/texas-police-group-puts-up-billboard-warning-enter-at-your-own-risk-saying-austin-defunded-police/.
17 Meena Venkataramanan, "Austin City Council Cuts Police Department Budget by One-Third, Mainly Through Reorganizing Some Duties Out from Law Enforcement Oversight," *Texas Tribune*, August 13, 2020, www.texastribune.org/2020/08/13/austin-city-council-cut-police-budget-defund/.
18 Security.org Team, "Police Brutality Statistics & Analysis for Cities and States: 2013–2021," *Security.org*, June 15, 2021, www.security.org/resources/police-brutality-statistics/.
19 Aydelotte et al., "Traffic Safety Impacts of Marijuana Legalization," *American Journal of Public Health, Research and Practice*, June 22, 2017, https://komornlaw.com/wp-content/uploads/2018/01/drvp-aydelotte2017.pdf; Benjamin Hansen, Keaton Miller, and Caroline Weber, "Early Evidence on Recreational Marijuana Legalization and Traffic Fatalities," *Economic Inquiry*, 58(2), 2020, pp. 547–568.
20 Kiannah Sepeda-Miller, "Downstate Republican Wrong about Wage Hike Costing 50,000 Jobs," *The Chicago Sun-Times*, 05/05/2019, https://chicago.suntimes.com/2019/5/5/18620714/fact-check-downstate-republican-wrong-about-wage-hike-costing-50-000-jobs.
21 Ibid.
22 Ryan Fazio, "NY and CA Spend Billions More in Taxes than TX and FL—And Get Worse Results," *New York Post*, February 1, 2020, https://nypost.com/2020/02/01/ny-and-ca-spend-billions-more-in-taxes-than-tx-and-fl-and-get-worse-results/.
23 Danilo Trisi and Matt Saenz, "Economic Security Programs Reduce Overall Poverty, Racial and Ethnic Inequities," July 1, 2021, www.cbpp.org/research/poverty-and-inequality/economic-security-programs-reduce-overall-poverty-racial-and-ethnic.

9
SURVEYS

Importance of Surveys

Much of what we read each day is based on surveys. What percent of the population approves of the president? What do people think about Black Lives Matter or its proposals for police reforms? How much confidence does the public have in the economy? Does the public support President Trump's anti-immigrant policies? In addition to attitudes or opinions, surveys also try to uncover facts, such as how many people know someone who has died of the covid-19 virus, how many people are unemployed or have been victims of crimes. Companies do surveys to find out what brand of bread you buy at the supermarket. Non-profit advocacy groups sometimes ask you to tell them what issues are most important to you.

Surveys have impact. Predictions of election outcomes can influence campaign contributions and voter turnout. Household surveys determine unemployment rates that are sometimes used to determine eligibility for federal grants. The Census is a constitutionally mandated survey, and the number of representatives each state sends to Congress depends on the head count. Public policy is sometimes determined or rejected based on the opinions expressed in surveys. If you want to know what consumers think about your product and how you might change it, you are likely to use a survey. If you are in the field of public health and need to know how many people are planning to have their children get routine vaccinations, you will have to rely on a survey of parents.

How to Analyze Surveys (Without a Degree in Statistics)

Before you accept the results of a survey, before you repeat them, before you use them, you should do some checking. Some surveys are well done, but others are done by people who don't know how to do them and don't realize how much skill and knowledge is required. More disturbing, sometimes the methods and design are intentionally biased or the results are purposely misrepresented. Fortunately, you don't have to be a statistician to see the weaknesses or spot intentional misinterpretation of survey results.

- You can check out the reputation, reliability, and methodology of the firm or organization that was responsible for the survey.
- You can look at the survey design, including the wording of questions, the suitability of the answer categories, and how respondents were selected.
- You can look for fact-checks of the survey results you are examining.
- You can compare the answers in different surveys that have asked similar questions. If there is a wide variation between different surveys, you want to be cautious in accepting the results of any one of them.

Examine the Reputation of Company Doing the Survey

Some survey companies and institutes have been around for years, with a long track record of using the gold standard of methodology. Often, they have successfully predicted winners and losers in elections. Other polling companies may not be as reputable or reliable. One of the first questions you might ask yourself is, who did this survey? Is it a company or institute I should trust?

A report based on a survey that doesn't tell you who designed and fielded it should make you immediately suspicious. There is no way to check the reputation of a firm that hides its identity.

The website FiveThirtyEight.com rates political polling outfits, evaluating their methodology and their record of accuracy in predicting election outcomes. The site lists not only how many times a polling company has predicted the winner, but how close the pollsters were to predicting the actual spread, who won or lost by how much. Among FiveThirtyEight's favorites are SurveyUSA, the Marist Institute for Public Opinion, Monmouth University Polling Institute, Suffolk University Political Research Center/USA Today, ABC News/Washington Post Poll, and CBS/New York Times.

Though the track record on predicting election outcomes is a useful indicator of quality, you should also look for the stated goals and methods of a survey outfit. Good survey companies and institutes often have a methodology section on their websites describing how they design and carry out their surveys. Several of the best ones pride themselves on their role as teachers, not only for students but also for the public, for policy makers, and for other survey research outfits. Looking at their websites can help you discern the characteristics of well-done surveys, and hence learn to recognize surveys that are seriously flawed.

Among the best survey centers are the Marist Institute and Monmouth University Polling Institute, which were chosen by FiveThirtyEight, the

Roper Center for Public Opinion research, the Pew Research Center, the Gallup Poll, and NORC.

The Marist Institute, known for its accuracy on election polling, is a university-based polling institute with a strong teaching mission. As part of that mission, it offers free, online short courses on surveys, and describes on its website the methods it uses in its surveys.[1] The website says it uses live interviewers (as opposed to recordings), randomly calls both landlines and cell phones, and interviews only one person per household. Interviewers are thoroughly trained, and quality controls and checks are built into the procedures.

If a survey company only uses telephone numbers for landlines, it misses all those people who only have cell phones, so the Marist Institute tells you that it uses both. Everyone in a given target population should have the same chance to be chosen for the survey sample, so respondents are chosen at random from a list that includes everyone who is relevant to the study, such as all registered voters. If the people who are in the sample and asked questions are chosen at random from the larger population, they should be very much like the larger population. If survey researchers do not pick their respondents at random, their sample might be quite different from the population. When they try to apply the survey results to the whole population they may be off the mark.

The Roper Center describes its mission as

> to collect, preserve, and disseminate public opinion data; to serve as a resource to help improve the practice of survey research; and to broaden the understanding of public opinion through the use of survey data in the United States and around the world.

It maintains an archive of surveys done by others over the years, surveys that use traditional and tested methodology. You can get access to its library of surveys by becoming a member of the Center, but you have to pay for such access unless your employer or school is already a member and provides access for you.

The Roper Center website includes a section called polling fundamentals that explains in straightforward language the basics of random sampling. More generally, the site describes the sources of error in surveys: sampling error, non-response error, measurement error, and coverage error. Sampling error means that those chosen to answer the survey question were not randomly selected or are otherwise not typical of the population at large. Non-response error happens when some respondents chosen for a survey don't answer, so the respondents who do answer may no longer be typical of the whole population. Measurement error means the survey didn't measure what it was supposed to measure. This can happen if questions are worded badly or were asked in the wrong order (so that the answer to one question biases the answer to another one) or the possible answer choices were too limited or biased. Coverage error refers to the idea that not every element of the population has an equal chance to get into the survey, such as people without telephones, people living overseas, or under bridges.

The Pew Research Center defines itself as a non-profit, non-partisan, and non-advocacy "fact tank" (as opposed to a think tank which is usually more advocacy oriented). It describes its role as informing the public rather than persuading the public or elected officials on any issues. It doesn't take policy stances. Allsides /Media Bias rates Pew Research Center not biased to the left or right.

In the discussion of its methodology, Pew notes that survey response rates are often low. Non-response error can easily creep in if only 10 or 15 percent of the randomly chosen sample actually responds to the survey. Survey researchers have to check the degree to which those who did respond are like those who didn't respond, and how well those who did respond match the characteristics of the broader population. If those chosen for a survey but who decided not to answer the questions are substantially different from those who did answer the questions, the data might end up being biased.

It is common to find that the sample that did respond no longer matches the population, in which case the researchers try to amend their data, weighting the responses of those who responded by their proportions in the population. If 15 percent of the population are rich, but only three percent of those in the sample are rich, the researchers might multiply the answers of the three percent to match the percent in the population. This is jury rigged, but it is a way around the typically low response rates to surveys. Pew suggests that you should pay attention to how low the response rates are and what techniques are used to address the resulting problems. If a study relies on random selection of respondents but doesn't include information about response rates, it may not be a reliable survey.

While analysts note that Gallup doesn't always get political polling right and FiveThirtyEight describes the company as skewed slightly right, Media Bias/Fact Check rates the company as least biased and very high on factual reporting. Allsides /Media Bias rates Gallup as center. Gallup presents the results of its surveys without opinion or slanted words. The company prides itself on using scientifically proven and accepted methodologies.

Gallup, in its dual role as consultant and survey research firm, critiqued surveys done by employers of their own employees. Gallup claims that though well intended, company managers are generally amateur survey researchers and hence make a number of common mistakes. Some of those mistakes are outlined above, but some add to our list of mistakes to look for that can reduce the credibility of survey results. One is overly long surveys that wear respondents out so they lose attention, possibly eroding the quality of responses and probably eroding the number of responses. A second mistake is that these managers sometimes write questions that confirm their own biases.[2] These flaws are relevant when looking at any survey, by bosses of their employees or by anyone else.

NORC (formerly named the National Opinion Research Center at the University of Chicago) runs a number of different studies, some longitudinal, many sociological. The goal of this university-affiliated survey research center is to provide fact-based information for policy makers. In line with its university affiliation, it also has a teaching function, that is, it researches and innovates in methods and design, and carefully documents its own methodology for its surveys. NORC has partnered with the Associated Press so that its results can be publicized by a media company with a reputation for neutrality and for documenting its sources.

In recent years, NORC has relied in part on panel studies. A group of people form a panel and answer a series of surveys, not just one. Although some survey companies use panels that are self-selected, a kind of convenience sampling that is usually not representative of the public at large, the NORC panel, called AmeriSpeak, is randomly chosen from a national frame. Survey participants should be pretty much like the population and surveys can be fielded quickly.

NORC describes the process of selection of panel members in the following way:

> During the AmeriSpeak recruitment process, NORC contacts sampled households in English and Spanish by U.S. mail, telephone, and through field interviewers conducting in-person recruitment. Selected households can join the panel by visiting the AmeriSpeak Panel member website or by calling the AmeriSpeak toll-free telephone number. NORC obtains informed consent from study participants during the registration process.
>
> After providing informed consent, AmeriSpeak Panel members first complete an introduction survey asking questions about their background, household composition and characteristics, and interests. Afterward, the AmeriSpeak panelist may be invited to participate in surveys and other kinds of research regarding a wide variety of topics. AmeriSpeak Panel members typically participate in AmeriSpeak web-based or phone-based studies two to three times a month.[3]

Some survey shops don't have as good a reputation as those listed above. Harris Survey was a famous and trusted polling company for many years, but recently has changed ownership several times. The website FiveThirtyEight grants it only a grade of C based on the accuracy of its election predictions. Harris can do surveys quickly via the internet, but it sacrifices accuracy for speed.

Harris has a cooperative agreement with the Harvard Center for American Political Studies (CAPS): Harris does the surveys on political topics and the CAPS posts the survey questions and summaries of the responses online. The conclusions sometimes appear in locations such as The Hill, an online news site, and are often picked up by politicians who agree with some of the findings and want to claim that the American public agrees with their policies. Unlike most of the major survey companies, neither the Harvard Center for American Political Studies nor Harris provides much information on the methodology of their surveys.

Harris pays respondents who volunteer to be on a panel. Volunteers get points for each survey they fill out. When the total reaches a preset high level, the respondents can exchange their points for gift cards.[4]

Harris polls are described by Pew as "opt-in"; that is, the respondents choose to be on a panel and decide whether to fill out a survey that they are offered. Unlike NORC, Harris does not choose respondents randomly from the population at large.[5]

Langer Research Associates describes opt-in surveys in the following terms.

> Opt-in online surveys are completed by individuals who've been recruited to fill out questionnaires on the internet, usually in exchange for points redeemable for cash and gifts. Unlike probability samples, such as those used in good-quality telephone or face-to-face surveys, opt-in online surveys are based on non-probability or "convenience" samples. As such they operate outside the realm of inferential statistics, meaning there is no theoretical basis on which to conclude that they produce valid and reliable estimates of broader public attitudes or behavior.[6]

Harris notes that because its polls are not based on random samples, no estimates of sampling error are reported. Readers have no idea how accurate Harris's surveys are.

Though presumably Harris tries to choose a variety of respondents who look somewhat like the nation, or like registered voters, that effort may not be successful since they can choose only from a group that has self-selected. Harris acknowledges this issue when it reports that it routinely weights the respondents who do reply, so that the results more nearly approximate their distribution in the population at large.

Efforts to improve the match between the sample and the population by weighting the survey respondents by their proportion of the larger population (if you have too few of a category in your sample, just count several times the answers of those who did respond) only marginally improve the match between sample and population.[7]

Opt-in online polling normally signals a survey on whose results you should not rely.

Examine the Methods and Design of Specific Surveys

The descriptions of methodology on some of the better survey shop websites should give you a clue what to look for in survey design. Questions you should ask yourself include how many people responded to the survey and how were they chosen? As described above, most survey research is based on a sample of respondents from the universe of possible responders; analysts then try to generalize the survey results from that sample to the whole larger group. If the participants in a study are too few, or if the sample isn't representative of the larger group, the researchers cannot generalize accurately from their sample to the whole population.

You should look at the response rate, because even if the original sample is chosen at random, if only some of those selected answer the questions, the ones that do answer may not be like the ones that don't answer. The sample might no longer match the population very well. This problem of non-response is serious in survey research, as response rates are generally pretty low. Survey researchers try to work around this problem by comparing the characteristics of those chosen for the survey who do and those who don't respond; if there is a pretty good match, the researchers don't have a serious problem. If they don't know much about those who didn't respond, though, this technique does not work well. Instead, they might compare the characteristics of those who did respond to those of the whole larger group from which the sample was drawn; if there is a big difference, researchers can try to make statistical repairs, but as noted above, those repairs have limited effect.

If respondents have been chosen at random, researchers can assume that the proportion of the respondents in the sample who answer in a given way will be similar in the larger population. Since researchers are making a bit of a guess, they try to make clear the degree of their uncertainty. Reports are often worded to indicate a given probability that the real answer will be somewhere in a stated range. If the sample is small or the non-response rate is high, that range will be pretty big. This range is called the margin of error. If the sample hasn't been chosen at random, then researchers cannot calculate a margin of error, and the reader will have little idea of how accurate the survey results are.

Another element of the design is how the questions are asked, in person, over the phone, by mail, or by internet. In terms of likely accuracy of the results, in-person surveys are best, then mail, phone, and finally internet. For phone interviews, you want to know if both landlines and cell phones were used.

You also want to look at the questions asked. Is the wording clear? Are the questions biased toward one or another response? Do the questions provide sufficient context? Are people asked questions to which they ought to have answers or opinions, or are they asked things they are not likely to know? Are there filter questions to make sure that respondents are only asked questions that are relevant to them? (You should not ask people who are unemployed what their salaries are.) Are the answer categories appropriate, or do they limit and channel possible responses? The way the questions are worded and the way answer categories are framed can make a substantial difference in how people respond.

Harris and the Harvard Center for American Politics cooperated on a number of surveys that were summarized and discussed on the news website The Hill. One of the articles based on the surveys was headlined "Poll: Americans Overwhelmingly Oppose Sanctuary Cities."[8] Your concern should be raised by the description at the end of the article that it was based on an online survey rather than a telephone or face-to-face survey. Further, you should have been disturbed by the fact that there was no mention of a margin of error, suggesting that respondents were not chosen at random. The sample could be biased.

If you looked at various answers on the survey beyond the one question reported in the headline, you might wonder about the seeming lack of consistency between answers to related questions. Respondents supported an increase in border protection staffing but opposed the construction of a wall along the border. They overwhelmingly supported a path to citizenship for illegal immigrants but opposed sanctuary cities.

The codirector of the survey, Mark Penn, tried to explain the apparent contradictions saying that the public wanted to treat legal immigrants well but wanted to deport criminals. It seems more likely that respondents were reacting to the wording of the questions, which led them in different directions. For example, the survey asked registered voters (why ask only registered voters? what bias might that introduce?) if cities that arrest illegal immigrants for crimes should be required to turn them over to immigration authorities. They were asked to respond by agreeing or disagreeing, a little or a lot.

The question describes undocumented immigrants as illegal (many are here legally, if without documents), and then piles onto that, if they were arrested for crimes. There is no information about what crimes people were in jail for, no mention that people can be arrested for a crime but not convicted of it and still spend time in jail awaiting trial. It was up to the imagination of the respondent to fill in the blanks. Having been told twice that these people are criminals, the respondents are likely to imagine that they are dangerous, and of course should be turned over to the immigration authorities.

The question does not suggest any alternative to turning these criminals over to immigration, nor does it indicate what would happen to them and their families if they are turned over, or what would happen to them and to the community at large if they are not turned over. The question takes a complex issue, simplifies it into a yes or no question, where the only acceptable answer seems to be yes. If you say no, are you saying that violent criminals should remain at large in the U.S.?

Concluding that a large proportion of the sample, and hence the population, oppose sanctuary cities implies that the respondents are familiar with the term and understand the implications. In this case, however, respondents may have no more information about the issue than that embedded in the question. They may not be aware that controlling immigration is a federal responsibility, not a state or local function. They may not know that the president wanted to force the state and local governments to carry out its policies by threatening to withhold all federal funding from them if they didn't comply. State and local governments under our system of federalism are not the subordinates of the national government, to be ordered to do what the national government says to do. State and local governments have a legal right to not carry out laws that are the responsibility of the national government. The courts agreed that the president did not have the right to withhold all federal funds from states and cities that refused to carry out federal responsibilities. If survey respondents had all that information, would they still have answered the question the same way?

Well-worded questions are balanced and provide sufficient context so that even people unfamiliar with the topic can offer a sensible response. Further, well-written questions describe two or more sides of an issue and then ask which one more closely matches the opinions of the respondent. In this case, there should have been a second acceptable option. For example, less biased wording might be,

> Some people believe that state and local governments should turn over to the federal immigration authorities undocumented immigrants who have been arrested; others believe that immigration is a federal responsibility and that such cooperation would threaten immigrant communities and make them less willing to report crimes or testify in court. Are you more in favor of state and local cooperation with federal immigration authorities, or more in favor of letting the national authorities carry out immigration policies on their own?

In addition to problems with the wording of the question and lack of context, the headline could just as easily have been "Majority of respondents oppose Trump's wall," instead of "most support Trump's opposition to sanctuary states and cities." Reporting the answer to a different question on the same survey would have given exactly the opposite impression, instead of support for the president's policies, it would have shown opposition to them. A fair report would have included both and called attention to the differences.

There was another technical problem with the survey, mentioned here in case you run into it on other surveys. The story in The Hill merged the categories of slightly agree and strongly agree, (and slightly disapprove and strongly disapprove), a non-recommended procedure. The survey oversimplified the issue, allowed only a yes or no answer, and then combined slightly agree and strongly agree, stripping away not only subtlety, but much of the meaning of the answers. Slightly agree and strongly agree are not the same and should be reported separately. Many questions cannot be meaningfully answered yes or no, agree or disagree. It might be helpful to include an answer category of "I don't know enough about it." Limited answer categories offer a clue that you may not want to rely on such a survey.

When you are checking out the questions and answer categories, besides looking for biasing words and yes or no answer categories when a more nuanced and complete set of options is required, you should ask yourself whether the respondents are in a position to know the answers to the questions asked, or whether enough information is given in the questions to enable an intelligent and reasoned answer. If not, respondents are likely to try to answer, even if they don't know or understand the question, with the result that their answers might look meaningful, but in fact, be uninterpretable.

Checking the Fact-checkers

The *Washington Post* fact-checker looked into the claim that 80 percent of the respondents, and by inference the population, were critical of sanctuary cities and states and thought that state and local governments should turn over criminals to the federal immigration authorities. The *Post* fact-checker reminded readers that this was an opt-in poll, and hence probably not representative, and the wording suggested that the question was about people who had committed serious crimes, which may not have been the case. According to the *Post* fact-checker, the question wording may have led to the high figure.[9]

Comparing Responses to Similar Questions on Different Surveys

Fortunately, in the case of the question about sanctuary policies, the *Post* fact-checker did some work for you, looking at other surveys that asked similar or related questions and comparing the results. Note how the questions are worded in other surveys, with context or definitions, and with more than one reasonable option for answering.

One example came from a McClatchy-Marist poll.

> 'Sanctuary City' is a term used to describe U.S. cities which do not enforce immigration laws and allow undocumented immigrants to

live there and, in many cases, receive services. Which comes closer to your opinion? Undocumented immigrants should be deported so there is no reason to have sanctuary cities. Sanctuary cities are needed to provide services to undocumented immigrants while they are in this country." Response: 41 percent believed there was no reason to have sanctuary cities, and 50 percent believed they are needed.

A second example from the same survey asked, "Do you support or oppose the federal government cutting funds to cities that provide sanctuary for undocumented immigrants?" 43 percent agreed, 53 percent disagreed.

The Post Fact-checker also called attention to a Fox News Poll that asked "Some so-called 'sanctuary' cities refuse to assist federal authorities detain and deport illegal immigrants—do you favor or oppose penalizing those cities by taking away their federal funding?" 41 percent favored and 53 percent opposed.[10]

It is not at all clear that 80 percent of the public oppose sanctuary city or state policies. These other surveys indicate that more people approve than disapprove of sanctuary cities. The results depend on how the question is asked, and whether the respondents of the Harris Harvard poll are typical of registered voters.

If the fact-checker had not included a comparison of survey questions from other survey research outfits, you could have looked them up yourself. While a number of survey shops maintain databases for analysis, like Roper, they are open to members for a fee. Luckily, there are free sites as well. Pollingreport.com provides polling results from a variety of sources, which makes it an efficient place to check first. You can also check some of the individual pollsters, such as Reuters polling (polling explorer), news.gallup.com, and Monmouth University Policy Institute. Pew's database of surveys and the Marist poll (http://maristpoll.marist.edu/) are also free. NORC posts on its website reports and publications by its staff based on its survey data; the results of its longitudinal survey, the General Social Survey, are also available to the public. Whether or not you find the comparable questions you are looking for, these sites are fascinating to browse through.

Unintentional Bias? Hard-to-Get Respondents

Some people to whom a social scientist might want to ask questions are not readily available. They may hide if they are doing something illegal or are afraid of bill collectors, process servers, or rival gang members. Or they may not have telephones or a computer. Maybe they are homeless. Or there may not be a list of all those in the population with given characteristics so that a sample can be chosen from the list at random. Sometimes it may seem better to get some information from some of those folks even if researchers cannot know how representative their samples are. The problem is that when reporting the results, the degree of uncertainty about the degree of representativeness is not always made clear.

One example of a difficult-to-find set of respondents is undocumented immigrants. A recent study investigated whether stricter state laws helped stem the flow of undocumented people from Mexico into the U.S.[11]

The researchers used surveys taken by the Mexican authorities of undocumented workers passing through Mexican border towns and Mexican airports on their way to the U.S. How representative was this data collected from undocumented immigrants?

The Mexican government surveys are done at frequent intervals, conducted in eight border cities and five Mexican airports. "Within localities, the survey is conducted at different zones (bus stations, train stations, international bridges, and customs inspection points) and at different points (access doors, boarding zones, gates, and baggage claim areas) by which migrants must pass." Mexican authorities estimate that 94 percent of total border crossings occur through locations covered by the survey.[12]

U.S. researchers describing this data said that the sampling is done probabilistically, which is a good sign, but that its statistical properties had not been well documented. A study in 2009 compared the Mexican survey results to other sources of data, determining that by and large the survey was representative, although it was stronger for the more educated and less strong for the less educated Mexicans.[13]

As this example suggests, using data collected for other purposes sometimes provides a reasonable sample, but without follow-up studies looking at the accuracy of the available data, a reader would have no idea how good the data was. Using available data for hard-to-get respondents doesn't always work out so well.

Pew is generally a reliable survey outfit, but reputation alone should not be enough to convince you to accept the results of every survey Pew does. One of their studies compared the public's views of policing with views of the police.[14] One major finding was that police think that abuse of force is an occasional event by bad apples, having no systematic implications, while the public at large was more likely to argue that such abuse was reflective of broader societal problems. These results seem intuitive, and might not trigger any skepticism on your part unless you wondered how the respondents were chosen and how the study was actually carried out.

The opinions of the public presented no particular problems, respondents were chosen at random from the population, as occurs in most methodologically sound surveys. But what about the police? There is no national list of all police officers engaged in direct policing from which to choose respondents at random. The survey was carried out by the National Police Research Platform, which studies police and policing, and is not a survey research outfit. This opinion survey was only one of its activities. It turns out that there are lists of police departments, though not of police officers; so, departments of a given size or larger were selected at random to be part of a panel, and then several really large departments were added, not chosen at random; in addition, other departments could opt in if they chose. Not all the departments that were selected at random agreed to be on the panel, and of the departments that agreed to take the survey, not all the officers in those departments agreed to fill out the survey. There were large numbers of officers in the study, but it is not clear that they were representative of all police officers in departments of over 100 sworn officers, even after efforts to weight the sample according to a few characteristics. One wonders about which officers would be willing to take the survey and how they might differ from those who were unwilling to take it.

It was not possible to examine the responses by individual departments, only by size category. But it would be the individual departments that would be of interest. Ideally, one would want to know the characteristics of the city or county's population, its percent Black or Hispanic, its violent crime rates, and the racial composition of the department. One would also want to know the number of police abuse-of-force complaints, especially the number of unarmed suspects who had been killed by the police each year. Comparing police attitudes in cities where those figures were known to civilian attitudes in those same cities about whether police-civilian relations were due to a few rotten apples or systemic would have been more useful.

The researchers did the best they could with the data they could get, but it is not clear how meaningful the results are, especially whether the police responses are typical of police more generally, and whether there are marked differences in attitude in departments that are known for police abuse of force and those that are not, and in departments with higher or lower percentages of Blacks in the department and in the cities they police. The study leaves more questions than answers.

Intentional Bias

Readers need to watch out for unintentional bias, but a more serious problem occurs when the bias is intentional. This can occur because the survey itself is designed in such a way as to produce certain answers, or it can occur because those analyzing or using surveys distort or misrepresent the results.

Biased Survey Design

Bias can be written into the questions and answer categories if the people writing the questions have strong opinions and want respondents to confirm those opinions. This happens in so-called push polls, where campaign staff write questions in a leading manner, including information in the question that biases the response. Biased questions also can occur in opinion polls that are not directly related to elections.

For example, Mark J. Penn, a former pollster, was the codirector of the Harvard Harris poll of December 2017. The survey indicated the public was highly critical of the investigation of Trump for asking Russia's help in winning the presidential election in 2016. Penn had strong opinions against impeachment, and was a strong supporter of President Trump, which suggests that he may have biased questions and answer categories.

One of the questions was,

> Do you think that the part of the Justice Department responsible for the Hillary Clinton email investigations, and that is supervising the Mueller investigation, is resisting providing Congressional investigators information on payments for the Fusion GPS dossier, unmasking of officials and other issues, or is it cooperating fully with Congress?

Another question was

> Do you think that the Fusion GPS dossier that was paid for by Hillary Clinton's campaign was the source of the Justice Department investigation into Trump and Russia, or do you think the investigation was started on the basis of other information?[15]

Respondents would probably not have enough information to make an informed answer to the questions. There were no filter questions asking if respondents were familiar with the Russia investigation or with Fusion GPS, a company that gathered intel on opposition candidates and put that information in a dossier that may have played some role in initiating the investigation of President Trump. Respondents could have no way of knowing whether a part of the Justice Department was withholding information. The question wording might well be the first time that they encountered such a possibility. The suggestion that secret payments for the dossier were withheld from Congress to hide the source of the dossier was embedded in the question. Spelled out, the argument was that an anti-Trump cohort in the Justice Department intentionally withheld information from Congress, because if no one knew that the dossier was paid for by Clinton's campaign, the dossier might look legitimate, and hence be used to begin an investigation of the president. The designer of the question embedded a conspiracy theory in the question, making the whole investigation look corrupt. If a respondent was familiar with this conspiracy theory, he or she would understand the question, but otherwise would find it confusing. It is unclear what anyone who answered the question understood by it.

In the second of the questions, the question writer states as fact that the dossier was paid for by Clinton and suggests that the Fusion GPS dossier might have been the source of the investigation. The wording of the question implies that the dossier was just political opposition research and hence should not have been a basis for any investigation. Respondents would have no way of knowing what the basis of the investigation was. No evidence has ever been produced demonstrating that the GPS dossier stimulated the investigation, but in this question, the idea was planted.

These questions echo the published opinions and public presentations that Mark Penn was making. He was a frequent commentator on Fox News and contributed to the right-leaning editorials of The Hill, attacking the investigation of Trump as partisan and stimulated by Clinton foundation operatives. He publicly used the term "deep state" to describe democratic operatives in government trying to undermine the president, a conspiracy theory with no evidence behind it. It looks like Penn's personal opinions drove the survey questions.

You should be suspicious of survey questions that ask people questions about things they may not know, and doubly suspicious of questions that are so confusing their meaning is difficult to fathom.

You should probably be suspicious also of survey results that are intended to create fear or hate. While they may be accurate, you should check them out before accepting the results. For example, when Trump was a candidate, he used as a basis for his anti-Muslim immigration policy a survey that concluded that 25 percent of Muslim respondents agreed that "Violence against Americans here in the United States can be justified as part of the global jihad." The survey was done by the Center for Security Policy. As described by the Southern Policy Law Center which tracks extremist groups, "The Center for Security Policy (CSP) has gone from a respected hawkish think tank focused on foreign affairs to a conspiracy-oriented mouthpiece for the growing anti-Muslim movement in the United States."[16]

The source, in this case, should make you suspicious. It certainly roused the interest of a Politifact fact-checker. The study surveyed only 600 Muslims and used online polling. The response rate of the survey was not reported, another clue that the survey results should be treated with skepticism. Further, the survey asked leading questions with limited answer options. In other words, the survey was intentionally biased.

The fact-checker observed

> It's also worth noting that the head of the Center for Security Policy, Frank Gaffney, has articulated a variety of theories about Muslim extremists that verge on conspiracy, such as the idea that the Muslim Brotherhood has infiltrated the United States government and the false narrative that President Barack Obama is Muslim.[17]

Intentional bias sometimes occurs when a candidate is trying to delegitimize an opponent. Ocasio-Cortez is an outspoken, left-wing democratic congresswoman from New York. As such, she has often been the target of right-wing attacks and distortions. An anti-Ocasio-Cortez political action committee did a poll and found that she was unpopular in her district.

Beth Baumann, in an article on the conservative website Townhall, described the poll taken in Ocasio-Cortez's district. The poll takers "knocked on 10,556 doors and spoke to 22,546 voters."[18] The political action committee reported that:

- 58.2 percent of those surveyed were unfamiliar with Ocasio-Cortez.
- 50.8 percent of those surveyed had an unfavorable opinion of AOC.
- 56.6 percent of those surveyed said they were unsure if Ocasio-Cortez had their district's best interest at heart.
- 33.4 percent of those surveyed said they would oppose AOC running for reelection next year.[19]

If you didn't know that the purpose of the poll was to discredit a political opponent, you might be convinced by the apparently large size of the sample and the percent with an unfavorable opinion of her. But given the obvious political motivation behind the poll, you might decide to look further.

The first thing you might notice is that 58.2 percent of those surveyed were unfamiliar with Ocasio-Cortez, but 50.8 percent had an unfavorable opinion of her. How is that possible? If 58.2 percent of the respondents didn't know who she was, then only 41.8 had any idea who she was. How could 50.8 have an unfavorable opinion of someone they didn't know? Why would a survey researcher ask someone who has said they don't know the person they are talking about whether they had a favorable or unfavorable opinion of that person? The result is non-sensical. Well-designed surveys ask "filter" questions, that is, they ask some questions to see if the respondent is appropriate for the survey. If the survey is about which candidate a respondent is going to vote for, a filter question might be, do you plan to vote in the next election? If the answer is no, they should not be asked who they will vote for. "Do you know Ocasio-Cortez?" is a filter question, those who don't know who she is should not be asked any further questions about her.

A second problem that might have occurred to you is that many people in the same household were questioned. This is not a recommended practice for several reasons. First, it means that the interviewees were not chosen at random, and second it means that one person's answer might have influenced the answer of a second or third person.

To interpret the results, you need some context that was not supplied. As noted in the last chapter, you should ask yourself if these numbers are high or low. How many people know who their representatives are? Is Ocasio-Cortez different from other representatives in this regard? A Gallup telephone poll indicated only 35 percent knew who their representative was.[20] More than 41 percent of Ocasio-Cortez's constituents who were polled knew who she was. The opposition PAC suggested that her constituents didn't know who she was, but actually, Ocasio-Cortez did a bit better than most on this dimension.

Similarly, the poll result that indicated disapproval of Ocasio-Cortez lacked context because 33.4 percent of those surveyed by the PAC were not planning to vote for her. In context, a Pew poll found that 40 percent approved of their own member of Congress, while 47 percent disapproved.[21] And in 2013, a similar Pew poll found that 38 percent wanted their own representative to lose his or her job in the 2014 elections.[22] Thus, Ocasio-Cortez did better than the typical representative had done on this question several years earlier.

One might reasonably conclude that Ocasio-Cortez is more popular than other representatives on average, but you would not know that from an article citing a poll designed and fielded by an opposition political action committee. You need to ask who paid for and designed this poll and what was its purpose. And then you need the context to understand the answers.

Intentionally biased surveys are not designed to learn something from respondents. They may be aimed at influencing public opinion, as in the Ocasio-Cortez case, or planting or reinforcing opinions in the minds of those responding to their surveys. Trump and Pence did a survey of their supporters, people on their mailing lists, not randomly chosen, about media bias.[23] This survey was so biased it disturbed the legitimate survey researchers. NPR described it as "enough to make a social scientist cringe."[24]

The first question on the survey asks, "Do you trust the mainstream media to put the interests of Americans first?" That is an ambiguous question, what does the interest of Americans mean? First before what? It implies that somehow the mainstream media is not acting in the interest of Americans.

One question asks "On which issues does the mainstream media do the worst job of representing President Trump? (Select as many that apply.)"

- Immigration
- Economics
- Radical Islamic terrorism
- Pro-life values/social issues
- Religion
- Health care
- Second Amendment rights

That question assumes that the mainstream media do a bad job at representing President Trump on all these issues; the respondent has only to answer on which issues the press does the worst job.

The survey asks questions that respondents are unlikely to know the answer to, such as "Do you believe that the mainstream media does not do their due-diligence fact-checking before publishing stories on the Trump Administration?" How would a respondent know what kind of fact-checking media outlets use? The implication here is that the stories are not fact-checked, and hence are false. Respondents would not know otherwise.

The survey builds resentment with questions like "Do you feel that the media is too eager to slur conservatives with baseless accusations of racism and sexism?" As a respondent moves through the questions, resentment would continue to build, for example, another question was "Do you believe the media is biased when it covers people of faith and supporters of religious liberties?"

One of the questions reinforces the correctness of the administration's policies toward Muslims. "Do you believe the media is biased when it covers President Trump's restriction on immigration from countries compromised by radical Islamic terrorism?" By using the term radical Islamic terrorism, the question implies that of course the President's policy was correct, to keep you safe. The justification of the policy, along with the fright tactics, dictate the answer. Wording is important.

"Do you believe that the media has been too quick to spread false stories about our movement?" Note that in this question, the implicit argument is made that the media are spreading false stories, the respondent only gets to say whether these are spread too quickly. (Would it be better if they were spread slowly?).

Such surveys are intended to plant ideas, feed resentment, and build political support. They are often followed by a request for a donation. They are not a reliable source of information about anything other than the ideas of the politicians and their staff who design and send the surveys and what they want their followers to think and say. There is no substitute for looking at the actual questions asked.

Misinterpretation of Survey Results

Intentional bias isn't always the fault of the survey researchers. A survey may be well designed, but the results misinterpreted. One trigger that might indicate bias by misinterpretation is an argument from authority. A speaker or writer might claim that a survey from a trusted source reported something, so it must be true. If an argument seems to depend entirely on the reputation of the survey research outfit, it is a good idea to check out if that research actually said what the speaker or writer claims it says.

Factcheck.org pointed out that Trump claimed falsely that a Pew survey found that among the world's Muslims, "27 percent, could be 35 percent, would go to war" against the U.S. When asked about this result Pew responded that they had never asked such a question in a survey.[25]

Trump was making the broader claim that Muslims hate us and are willing to attack us in order to justify his policy of blocking Muslims from entering the country. When Fox News Sunday interviewer Chris Wallace told Trump that "at most, 100,000 people are fighting for jihadist causes. That's less than—it's a tiny fraction of 1 percent" of all Muslims. Trump responded that that number was wrong, that "27 percent, could be 35 percent, would go to war," against us, citing Pew as his source.

Trump was insistent that Pew had found that 27 or maybe 35 percent of Muslims worldwide would go to war against us. Where did such an idea come from since Pew denied having ever asked the question? What Pew had studied was militant Islam in various Muslim countries around the world. The study concluded that in a few countries substantial minorities expressed the opinion that sometimes violence against civilian targets could be justified to protect Islam from its enemies. Trump generalized the results from a substantial minority in a few countries to all Muslims everywhere, and further claimed that they would be willing to attack the U.S. Other Pew studies reported that the vast majority of Muslims in the U.S. oppose terrorism.[26]

Arguments from authority should trigger your curiosity, and the technique described in an earlier chapter of checking to see if a quoted source says what the speaker says it says should help you figure out whether or not to believe the argument.

Conclusion

If you think a survey might be biased, or poorly done, you can look at who did the survey, their reputation for accuracy and good methodology, and see if individuals who worked on the survey have expressed their views publicly. You can see if fact-checkers have questioned the results and can look at the wording of questions to see if they are clear, include context, and if the answer categories are appropriate or too directive. When you evaluate the survey methods, you should look for sample size and representativeness, response rates, and techniques for choosing the sample, and whether the survey was carried out in person, by phone, or by internet. Keep in mind that it isn't always the survey design that is weak; sometimes the problem lies with those who interpret, or misinterpret, the results. Comparing what the surveys actually asked with the conclusions cited by politicians or pundits is one way to check for intentional bias. In addition, when the numbers seem unlikely to be true, you can look for other surveys, comparing question wording, answer categories, and results.

Notes

1. http://maristpoll.marist.edu/methods/#sthash.eZwC9h72.dpbs.
2. Ryan Pendell, "10 Ways to Botch Employee Surveys," *Gallup*, August 28, 2018, www.gallup.com/workplace/241253/ways-botch-employee-surveys.aspx.
3. https://amerispeak.norc.org/about-amerispeak/Pages/Panel-Design.aspx.
4. www.harrispollonline.com/#homepage.
5. Claudia Deane, Courtney Kennedy, and Scott Keeter, "A Field Guide to Polling: Election 2020 Edition," *Pew Research*, November 19, 2019, www.pewresearch.org/methods/2019/11/19/a-field-guide-to-polling-election-2020-edition/.

6 Briefing Paper, "Opt-in Online Surveys," Langer Research Associates, August 2012, www.langerresearch.com/wp-content/uploads/Langer_Research_Briefing_Paper-Opt-in_Online_Panels.pdf.
7 Andrew Mercer, Arnold Lau, and Courtney Kennedy, "For Weighting Online Opt-In Samples, What Matters Most?," *Pew Research*, January 26, 2018, www.pewresearch.org/methods/2018/01/26/for-weighting-online-opt-in-samples-what-matters-most/.
8 Jonathan Easley, *The Hill*, February 21, 2017, https://thehill.com/homenews/administration/320487-poll-americans-overwhelmingly-oppose-sanctuary-cities.
9 Michelle Ye Hee Lee, "Do 80 Percent of Americans Oppose Sanctuary Cities? The Washington Post Fact Checker," *The Washington Post*, March 28, 2017.
10 Michelle Ye Hee Lee, "Do 80 Percent of Americans Oppose Sanctuary Cities?," *Washington Post Factchecker*, March 28, 2017, www.washingtonpost.com/news/fact-checker/wp/2017/03/28/do-80-percent-of-americans-oppose-sanctuary-cities/.
11 Mark Hoekstra and Sandra Orozco-Aleman, "Illegal Immigration, State Law, and Deterrence," *American Economic Journal: Economic Policy*, 9(2), 2017, pp. 228–252, www.aeaweb.org/articles?id=10.1257/pol.20150100.
12 Ibid, p. 231.
13 Michael S. Rendall, Emma Aguila, Ricardo Basurto-Dávila, and Mark S. Handcock, "Migration between Mexico and the U.S. Estimated from a Border Survey," May 7, 2009, www.researchgate.net/publication/228916062_Migration_between_Mexico_and_the_US_estimated_from_a_border_survey (accessed July 8, 2020).
14 Rich Morin, Kim Parker, Renee Stepler, and Andrew Mercer, "Police Views, Public Views," January 11, 2017, www.pewsocialtrends.org/2017/01/11/police-views-public-views/.
15 harvardharrispoll.com.
16 The Center for Security Policy, Southern Poverty Law Center, www.splcenter.org/fighting-hate/extremist-files/group/center-security-policy.
17 Lauren Carroll and Louis Jacobson, "Trump Cites Shaky Survey in Call to Ban Muslims from Entering US," *Politifact*, December 9th, 2015, www.politifact.com/truth-o-meter/statements/2015/dec/09/donald-trump/trump-cites-shaky-survey-call-ban-muslims-entering/.
18 Poll Reveals Just How AOC's Constituents Feel About Her … And It's Enlightening, June 17, 2019.
19 Beth Baumann, "Poll Reveals Just How AOC's Constituents Feel About Her … And It's Enlightening," Townhall, June 17, 2019, https://townhall.com/tipsheet/bethbaumann/2019/06/17/progressive-darling-aoc-faces-trouble-in-her-own-district-n2548423.
20 Elizabeth Mendez, "Americans Down on Congress, OK with Own Representative," *Gallup*, May 9, 2013, https://news.gallup.com/poll/162362/americans-down-congress-own-representative.aspx.
21 Pew Research Center, "Section 2: Public Views of Congress; Voters' Views of Their Own Representatives," July 24, 2014, www.pewresearch.org/politics/2014/07/24/section-2-public-views-of-congress-voters-views-of-their-own-representatives/.
22 Pew Research Center, "Record Anti-Incumbent Sentiment Ahead of 2014 Elections," October 15, 2013, www.pewresearch.org/politics/2013/10/15/record-anti-incumbent-sentiment-ahead-of-2014-elections/.
23 Trump-Pence Mainstream Media Accountability Survey available here: https://gop.com/mainstream-media-accountability-survey/.
24 Danielle Kurtzleben, "The Trump Media Survey Is Phenomenally Biased. It's Also Useful," *NPR*, February 17, 2017, www.npr.org/2017/02/17/515791540/the-trump-media-survey-is-phenomenally-biased-it-also-does-its-job-well.
25 Robert Farley, "Trump's False Muslim Claim," *Factcheck*, March 16, 2016, www.factcheck.org/2016/03/trumps-false-muslim-claim/.
26 Pew Research Center, "Little Support for Terrorism Among Muslim Americans," *Pew*, December 17, 2009, www.pewforum.org/2009/12/17/little-support-for-terrorism-among-muslim-americans/.

10
RESPONSE
Fighting Back

Once you have figured out that an argument or ad is misleading, if it is likely to hurt people or cause serious damage, you should do what you can to stop or counter it.

You might feel like Sisyphus in Greek mythology, condemned to roll a huge rock up a hill only to see it fall back down again. In reality, your task is not impossible. Success should be measured in terms of friends, relatives, or strangers whom you convince not to pass along misinformation and in terms of people you teach how to recognize and analyze lies, exaggerations, and distortions. In some cases, success can be measured in lives saved.

You don't have to convince the world all by yourself. Others will fight alongside you, including some you persuade. Unlike Sisyphus, when you roll a rock up the hill, it stays there, and you can go back down and roll up another one, until you, your friends, your acquaintances, and strangers you have persuaded, have built a wall to keep out misinformation, distortions, and lies.

Taking action is necessary because misleading information has consequences. The policeman described in an earlier chapter lost his job when he believed a false quote and acted on it. When President Trump talked about the possibility of injecting or swallowing bleach as a cure for covid-19 (it isn't), poison hot lines got a rush of telephone calls. Misinformation on Whatsapp led to a mob killing in India. Conspiracy theories about 5G networks led to people attacking communication towers in the United Kingdom. Denial that AIDS was caused by a virus susceptible to treatment in South Africa led to a marked reduction in average life span and left many orphans.

What can you do about what you discover? First, of course, refrain from passing it along. That is important by itself. But there are also other avenues for response, depending on how much time and energy you are willing to devote to the effort.

Success Is Possible

Efforts to respond to fake news, conspiracy theories, distorted stories, or so-called alternate facts do sometimes work.

In Italy, the anti-vaxxer movement had taken root, with the predictable outcome of an outbreak of avoidable illness, including deaths. As reported in the *Washington Post*, an Italian doctor, Roberto Burioni, decided to take action. He wrote on social media, countered the arguments of the anti-vaxxers, and discussed the harm caused by the diseases that were being allowed to flourish. He followed up with a book *Vaccines Are Not an Opinion*. He joined a movement that successfully pressured the government to require vaccinations for children before they would be permitted to attend school. Most importantly, he was not alone; others also felt a personal responsibility to help reduce the spread of anti-vaxxer sentiment.[1]

Another successful campaign against false information occurred in South Africa, when, confronting a massive epidemic of AIDS, the president denied that AIDS was caused by a virus and could be treated with anti-virals. Instead, he blamed poverty and general poor health conditions. Consequently, he worked to cut off funding for those who were working on strategies to reduce the transmission of AIDS. Health workers and academic researchers took part in a campaign of research, testing, and advocacy. As two of the participants in that struggle described, the health workers "were faced with a horrific epidemic and did the right thing. En masse they spoke truth to power. They were relentless in their pursuit of scientific evidence and ruthless in their implementation." It took years, but with the public and eventually the government on board, they turned the tide, improving public health, saving many lives.[2]

You don't have to be a doctor saving young people from disease to be successful. You don't have to engage in a long-term campaign, though you can if the stakes are particularly high. Small efforts also count. Each time you discourage someone from passing along false information, you are helping build the wall against lies and distortions.

What To Do?

One approach to fighting denialism and distortions is to present accurate information, even though not everyone is open to straight factual material. The people who start such campaigns are least likely to listen to opposing arguments, but some of those who repeat that misleading information are likely to become more cautious about it in the face of contradictory information.

When California's governor, Gavin Newsome, offered emergency funding to the state's undocumented workers to help tide them over from the covid-19 pandemic, right-wing opposition to Newsome flared on Twitter, with a renewed effort to recall him, that is, remove him from office through the formal mechanism of a recall election.[3]

Opposition to Newsome was based in part on factual misinformation, such as that the undocumented don't pay taxes but receive government support. Some tweets argued, also incorrectly, that the undocumented were getting financial help while other Californians were not.

Some of the reactions to the recall effort illustrate possible strategies of response. These responses were less aimed at the diehard Newsome opposition and more to others open to persuasion by clear, fact-based arguments. For example, one tweet mentioned the dependence of the whole country on the food produced and distributed by undocumented workers. One mentioned the contagion effect of covid-19; if the undocumented got sick, others in the community are also likely to get sick. A different response was to support the governor rather than the undocumented by noting that, based on the governor's leadership, the death rate in California was way lower than it was in New York State. Most directly, many tweets pointed out that the undocumented do pay taxes, including social security, which they are not eligible to receive after retirement.

You might not want to get involved in a whole campaign but want to react constructively while you are still irritated at an attempt to cheat or deceive you. What could you do about that? There are many ways to respond, some requiring less and others more effort and time.

Report What You Found

The quickest and easiest response is to give the problem to someone else whose responsibility it is to follow through. You can often report your findings to fact-checking sites, letting them investigate further and publish their findings. Common Cause, a good government group advocating and supporting democracy, recruits citizens on a non-partisan basis to watch for false claims on social media, especially about elections. Volunteers are trained and report misinformation or disinformation to them so that they can put out corrections.

A number of social media sites allow users to report stories they consider fake. The following paragraphs offer a snapshot for how to report your findings. The details of how social media handle user complaints could change but the chance is good that they will continue to allow user comments on the truth value of posts.

Many fake news stories appear on Facebook, and lots of users fall for them. If you discover one that seems to you to be false news or a hoax, you can report it by tapping the upper right-hand corner of a post on a Facebook app and selecting "It's a Fake News story." Facebook promises to send items identified by users to independent, third-party fact-checking organizations. Facebook does not promise to immediately remove those articles verified by fact-checkers as false, but "If the fact checking organizations identify a story as fake, it will get flagged as disputed and there will be a link to the corresponding article explaining why. Stories that have been disputed may also appear lower in News Feed." Their idea is to allow people to make their own choices about whether to read or believe a story once it has been flagged as false or misleading. Though this could change, at present you have the option of recommending what Facebook should do about the article, just flag it, send a message to the author, or block the author.[4]

YouTube, another frequent source of false news, has a policy called "community guidelines." If you find an instance of a video that contradicts those guidelines, you are invited to report it. These guidelines include various kinds of scams and manipulated videos, as well as efforts to discourage people from voting or participating in the census. Forbidden content includes exaggerated promises, such as get-rich-quick schemes and false cures for illnesses. Pyramid schemes, a form of financial scam, are also forbidden. Violators of community guidelines will get an initial warning but will not be banned until they have three violations.

Instagram also allows users on mobile apps to report false news when they find it. Click on the three dots in the upper right corner, click on "report," then "inappropriate," and then on "false information." Instagram won't delete a flagged post, but will demote it and remove it from the explore tab. U.S.-based fact-checkers will look at flagged posts. Instagram aims to use this data to train artificial intelligence programs and reduce dependence on human fact-checkers.

You can report false advertising to the appropriate federal or state agency.

False advertising is illegal. At the federal level, the Federal Trade Commission (FTC) is responsible for monitoring advertising claims. If the FTC is alerted to an instance, it can initiate a civil investigation or even sue the accused. The Federal Trade Commission maintains a webpage for reporting scams to them. You click on a topic and subtopic, then write and submit a report online. The webpage ReportFraud.ftc.gov gives hints about what to include. There is a separate link for scams or misleading ads about the coronavirus.

After the FTC has studied your report, it may send a warning letter, advising the recipient to stop immediately making those false claims and "requiring the recipients to notify the FTC within 48 hours about the specific actions they have taken to address the agency's concerns." The letters contain the threat that if companies don't stop making false claims, "the Commission may seek a federal court injunction and an order requiring money to be refunded to consumers."[5]

The Food and Drug Administration (FDA) monitors false claims about drugs, medical devices, and proposed medical cures. The FDA describes its jurisdiction as

> ensuring that foods are safe, wholesome, and correctly labeled. It also oversees medicines, medical devices (from bandages to artificial hearts), blood products, vaccines, cosmetics, veterinary drugs, animal feed, and electronic products that emit radiation (such as

microwave ovens and video monitors), ensuring that these products are safe and effective. FDA also regulates tobacco products.

The FDA solicits reports from the public, along with those of the medical professionals and companies. It warns the public about scams and sends warning letters to companies. If you suspect some illegal scam, you can report it to the FDA. Unless they change its location, the reporting form is online at https://www.accessdata.fda.gov/scripts/email/oc/oci/contact.cfm. You can also call or email the agency. You get to choose the topic from a drop-down menu. When accessed recently, the drop-down oddly included the option of reporting a fugitive. (That option brings some funny images to mind, of fleeing microwave ovens or bad carrots hiding underground, undoubtedly not what the agency had in mind).

The Federal Communications Commission (FCC) receives citizen complaints about broadcast advertising, including false or misleading ads. It has an online complaint form (https://consumercomplaints.fcc.gov/hc/en-us). The site encourages informal complaints, and has separate buttons for complaints about televisions, telephones, radio, and the internet. There are also links for complaints about accessibility and emergency communications. They promise to deliver your complaint to the service you complain about and require that the company answer you within 30 days.

Many states also have laws against false or misleading advertising. For example, Connecticut has a Department of Consumer Protection where people can file complaints (https://portal.ct.gov/DCP/Complaint-Center/Consumers---Complaint-Center).

Comment on Social Media

With a little more effort, you can engage briefly with false arguments on social media. You can add a tweet, as many people did in California defending the governor. It helps if you have a lot of friends and they have a lot of friends. The more people who follow you, the more likely your cogent, evidence-based argument will have an impact.

If you are a regular contributor to Twitter and your tweets always sound reasonable and are based on expertise and evidence, you can develop a following. Dr. Angie Rasmussen, a virologist, posts regularly about the coronavirus, responding to exaggerations or misinformation. She recently attacked a newspaper article in the *Los Angeles Times* that reported the covid-19 virus had mutated and was more transmissible, and therefore people should be warned, and presumably, be frightened. Rasmussen's response was factual, that there was a change in one acid for another in one location of the virus, and that no one had any idea [yet] what the implications were for humans, whether transmissibility was enhanced or not, and hence there was nothing about which to warn people. "However, when the mutation was tested in animals, it had no effect on pathogenesis or viral shedding."[6] The takeaway message is that the original story was alarmist, exaggerated, and the evidence for the conclusion was missing.

You don't have to have that kind of knowledge base to post on Twitter, but it is great if you do.

Letters to the Editor and Comments on Stories

Responding to falsehoods or misleading information on social media is not the only way to have an impact. If you are willing to take a little more effort, options include writing a letter to the editor of a newspaper about a recent story that included a false statement and commenting on news stories. These can be one-time efforts on your part, or you can write letters or comments more frequently.

When President Trump claimed he had the necessary authority to reopen the states for business during the covid-19 pandemic, a constitutional lawyer, Floyd Abrams, sent a letter to the *New York Times* arguing that under the constitution, the president does not have the authority to open up the states. He gave the example of the courts prohibiting President Truman from taking over the steel mills during the Korean War and argued that the courts today would say something similar if President Trump tried to act on his claim to near universal power.[7]

Newspapers have limited space to print letters to the editor, so they try to pick the ones that are brief, informative, and well written. If your letter is not accepted for publication, you can send it to another newspaper and try again and keep trying until the newspaper story and your letter are no longer relevant. Try to refer in your letter to an article or articles that were published in the newspaper where you are sending your letter.

While asking for reader feedback on stories has a long history, many newspapers around the world dropped this feature as debates and discussion moved to social media, and comments sections were prey to trolls and bots. The sheer volume of such responses made it difficult to monitor them, but in recent years the direction has been to restore this feature in an effort to engage readers and keep their attention for a longer period of time, a difficult task while competing with cell phones. Keeping the comments and debate sections for paid customers is intended to help reduce the trolls.[8] This trend means you should focus on the newspapers to which you subscribe.

By now many newspapers allow readers to make comments on individual stories or invite debate on controversial themes. You can use this opportunity to call attention to exaggerations, distortions, deceptions, and lies in the stories you read. Comments on stories are less like a letter to the editor and more of a dialogue among readers, and between readers and authors of articles and opinion pieces.

For example, a perspective piece in the *Washington Post*, "Some may have to die to save the economy? How about offering testing and basic protections?" by columnist Sally Jenkins, evoked a large set of comments. Many agreed with the essay or some part of it, others disagreed.[9]

Some readers mentioned the difficulties of opening up the economy when many are still reluctant to mingle with others even when it is declared legal to do so; some claimed that exposing people to needless risks would not accomplish anything; several readers suggested that Trump, Pence, and their supporters make the sacrifice (of their lives) rather than asking others to do so for the sake of the economy. Key, however, was the rejection of the false dichotomy, the framing of the argument as two mutually exclusive alternatives, the economy or people's lives. More testing could provide a safer way to reopen the economy without requiring people to sacrifice their lives.

The opportunity for readers to comment in the newspaper is not limited to English language papers. For example, the prominent Spanish newspaper *El Pais* solicits polite reader comments on a selection of stories and moderates the comments. *El Pais* maintains a reader forum called "And You, What Do You Think?" It is not focused on particular stories so much as themes, such as immigration, feminism, environmentalism, and education. The paper presents information on each of those topics and then invites responses via email. In 2020, the public editor (defensor de lectores) had observed that the forum had been taken over by right-wing ideologues and bots, often posting under false names, who had turned it into a swamp, submitting thousands of comments daily, many of which were rude. Now the comments are behind a paywall and the ground rules demand courtesy. If you subscribe, you can post your reactions.[10]

Comments you make on a story should be brief; you have space for only one idea at a time, but since many people write, together the comments cover the ground. Your comments count even if you are the only one to comment, but when many people write on the same side of an issue, they have more impact together.

You can agree or disagree with an article or opinion piece, but it is usually a good idea to avoid sarcasm and name calling, even when others engage in it. You can make a short statement of fact, relating to the article or theme; sometimes you can rebut someone else's comment on the same article or essay.

Op-eds

With somewhat more effort, although still a one-time commitment, you might submit an op-ed to a newspaper. If you have any first-hand knowledge or experience on the topic being discussed, it is especially valuable. An op-ed is a kind of editorial or opinion piece that is not written by a journalist, but by someone with deep knowledge of the subject, who can give some context, history, or facts. If such an essay is accepted by a newspaper, it appears opposite the editorial page, hence the name op-ed.

Someone with knowledge of biology can explain how one can determine whether covid-19 was engineered as a weapon in a laboratory. Someone with knowledge of constitutional law can respond to claims that reprogramming funds for Trump's anti-immigrant wall along the southern border was legal. Someone who works in a hospital can respond to charges that covid-19 is a hoax.

One example occurred with the resignation of a foreign service officer, Chuck Park. Writing in an op-ed published in the *Washington Post*, he argued against the conspiracy theory of the "deep state." The deep state is supposed to be a cabal of bureaucrats inside government that secretly opposes the president's will. Park, based on his experience inside government, claimed that far from being a source of resistance inside government, the bureaucracy he saw was passive; he called it the complacent state. He saw no resistance to Trump's policies and was warned that his career was at risk for signing a cable opposing the ban on travelers from mostly Muslim countries. "Among my colleagues at the State Department, I have met neither the unsung hero nor the cunning villain of Deep State lore."[11] A day after his op-ed appeared, Park was interviewed on National Public Radio. After that, he was interviewed by Anderson Cooper on CNN, reiterating that he had seen no evidence of a deep state.

If you are writing an op-ed for submission to a newspaper, you need to stick closely to the subject. Think of an accurate but catchy title. Don't attach anything else to your email, (assuming you submit your essay electronically), and be sure to check on the submission requirements and follow them carefully. You should submit your essay to only one newspaper at a time. Each paper may have a different policy about whether and when it will respond. The *New York Times* says it will respond within three days, and if you haven't heard by then you are free to submit your essay elsewhere.

Blogs

If you really get into deciphering the twists, dog whistles, exaggerations, frauds, lies, and distortions, public and private, and begin to feel good about what you are doing and the importance of it, you might want to set up your own blog. You don't have to make it an overwhelming task, your blog posts can be reasonably short and you may decide to post only once or twice a week. There is plenty of false, exaggerated, and misleading information out there to choose from, depending on your interests and experience. You need to have something to say that is somewhat different from the fact-checkers and you need to find a niche that will differentiate your blog from others out there in cyberspace. Some existing blogs focus on legal issues, journalistic norms, or free speech issues. Some follow and report on what social media sites are doing about false news. You could specialize in some area and aggregate stories on that topic, such as health care or health scares, or you could focus on political arguments attacking opponents or on blame shifting.

Whatever way you cut the material, it needs to provide information in an easily digestible manner, be interesting and useful, that is, it needs to go further than just the short discussions on fact-checking sites. You could set up a panel of friends and family and report on how they reacted to various stories you have figured out are distorted in some way. One site has described and ranked the ten most striking or important fake news articles of the year (Radio Free Europe Radio Liberty, a private non-profit funded by a U.S. government grant). You could do something similar but a little different, for example, focusing on the U.S., or on a particular state, or you could have a substantive focus, such as immigration or health—the ten most egregiously misleading stories in health care this year, or the most serious misuse of survey data in policy advocacy. You could write a blog about which distortions or lies were most important, most effective, or most destructive. You need an angle of some sort, but fortunately, there are lots of possible angles to choose from. In fact, the possibilities are nearly inexhaustible. You need to make sure that the topic you choose is broad enough that you will have enough to write about week after week; you also need to make sure you are interested in the topic and won't get bored with it after a few issues of your blog.

If you decide to go in this direction you need to learn how to set up a blog. Different vendors provide different sets of services and vary in how much you have to do yourself. They also differ in the degree of flexibility they provide if you want to change the appearance of your blog or attract advertisers. Websitesetup.org has some suggestions for criteria to use as you select the platform for your blog.

1. Is it free, and if so, what does that mean you have to do yourself, and are you prepared to do that, what do you get for no dollars?
2. If it costs money, can you afford it, and what comes with that fee, are they features you need and want?
3. Is it easy for a beginner to use?
4. If you are thinking of making the blog pay for itself, or give you some income, does the site allow for that?

The most popular site for blogs is Wordpress.org; all you have to pay for is a domain name and a web host, both inexpensive. However, there are many other alternatives, including blogger and Tumblr. The advantage of Wordpress.org is that it is easy to set up and you can concentrate on your content. There are step-by-step directions on the web to guide you.

Protests

A different approach is to protest the sites that create, promote, and circulate false news. One of the most effective ways to do this is to complain to the advertisers on these sites. In 2019, Media Matters for America launched a campaign against Fox News advertisers, calling the campaign Dump Fox. It listed the major advertisers for each of the major prime time programs, making it easy for the public to complain to the advertisers. Those who protested Fox had a variety of complaints, but prominent among them were the network's promotion of false news and conspiracy theories.

Protests against the right-wing news site Breitbart included charges of racism, misogyny, and xenophobia, but the site also published conspiracy theories and intentionally misleading stories. The chosen protest technique was to target the site's advertisers, which was successful in hurting Breitbart's revenues. The campaign, orchestrated by Sleeping Giants, suggested that protesters get on the site and take a screen shot of an ad there, and tweet it to the advertiser with a polite note so the company paying for the ad would know on what kind of site their ad had ended up. Companies sometimes buy ads through aggregators who place them and the company doesn't know where they land. Companies prefer not to have their ads in places that foster hatred and promote false news. Once you have told them, they may withdraw their advertising dollars.

Another avenue for pressuring those perpetrating false, and in some cases downright dangerous, narratives is pressuring their credit card companies, the ones that allow them to collect donations. Jim Bakker, a televangelist who tried to peddle a false elixir (a colloidal silver solution) as a remedy for covid-19, was chastised by states attorneys, the Federal Drug Administration, and the Federal Communications Administration. With civil suits against him, his credit card processing company dropped him.

Join Groups of Activists

You can join with other activists in organizations pressing campaigns. Faithful America is one group and Sleeping Giants is another. Truth in advertising.org is a private non-profit dedicated to education of the public and advocacy efforts to keep advertising honest. They solicit complaints about advertising and investigate them; those found to be significant frauds are then listed on their website. They ask you to sign their petitions, post comments on articles, subscribe to their feeds, follow them on Twitter, and like them on Facebook.

In January 2020, a small group of protesters demonstrated outside Facebook's headquarters in Menlo Park, California, complaining about the company's policy of allowing falsehoods in political advertisements. The protest was carried out by activists from organizations including Media

Alliance, Global Exchange, and the Raging Grannies Action League.[12] Media Alliance has a broader mission than just opposing false and distorted news, but its aim of excellence and accountability in media includes such activities. Global Alliance is an organization of Public Relations professionals that works toward raising the standards, including the ethical standards, of the profession.

An organization on the left called Indivisible has started a campaign called The Truth Brigade. Indivisible recruited a number of experts to monitor important mis- and disinformation on right-wing websites and send notices every two weeks to a group of volunteers across the country, asking them to counter that mis- and disinformation in their own networks of friends, associates, neighbors, and relatives. They provide suggestions on what the volunteers could say to offset the factually incorrect or misleading material. Volunteering for The Truth Brigade is an easy way to fight back against some of the truth decay. The advantage is that it adds your voice to that of many others, and it addresses people with whom you have the best chance of being persuasive. An obvious disadvantage is that the approach is one-sided, attacking only stories circulating on right-wing sites. You could use a similar approach with misleading material you find yourself on left-wing sites.

You can help fund some of the organizations that are fighting false news, conspiracies, misleading advertising, or faked photographs and videos. Fact-finding organizations welcome financial support that comes from grassroots readers.

What Do You Say to Convince Others?

By now, you know where and to whom to respond to a misleading or false story or scam, but what do you actually write or say? You want to respond to the uncle who claims that immigrants are rapists or bring diseases, like Hansen's, to the U.S.; you would like to stop people from advertising quack cures for covid-19. You know very well that Kiev doesn't have Hillary's "missing computer," but how do you convince those who are certain it is true?

What to Avoid Saying

It is easier to talk about what does not work than what might work. People who have bought a false or misleading narrative can become defensive if you attack their views, and those beliefs can become even more firmly entrenched. Your social instincts should tell you that mockery is not a good strategy, even if you think what you are hearing is crazy. Mockery humiliates people and makes them angry but doesn't change their minds.

Comparing what they have been told or what they read and what you know to be facts doesn't work well either. People tend to remember not the facts that you cite, but the false narrative you are reacting to. Hearing it again reinforces it in people's minds. Just listing what you know to be true without repeating the false narrative might be more effective, but for a deeply held belief, facts alone are not likely to be effective.

Try to keep your own emotions out of the argument. I personally find this very difficult, I get too excited, but I know this is not a winning strategy. I am better at writing. If you can, get your emotions out first, write your angry comments down, and then tear them up or erase them without sending them. It is especially important to stay cool when you are online. Face to face, if you lose an argument or offend someone, it is only one person; online you can lose hundreds or even thousands of people.

Why Do People Accept False or Misleading Stories?

Why do people accept stories, advertisements, and political claims, why do they accept conspiracy theories that have been widely debunked? If you understand the why of it, you can sometimes figure out how to substitute a different narrative.

People accept some false narratives because they are looking for explanations, even though there may not be good ones. We don't know why some children develop autism. Several months into the covid-19 pandemic, we still didn't know how to prevent or treat covid-19. When the World Trade Centers in New York City were hit by airplanes, it was a shock, and people searched for some satisfying explanation for why it happened, what it meant.

Some people are distrustful of doctors and the medical profession more broadly, of news media, and of government. We are told that hospital mergers will bring down the costs of medicine, but when consolidation occurs, the main thing that happens is that prices go up. Drug companies suddenly vastly increase the costs of medicines needed by millions of people and work hard to sell addicting drugs, contributing to an epidemic of overdoses. Insurance companies sometimes contest legitimate requests for bill payment. It is not surprising that some people develop suspicion of the medical profession and think that doctors, drug companies, and insurers are out to make a profit when people need them most.

President Trump routinely attacked the media, calling it false news—why should people believe the media? Distrust of government is understandable, given that in some cities, police charge the poor for minor violations, ensnare them in debt, and sometimes shoot and kill unarmed people. At the national level, reasons for going to war sometimes seem to be made up excuses—the claim that Iraq had weapons of mass destruction turned out to be false but was sufficient to start a war.

People are programmed to look for patterns where there may not be any, grasping for understanding. Once they see what looks like a pattern, they are reluctant to give it up. Once you look at a cloud and see a shape in it that resembles a rabbit, it is hard to say it has some other shape or none at all, you continue to see the rabbit. Once it became known that some government insiders wanted to go to war to protect oil interests in the Middle East it was easy to accept the idea that these same people bombed the World Trade Center and blamed it on militant Muslims as an excuse to go to war.

Important for nearly everyone is a bias to accept information that agrees with their beliefs and rejects information which contradicts them. If you oppose abortions, then you may be willing to accept without evidence claims that abortions cause mental instability and possibly suicide among women. You want to believe it because it strengthens your argument. If you favor marijuana legalization, you may reject out of hand—without looking at the data—charges that smoking marijuana increases automobile accidents.

Finally, people tend to accept the ideas of those in their immediate circle of contacts. As a group, they collectively construct meaning and seek social approval. Especially because repetition is powerful, if we hear the same arguments over and over in our networks, from our friends, from our families, we are more likely to take their truth for granted. If we are praised for repeating those arguments, we are more likely to continue to repeat them.

Approaches That Might Work

So, what does all this suggest about what kinds of arguments might work to stop so many people from accepting false or misleading claims?

First, don't hesitate to get involved because you are afraid of a fight; there are ways to argue that leave you and your friends and family still talking to each other without reinforcing opposing views. While you might get some pushback online, most of it is harmless name calling. When you evoke that kind of response, it means you are making effective arguments; those who hold tightly to opposite views are trying to undermine your authority rather than reply to your arguments.

Use your networks, family, friends, coworkers, club members, and members of your religious congregation. Some of them need to hear your narrative, your point of view, your evidence. If they hear it from you, whom they know and may trust, they may be more inclined to believe it.

Acknowledge the mistrust that your audience has learned from experience. If they mistrust the media, find some source they do trust; if they mistrust doctors, find a source other than doctors, some source that doesn't benefit financially from pushing a false narrative.

Don't repeat the false information. You don't need to talk about whether the preservatives in vaccines cause autism, but you can talk about the increase in disease incidence and consequences as fewer people get vaccinated.

If possible, be proactive, get a better version of events into their hands before they hear and accept some made up, twisted version of those events.

Because it is so hard to get people to give up a false or misleading narrative once they have accepted it, once it has become part of their persona or identity prevention is a better strategy than cure. You can take the initiative with friends, relatives, and acquaintances, taking advantage of people's embeddedness in a network and their desire to fit into that network. If they hear the argument a lot, from different sources or from the same source, they are more likely to accept it. So, if you have found something of interest that is circulating widely, you might want to warn your friends and relatives, even acquaintances, before they are exposed to it, a kind of inoculation.

I imagine a conversation being something like this:

> Hey guys, guess what, I ran across this really intriguing data this morning, that showed that some police departments were able to reduce the number of unarmed blacks they shot and killed by adopting a series of policies about the use of deadly force. And the really interesting kicker? The police were less likely to get shot or hurt afterward. It didn't make them more vulnerable to violent criminals.

You might get some questions based on your initial presentation, such as what kind of policies did the police adopt? Or did that make them less aggressive in arresting bad guys and clearing crimes? Be prepared to answer such questions, but you can do this in advance since this is your narrative and you control the topic. Someone might ask you a question you don't know the answer to, such as what kind of enforcement was there, how did that work? Great question, I don't know, maybe I can find out.

Going first gives you a strategic advantage, you get to set the agenda, you are not challenging their beliefs on their turf, they are, hopefully politely engaging with you on yours. You won't win everybody, but you may win some, and with each case, you strengthen that person's ability to question and think about what they read or hear. They may realize there is another side they didn't see before.

You can also help friends, relatives, and acquaintances by alerting them to the sources that rate news sites in terms of the levels and direction of bias. People sometimes find it fun to try their own hand at rating a website and comparing their own evaluation of bias to that depicted on the sites that evaluate them. These sites explain how they do the rating, which subtly teach readers what to look for in terms of choice of content, style, and presentation of evidence.

In making conversation, you can raise topics that illustrate how you analyze a story. They may not have run across the example you are using, which is of general interest, and so have no prior opinion, but what you are indirectly teaching is not so much your conclusion as your method of thinking. You could say, are you following the case of the women's soccer team claiming they are getting paid less than the men? A judge just ruled that the women have no case because they earned the same amount as the men last year. But their base pay is a lot less than the men's; the women's team won a lot of their games, and got bonus pay for each victory. The men also get bonus pay for victories, but they didn't win many games. The judge didn't pay any attention to the difference between bonus pay and base pay. Kind of an interesting case, it will probably be appealed. It doesn't matter where the conversation goes from there, some may think the judge was right, others that the judge was wrong, or that women's sports get lower attendance, whatever. The message is not in your conclusion, but in your process of looking beyond the first paragraph of a story, looking for what might be missing.

You could recommend the University of Washington's free online course, Calling Bullshit, The Art of Skepticism in a Data Driven World, by Carl T. Bergstrom and Jevin D. West, online at callingbullshit.org. The title alone is intriguing to those who tend toward skepticism, and the course itself is delightful and stress free. Or if you have enjoyed this book, you could recommend it to others in your network. You might want to use teasers, repeating particularly fun examples to engage (or enrage?) them.

You are not always going to be able to go first. Sometimes you are going to want to react to some specific story that is out there, maybe one that friends have sent you, or one that a friend or colleague is spouting. There is disagreement among analysts as to the relative effectiveness of a straight debunking, listing the facts of the matter from your point of view versus a more indirect and gentler approach. Each may be effective at reaching different groups of people. Some people might be persuaded by hard facts from a knowledgeable professional, while others need a softer, more sympathetic approach that clearly acknowledges their legitimate concerns.

The straight factual approach relies on knowledge and experience. You may need to state your credentials before presenting your argument. What kind of training have you had before you say the coronavirus jumped from animals to people and was not intentionally made in a laboratory? Have you worked in a laboratory? Are you familiar with the DNA or RNA of viruses? Or are you privy to intelligence reports on the subject? Do you have first-hand experience with the strength of metal beams that have been heated by fires so that you can speak knowledgeably about 9/11 conspiracies? Do you teach statistics or survey design when you are about to describe the weaknesses of a study that misuses surveys?

A brief tag, phrase, or clause before you start your argument is usually all that is needed. Here are some possible examples. "Having taught methods and design to PhD students for years, I found this study fatally flawed because of the way the author chose the sample." "I have been an architect for all my professional career, I know the strength of steel beams, and it is perfectly possible for beam to get hot and bend well before it melts."

If you don't have those kinds of credentials, you should probably refer to some trusted source, either one widely viewed as neutral and authoritative, or one that conforms to the bias of your audience. On medical issues, you might want to quote the *New England Journal of Medicine*; for news you can draw on sources like PBS (Public Broadcasting) and the AP (Associated Press) that are widely viewed as relatively unbiased. The *Wall Street Journal* has a slight lean to the right in its news stories but might appeal to some of your audience. A good right-wing source on immigration is the Cato Institute, which offers responses to arguments against immigration based on years of research. A mildly left-oriented source, the Brookings Institution, often researches shibboleths, such as "robots take people's jobs." Think about what sources your audience trusts more than others and try to find support for your argument in those sources.

The straight factual approach works best if you don't repeat the false arguments. Just state the narrative for which you have evidence without reference to what you think the reader or listener might believe.

When you make corrections in popular mistaken narratives, your audience, who believes them, may think that you consider them gullible or ignorant. That kind of derision often has the effect of making people dig in and get defensive. You might want to short circuit that assumption by suggesting that the information they are repeating has been widely reported or is a social norm, or was taught in school; you need some reason they are accepting this argument other than their own ignorance or prejudice, something that will get them off the hook. If you seem to blame them, you may never win them over.[13]

These days, I generally lean on the side of a gentler, more supportive approach. You can indicate that you understand and to some extent accept your audience's concerns, you can acknowledge those parts of the story that you have verified, while noting those parts that are just guesswork, that lack evidence, or that are really wrong. You can acknowledge your audience's distrust and go from there.

It is easy to agree, for example, that the medical industry is not always to be trusted. You can agree that people need to use their own judgment sometimes, that doctors do de-emphasize side effects and should be more up front about them. Then you can move on to the idea that prevention is better than suppression of disease, on which you might get agreement, and then you can discuss the importance of vaccinations in preventing disease and the consequences of a failure to get vaccinated. In one example cited earlier in this chapter, a doctor emphasized the disfiguring impacts of some contagious diseases. Getting the disease isn't risk free. You can even show friends how to check the nature, severity, and frequency of the side effects of various medications. Everyone might not believe you or the sources you cite, but for others you will have given them the tools they need to make rational decisions.

Sometimes there is a misunderstanding involved that you can gently correct without sounding critical. I remember one discussion in which the person I was speaking to archly claimed that the temperature was so cold and snowy that day, clearly global warming was a hoax. If I had had my wits about me, I would have said, I know, I hear that argument often, but the pundits on TV mistake weather for climate. Weather is local and highly variable day to day, sometimes hotter and sometimes colder, but climate change means what is happening over years, not days or weeks, and over great distances, around the globe, not just locally. On average, around the world climate is getting hotter.

You could then suggest that they look at NOAA's website (the National Oceanic and Atmospheric Administration) which tracks global temperatures. The page, Climate Change: Global Temperature (https://www.climate.gov/news-features/understanding-climate/climate-change-global-temperature) has a dramatic graphic of average global temperatures each decade from 1880 to 2020 compared to the long-term average from 1901 to 2000. If they find this data themselves, they are more likely to believe it than if you show it to them. If they don't trust NOAA or if NOAA takes down this graphic at some point, other sites around the world present similar data, such as the Hadley Centre for Climate Science and Services in the United Kingdom.[14] If your argument works, every time the person you are arguing with hears a talking head repeat the mistake of substituting weather for climate, it will make them feel smarter, they now know better.

Your argument is sympathetic, includes the possibility that the weather on any given day may be cold and snowy, while offering an alternative conclusion. You are not repeating their arguments in a way that will reinforce them, you are not even indirectly saying they are ignorant, you are leading them from where they are to a different conclusion.

Conclusion

Regardless of which model we use, the more straightforward, authoritative fact presentation or the more sympathetic one, we need to put forth counternarratives, on the web, in news media, and with acquaintances, friends, and family. If our comments encourage others to post critical analyses of speeches, articles, or advertisements, together we may drown out the voices of distortion, exaggeration, and lies. While there are undoubtedly a few bad actors out there, who make up stories or twist facts for their own ends, most of the people who pass such stories along do so unwittingly. They do not want to pass along false or misleading information. Those are the people we need to reach.

Notes

1 Anne Applebaum, "Italians Decided to Fight a Conspiracy Theory. Here's What Happened Next," *The Washington Post*, August 8, 2019.

2. Glenda Gray and James McIntyre, "South Africa's Remarkable Journey Out of the Dark Decade of AIDS Denialism," *The Conversation*, July 13, 2016, https://theconversation.com/south-africas-remarkable-journey-out-of-the-dark-decade-of-aids-denialism-62379.
3. Office of Governor Gavin Newsom, "Governor Newsom Signs Suite of Legislation to Support California's Immigrant Communities and Remove Outdated Term 'Alien' from State Codes," September 24, 2021.
4. Adam Mosseri, "Addressing Hoaxes and Fake News," *Facebook*, December 15, 2016, https://about.fb.com/news/2016/12/news-feed-fyi-addressing-hoaxes-and-fake-news/.
5. "FTC Sends 21 Letters Warning Marketers to Stop Making Unsupported Claims That Their Products and Therapies Can Effectively Treat Coronavirus," April 23, 2020, www.ftc.gov/news-events/press-releases/2020/04/ftc-sends-21-letters-warning-marketers-stop-making-unsupported.
6. Twitter, May 5, 2020.
7. Floyd Abrams, "Trump's Claim of 'Total' Authority Over Reopening," *The New York Times*, April 14, 2020, www.nytimes.com/2020/04/14/opinion/letters/coronavirus-trump-governors.html.
8. Cyril Sam, "As Advertisement Revenues Dwindle, There Is a Pressing Need for Digital News Platforms to Generate Revenue Directly from Readers," *News Laundry*, September 27, 2019, www.newslaundry.com/2019/09/27/why-some-indian-news-outlets-are-bringing-back-the-comment-section.
9. April 18, 2020, www.washingtonpost.com/sports/2020/04/18/sally-jenkins-trump-coronavirus-testing-economy/#comments-wrapper.
10. Carlos Yárnoz, "La ultraderecha invade el foro de los lectores," *El Pais*, April 12, 2020, https://elpais.com/elpais/2020/04/10/opinion/1586555098_746716.html.
11. Chuck Park, "I Can No Longer Justify Being a Part of Trump's 'Complacent State.' So I'm resigning," *The Washington Post*, August 8, 2019, www.washingtonpost.com/opinions/i-can-no-longer-justify-being-a-part-of-trumps-complacent-state-so-im-resigning/2019/08/08/fed849e4-af14-11e9-8e77-03b30bc29f64_story.html.
12. Salvador Rodriguez, "Protesters Gather in Front of Facebook HQ to Decry Its Policy of Allowing Lies in Political Ads," *CNBC*, January 9, 2020, www.cnbc.com/2020/01/09/facebook-protestors-decry-policy-of-allowing-lies-in-political-ads.html.
13. Barry Davret, "How to Change Someone's Mind in 10 Steps; Getting Your Emotions Involved Doesn't Work. Here's What Does," *The Forge*, July 2, 2020, https://forge.medium.com/how-to-change-someones-mind-in-10-steps-e73d1f2d1e63.
14. www.metoffice.gov.uk/weather/climate-change/effects-of-climate-change.

AFTERWORD
The Responsibility Is Ours

Why Do We Have to Do This Ourselves?

Why doesn't someone shut down the fake accounts, catch the bad guys generating these false stories and altered videos, and/or force social media to prevent or take down threatening and damaging material? Between election tampering, false news about the coronavirus and vaccinations, and hate campaigns, the stakes could hardly be higher.

The Russians interfered in the U.S. presidential election in 2016. They set out to influence voter behavior and turnout in recent European Union parliamentary elections, undermining democratic institutions. A European Union report concluded that "There was a consistent trend of malicious actors using disinformation to promote extreme views and polarize local debates, including through unfounded attacks on the EU."[1]

Russian President Vladimir Putin has said the liberal idea including multiculturalism, the rule of law, and respect for human rights, is obsolete and has outlived its purpose.[2] He wants to take all these things down and one of his major tools has been disinformation and polarization through social media.

Misinformation about covid-19 has turned many people against vaccinations, leading to increased hospitalizations and deaths, and contributed to supply disruptions, unemployment, and political turmoil. Health workers have been attacked because of opposition to vaccinations. According to an article in the medical journal the *Lancet* in September of 2020, "More than 600 incidents of violence, harassment, or stigmatization took place against health-care workers, patients, and medical infrastructure in relation to the COVID-19 pandemic." The numbers would undoubtedly be much higher today.

> The incidents included doctors at a hospital in Pakistan being verbally and physically attacked after a patient died of COVID-19 and relatives entered a high-risk area while shouting that coronavirus was a hoax. In Bangladesh, bricks were thrown at the house of a

doctor after he tested positive for COVID-19 in a bid to force him and his family from the area.³

Hate messages attack immigrants, Asians, Jews, and Blacks. White supremacists spread their propaganda online, and online hate sometimes turns into real-life violence.⁴

Some of the people circulating false information have been identified. According to a recent study, just 12 people produce 65 percent of the shares of anti-vaccine misinformation on social media platforms, according to a study by The Center for Countering Digital Hate.⁵ It should be possible to close their accounts and those of people and organizations like them.

The problems resulting from the creation and circulation of false and distorted information are enormous. It looks like we should be able to find the perpetrators, and even if we can't, the social media companies that post false and misleading news are in plain view. So, what is being done to control it? Why are we more or less on our own to figure out what to accept and what to reject from what we read or hear?

Control Is More Difficult Than It Looks

Perhaps our expectations are too high about what can be done by others. Social media companies claim it is too difficult to monitor videos, requiring many hours of staff time to view and examine each one. Defenders of free speech object to proposals to prevent or remove false posts from social media, often arguing that the criteria for doing so are too vague and will lead to censorship. And while some perpetrators of false and misleading stories are out there in plain view, others hide their identities.

In democracies, fear of government censorship has prevented most countries from passing and enforcing strong laws. In addition, influential social media have been effective in opposing or shaping proposals, arguing against making themselves responsible for misleading material posted on their platforms. In the U.S., during congressional hearings after the attack on the Capitol on January 6, 2021, the CEOs of three major platforms were asked if they should be held accountable for the posts on their sites that fed the violence that day. All three skirted the question.

Facebook's Mark Zuckerberg suggested instead that social media should demonstrate that they have systems in place to police clearly illegal posts.⁶ In the absence of strong and clear laws, much of the problem is not with clearly illegal posts, so Zuckerberg wasn't offering much cooperation. It is not clearly illegal to claim that Donald Trump won a second term in office. It is false, and dangerous, but not clearly illegal in the U.S.

A *New York Times* article described a shadow industry of disinformation for hire, in which companies or countries hire thousands of influencers to disseminate false news stories in specified locations. Some of these companies sound real, but if you look up their addresses, there is nobody and nothing there. The clients who pay the intermediaries are completely invisible. How can one capture the perpetrators and stop such efforts? If you publicize their recruitment efforts, they seem to stop, but can easily reappear somewhere else under a different made-up name. They are phantoms.[7] Catching ghosts is difficult.

As social media work harder to control false and misleading news, those spreading disinformation also work harder to hide their identities and that of their funders. While some of these linkages can be traced by trained analysts, many of them go undetected.

Governments around the world have been studying the issues, but so far only a few have passed laws to curtail foreign interference in democratic institutions or the lies of politicians, although some have passed laws to reduce the amount of misleading or false information about the coronavirus pandemic. Some more authoritarian regimes have passed vaguely worded laws that are more about controlling opposition to the regime than about controlling false and misleading information.

Media Control Laws

What many governments have done or are doing is studying the problem. After one extensive study, the European Commission recommended *against* taking regulatory action. Despite such advice, some governments have passed laws prohibiting false or misleading stories. Some of these laws have been strong and broad, while others focus more narrowly on one aspect of the problem, such as doctored videos or coronavirus misinformation. And then there have been countries that have passed laws that seem less concerned with false or misleading news than with political opponents or criticism of the regime. Not all of the laws that have been passed have actually taken effect or have remained in effect for long, and some are under legal challenge.

Broad Laws That Have Been Passed

France's law against hate speech, broadly conceived, passed in May 2020. It required online platforms to remove flagged illicit content within 24 hours or pay hefty fines for each instance. Terrorist content and child pornography were to be taken down within an hour. The Constitutional Council determined the law was invalid because it was difficult to determine what is illicit and that, due to the short time allowed, the law would encourage over censoring the taking down of any questioned post quickly, whether truly false or not. The law never took effect.[8]

The internet is controlled in China. Internet users have to provide their real names to service providers and companies are responsible for taking down forbidden material and for reporting such material to the government. China's new policy attacks false news, especially deepfakes, such as videos created by artificial intelligence or virtual reality technology. The new rules require the media to reveal that the videos or recordings were faked using such technology. Failure to disclose such distortions is now a crime. The focus is on both the users and the media platforms.

Kenya's law, The Computer Misuse and Cybercrimes Act of 2018, includes cyber-bullying, child pornography, false publications, and illegal monitoring of data. Supporters argued that it would criminalize false financial schemes and prevent the radicalization of young people into terrorism.[9]

Germany has long had laws against hate speech. Section 130 of the Criminal Code prohibits incitement to hatred and insults that assault human dignity against people based on their racial, national, religious, or ethnic background. Malicious gossip against private citizens and defamation of politicians are also outlawed, including defiling the memory of the dead. Holocaust denial was explicitly included in 1994. Violations are punishable by up to five years in prison. Glorifying or justifying Nazi rule was included in 2005.[10]

Recently, Germany has strengthened its existing laws in an effort to curtail the resurgence and violence of the far right. Those engaging in violence have often been recruited online. In 2017, Germany required social media platforms to remove questionable posts within 24 hours for simple cases or face large fines. An addition in 2018 required media platforms to send suspected criminal content directly to federal police when it is reported by a user.[11]

The Italian Criminal Code focuses on domestic peace and election security. It makes the publication and dissemination of false, exaggerated, or biased news that may undermine public order punishable by arrest and detention. In January of 2018, the Interior Ministry announced a protocol aimed at election misinformation, allowing Postal Police to fact-check communications and report alleged crimes to the judiciary. The police could initiate their own searches and also respond to citizen complaints but the portal for receiving citizen complaints was eliminated after the election. The standard was for information that was biased, unfounded, or defamatory.[12]

Laws Targeting Virus Misinformation and Scams

Some countries have tried to deal with false news related to the pandemic. The health crisis provided an opportunity to rush laws through, often without sufficient scrutiny, though some of them were withdrawn later or limited to the period of the health emergency. Laws or regulations with a focus on the pandemic have been hard to justify over the long term.

Malaysia passed a strong law, then repealed it, reestablishing portions of it in 2021 to deal with the pandemic. Publishing or sharing any "wholly or partly false" information about either the pandemic or a state of emergency that took effect in January is punishable by up to three years in jail.

In March 2020, the Philippines passed a law granting the president extra powers to manage the coronavirus pandemic. Republic Act No. 11469 Section 6 (F) penalizes individuals or groups creating, perpetrating, or spreading false information regarding the COVID-19 crisis on social media and other platforms. The law bans information about the virus that has no valid or beneficial effect on the population. The law also prohibits information intended to promote chaos, panic, anarchy, fear, or confusion, and criminalizes those taking advantage of the crisis through scams, phishing attacks, and fraudulent emails. Intended as a crisis response, this part of the law addressing false and misleading news about the virus was not renewed when its short life was over. Several prior efforts to control false and misleading news met with immense resistance for fear that they would prevent or curtail free speech unconstitutionally and would be used to target opponents of the administration.

Laws Targeting Opponents or Criticism of the Regime

Unfortunately for those wishing to see a stronger collective response to falsehoods spread on social media, when governments police the social media the results have often been targeted not against the lies or even the liars, but against political opponents and news media critical of regimes. Claiming threats of destabilization, some governments have made opposition or criticism illegal.

India has recently passed strong rules for social media, effective in 2021. The rules mandate traceability of encoded messages and require acknowledgment of takedown requests within 24 hours and redress within 15 days, for material that is unlawful, misleading, or violent. In cases dealing with sensitive matters such as sexual content, the social media have only 24 hours to take down the messages. Companies are required to submit a monthly report on the number of complaints and what action they took on each one.[13] Pornography must be taken down using automated processes. The companies are threatened with removal of protection from lawsuits and criminal prosecution for failure to comply.

In addition to complaints by users, government agencies may flag particular posts as illegal or harmful. If that happens, the post must be removed within a day and a half.[14]

Struggling with a second wave of covid-19, the Indian government forced Facebook, Instagram, and Twitter to take down dozens of posts, not those promoting false information, but those critical of the government's handling of the crisis.[15]

Twitter was also under pressure for failure to take down the posts of government opponents, including criticism of the prime minister's response to a massive farmer protest.

Whatsapp sued the Indian government over the privacy violations and legal experts tended to side with Whatsapp. Other court suits were pending. The fate of the new rules is thus unclear.[16]

Russia's law criminalizes the spread of online news that criticizes the government.[17] An addition in 2021 condemns social media that refuse to post Russian official media content.[18] This portion of the law is more about what must be posted than about what should not be posted and does not appear to be aimed at misinformation.

Russian authorities have objected to political opponents of the Kremlin using foreign social media platforms to organize protests and to publicize investigations into alleged corruption.[19]

Belarus, which lacks basic press freedoms, passed controversial amendments against false news in June of 2018. The law requires all authors of posts to be identified and comments must be moderated by site owners. Sites can be blocked for failure to comply. The definition of false news is vague. The law has been used to block popular sites like TUT.BY that report on news, including police abuse of peaceful protesters. "Belarus' Ministry of Information claimed TUT.BY published fake news discrediting the work of governmental institutions and 'damaging state interests in the current socio-political context.'"[20]

In Cote D'Ivoire, the law has been used against journalists and a minister was imprisoned on false news charges. The law has been used against journalists in Myanmar as well, where the law is vaguely worded to include incorrect information that causes fear or alarm to the public. The use of law also has been problematic in Thailand, where a longstanding prohibition on criticism of the King has been expanded to criticism of the government. Sharing or liking particular posts is sufficient to warrant arrest.

In 2018, Egypt passed a strong and vaguely worded law giving the state power to block or suspend media sites and penalize journalists whom the government claimed were publishing fake news. Websites require a government license. Fines can be imposed on editors. Filming can only occur in approved places, though no definition of approved places was included. Journalists and government critics have been arrested and charged with publishing false news.[21]

Charges against journalists have included spreading false news with intent to topple the Egyptian regime, damaging public order and harming the national interest, membership in a terrorist organization, and using the internet to promote ideas and beliefs calling for terrorist acts.[22] An Al-Jazeera producer was charged with "incitement against state institutions and broadcasting fake news with the aim of spreading chaos" after the network criticized Egyptian military conscription.[23]

Nicaragua passed a law in the fall of 2020 against digital crimes, including criminalizing the spread of false or misleading information on the internet. The law includes information that could raise alarm, terror, or unease among people. The government decides what fits in that category. Penalties increase if the information incites hatred or violence, or threatens economic stability, public health, national sovereignty, or law and order.[24]

The Iranian computer crimes law, passed in 2009, provides for punishments for spying, hacking, piracy and publishing materials deemed to damage "public morality" or to be a "dissemination of lies." Punishment is imprisonment for up to two years and a hefty fine is given for disseminating false news likely to "agitate public opinion."

Opponents argue that the law has been used for the suppression of critics of the administration.[25] Bloggers, online journalists, activists, and citizens have been "arrested and prosecuted for content posted online. The government continued to block websites and ban content deemed as critical of the state."[26]

Pakistan's law, passed in 2016, aims at controlling and punishing cybercrime of all sorts.

> Whoever intentionally and publicly exhibits or displays or transmits any information through any information system, which he knows to be false, and intimidates or harms the reputation or privacy of a natural person, shall be punished with imprisonment for a term which may extend to three years or with fines which may extend to one million rupees or with both.

Harmful or fraudulent email is included. Critics argued, "In the name of protecting the people, what the state did through PECA was amass powers to protect itself from criticism, strip citizens of speech and privacy rights, and subject them to the discretionary powers of investigative agencies."[27]

Legislation Proposed but Not (Yet?) Passed

Legislation that has been passed tells a story, but so does legislation proposed that has not become law.

Legislative proposals in the U.S. have been modest in scope, such as banning fake accounts or requiring social media platforms to make public their policies for what is acceptable or unacceptable content. Another proposal would require social media to make clear to potential users what personal information it will collect. Still another proposal required reports at intervals on advertisers. None of these proposals sought to ban false or misleading news or make social media companies responsible for monitoring the content on their sites. Some had no cosponsors, suggesting a lack of legislative support, but one proposal had garnered 47 cosponsors: It was aimed at preventing terrorists from having social media accounts. In 2019, a proposal by Senator Amy Klobuchar managed to get seven cosponsors for a program to offer grants to encourage digital citizenship and media literacy, but the legislation went nowhere. In fact, it is not clear any of these proposals will become law, as none of them have passed out of committee, let alone passed both houses of Congress.

What is especially striking about this mild legislative response is that it occurred after the January 6 attack on the Capitol by Trump supporters who were trying to overturn the election results. During hearings in March of 2021, members of Congress *threatened* to pass legislation to prevent online content that could lead to further violence, but there was little follow up.

Instead, toward the end of July 2021, democratic senators introduced a bill that would hold social media responsible for posting false material about vaccines, fake cures, and other harmful health-related claims during a health crisis. Called the Health Misinformation Act, it would slightly weaken the immunity of the social media companies granted by Section 230 of the Communications Decency Act, the section that says that social media is not liable for material posted on their sites. Shortly after it was introduced it had only one cosponsor and would undoubtedly meet opposition from social media company executives determined to protect their immunity from liability for circulating false or misleading information.

A law was proposed in Brazil called the Brazilian Law on Freedom, Responsibility and Transparency on the Internet. Its wording was vague, opposing false or deceptive content shared with the potential to cause individual or collective harm. A key provision reversed the protections of the social media companies, making them responsible for the content posted by users, rousing fears that companies would take down posts that might displease the government.

The bill was proposed because supporters of President Jair Bolsonaro's government were being investigated for spreading fake news during elections about rivals and journalists. The fake news was blamed for encouraging attacks on journalists and an attempt to invade the National Congress.[28] Bolsonaro indicated that he would veto a bill to control false information if it came to his desk in its current form.[29] It is a safe bet that this bill will not become law as long as Bolsonaro is president.

In Chile, a bill proposed in 2019 would cause politicians to lose their seats if they funded, promoted, or shared false news aimed at other candidates during an election campaign. In 2020, three bills were under discussion, aimed at various aspects of the problem. One proposed adding to the criminal code the crime of "spreading false news that disturbs the social order or causes panic in the population"; one proposed fines for those who propagate false news aimed at harming the work of the authorities in periods of the health crisis, and one proposed both a prison sentence and a fine for accusations, allegations, or news that refer to facts that could alter the sincerity of the electoral process. Given the still raw memory of the dictatorship of Augusto Pinochet and the anti-authoritarian tone of recent mass protests, it seems unlikely that such proposals would become law, and if they did, it seems likely that such a law would be rescinded or revised.

A number of other Central and South American countries have also proposed legislation. In Colombia, a ban on speaking ill of politicians was removed from a proposal. A proposal in El Salvador included up to five years in prison for raising alarm among the population through announcing disasters, accidents, or non-existent dangers. In Panama sentences of one to two years in prison were proposed for anyone disseminating disinformation "harmful to any electoral process or to the services provided by the Electoral Court." Peru also proposed to protect its elections through penalties for false information. In Paraguay, legislation was proposed to curtail false information about the pandemic but met such opposition that it was withdrawn. Legislators in Uruguay tried to prevent election disinformation but ended up withdrawing the proposal in favor of an informal agreement between political parties to refrain from such tactics. (This list may not be inclusive of all legislative proposals, but it gives you the idea.[30])

South Korea, which has been struggling for years to control fake news, recently proposed a revision to its media arbitration law, making the media companies liable for content deemed fake news. The proposal includes damaging someone's property, infringing on personal rights, or causing mental distress due to false or manipulated reports on purpose or due to negligence. Those claiming to be hurt by such posts would be owed five times the financial harm they suffered. This proposal was scheduled for a vote toward the end of August 2021 but was withdrawn due to a major backlash by critics claiming it would curtail free speech.[31]

The Media Literacy Approach

Rather than passing laws against false or misleading online material, some countries have opted for a policy of improving media literacy, including Australia, the Netherlands, and Nigeria. A 1998 report noted that France, Finland, and England had incorporated into school curricula material about the preparation, impact, and interpretation of news.[32] Sweden and Ontario, Canada have also integrated media literacy into their school curricula. In 2019, Finland was ranked first in Europe for resistance to disinformation. Sweden and the Netherlands also rank high, so this educational approach does work.[33]

Generally, however, central governments have not mandated education for adults or children that would make them more media savvy. The efforts that have been taken have often been by fact-checkers, by journalism schools or associations, and other private non-governmental organizations. Decentralized governments have been reluctant to dictate what should be in school curricula, and the need to reach adults as well as children has supported a more diverse set of approaches, through schools, libraries, and websites. While media literacy offers an approach that does not hamper free speech, it is difficult to achieve on a national basis.

When national government fails to act, sometimes states step in. In 2019, California passed a law prohibiting deep fakes during elections, raising questions about speech protection. AB730 applies to any politician within 60 days of an election. News media are exempt, as is satire or parody. Deepfakes are allowed if the authors acknowledge that they are faked. The law sunsets in 2023. Thus, it is of short duration and limited coverage.

Self-Regulation by Media Platforms

The legislative response has generally been soft and muffled, and while some countries have relied on education, the response in the U.S. has been to pressure social media platforms to police themselves. As a result, there has been a patchwork of responses from social media companies, often relying on fact-checkers to warn readers of material that has been judged misleading, without taking it down or preventing anyone from reading it.

There have been a few exceptions in which flagrant and dangerous violations of the media platforms' rules have resulted in temporary or longer-lasting expulsions from the site.

After years of allowing deceptive posts, a number of social media sites took some action against the most egregious violations after the January 6 attack on the Capitol, which had been supported by denialists claiming that Trump had actually won the election, and that the election had been stolen from him by the Democrats. Twitter labeled Trump's claims of election fraud "disputed" but didn't take them down or close Trump's account until after January 6. After that event, Twitter locked Trump out of his account for 12 hours. The platform informed him that his access would not be restored until he took down some inflammatory tweets; instead, he continued posting them and was ultimately locked out.

President Trump was eventually banned from Facebook for two years after the attack on the Capitol on January 6, 2021. Facebook announced that Trump would not be reinstated until the risk he posed to public safety had receded.

Some of Trump's closest allies also had their accounts curtailed, if not withdrawn, because of the fear of encouraging more violence. Rudolf Giuliani, Trump's attorney who had actively promoted the false news of Trump's election victory, found that his posts were labeled "disputed" and no replies or retweeting or likes were allowed because of the risk of violence.[34] The link between the inflammatory and misleading posts and violence in the Capitol had been established, and motivated social media to take some action.

Conspiracy theorist Marjorie Taylor Greene posted for years with complete freedom. She is now an elected representative who has argued that the

Parkland school shooting was a false flag operation. She harassed one of the survivors of the school shooting, calling him a coward and claiming that George Soros had paid him to advocate for gun control. She also charged the Speaker of The House, Nancy Pelosi, with treason, and predicted that Pelosi would suffer death or imprisonment.[35]

In 2021 she was finally kicked off Twitter, but only for 12 hours. Then, after she continued to post misleading material violating the platform's rules, she was kicked off for a week.

The gentle treatment of politicians, no matter how harmful their online posts or tweets, has created a loophole of gigantic proportions.

Moreover, when some people have been booted from media platforms, they create new accounts or shift to other platforms. For example, Alex Berenson, a former *New York Times* reporter and Yale educated novelist, was kicked off Twitter for posting misinformation on the coronavirus.[36] He had claimed that the Pfizer vaccine did not prevent death and that vaccination was like the Holocaust. He also had predicted that the vaccines would cause an uptick in cases and deaths from the coronavirus. After he was booted from Twitter, he set up an account on a lesser-known site, Substack.

Trump's first reaction on being terminated from Twitter for instigating violence was to work through alternate accounts, such as @TeamTrump. Twitter limited access to, but didn't take down, @potus and @whitehouse. @realDonaldTrump was the account that was blocked.

In the absence of concerted governmental efforts to regulate social media, we have become more dependent on social media sites to police themselves and act when their terms of service are violated. But so far they haven't done a very good job, even when the case does not involve politicians. Efforts to remove posts that violate their rules often meet with charges of censorship or bias.

Social media companies often are slow to respond or do not take down posts flagged as hate speech. One study tracked hate posts against Jews, including widely circulated conspiracy theories. The Anti-Defamation League evaluated eight social media platforms for how well they handled such complaints. Twitter and YouTube did best with an overall grade of B–; Facebook and Instagram earned a C–.[37]

A study by The Center for Countering Digital Hate reported that researchers filed 714 reports of digital hate; only one in six reported posts were taken down by the five major social media companies. Much of the flagged material contains false charges, for example, that Jews made a declaration of war on Nazi Germany, that the Jewish banking family Rothschild was involved in 9/11, and that the coronavirus was created in an Israeli laboratory. Another post that Facebook did not take down linked the Rothschilds to mind control, eugenics, and child sacrifice and abuse.[38]

The Center for Countering Digital Hate also reported that social media platforms failed to remove 95 percent of the anti-vaxx misinformation reported to them. One of the posts that remained on the sites claimed that the vaccinations against coronavirus were poisonous and could kill you either quickly or more slowly because it harmed one's DNA. Other posts linked covid, 5-G, and vaccines to a plot to track and control the world's population.[39]

The Center for Countering Digital Hate invites researchers to examine its data. Facebook, by contrast, only reluctantly allows researchers to look at its data. The company has withheld a quarterly report that made it look bad, and recently cut off access to researchers from New York University who were studying disinformation. The research team focused on political ads and covid-19 misinformation. Around 16,000 users installed an extension that allowed them to share with the researchers to which ads they were exposed. Facebook claimed that this data collection violated the users' privacy, although it is hard to see how, since the users had to install the extension that allowed them to share the information with the researchers. The researchers were gathering information on advertisers, not on users. Facebook allows researchers to study how advertisers target users, but only allows researchers who participate in a Facebook controlled program. It gets to choose who studies it.[40] Without full transparency, Facebook can claim it is doing a better job than it is actually doing to police false and misleading information.

Conclusion

The U.S. and other democratic countries have been hesitant to pass laws controlling the media. The model of less democratic countries passing laws to control the internet and using those laws against political enemies or critics of the regime has reinforced the fear of criminalizing lies, exaggerations, and distortions online. Only when there seems to be a clear and present danger, such as from terrorists or disease, does a consensus build to take legal action. And even then, many of the actions are temporary, or thrown out by the courts.

Instead, we have become dependent on social media companies to patrol their own space, relying on users, computerized algorithms, and human fact-checkers to call attention to problematic posts and news stories. The threat of regulation if they fail may have motivated some of them, and the obvious connection between false and misleading news and real-world violence and threats to health and democracy may have prompted the closing of a few accounts.

Self-regulation by social media companies has had mixed results. Bias in favor of free speech has allowed elected officials broad license to lie and distort, and reluctance by the private companies to take down popular posts has often resulted in warnings to readers rather than in removed material or closed accounts. Some platforms are just not motivated to police themselves, so bad actors stricken from one site can and sometimes do move to another one.

Further, as in arms races, actions by one party produce adaptations by the others. To the extent that social media platforms do actually police themselves, those spreading false and misleading news adapt and become less visible, harder to trace, and much harder to control.

Consequently, if we run across a warning on Facebook or some other media that some story might not be true, we need to judge it ourselves. If we hear some pundit on television telling us that the vaccines against coronavirus will make us magnetic, infertile, or will kill us, we need to look at the evidence. The so-called experts we see and hear may be paid by foreign agents to spread particular lies and distortions, telling us who to vote for and who to fear. Those arguments too we need to judge for ourselves.

If we read that lizard people secretly rule the earth, we should be skeptical, and check it out. On its face, that claim seems unlikely to be true. Unfortunately, a man who murdered his children had read that there were reptilian lizard people who ruled the world; he told police he had a vision that his wife had serpent DNA and had passed it on to his children. He claimed that he had murdered his two little children so they would not grow up to be monsters.[41]

False news and conspiracy theories have real-world consequences. So, we have to get this right. Nobody else is going to do this for us.

Notes

1 "Report on the Implementation of the Action Plan against Disinformation," *The European Commission*, Brussels, June 14, 2019, https://eeas.europa.eu/sites/default/files/joint_report_on_disinformation.pdf.
2 Lionel Barber, Henry Foy, and Alex Barker, "Vladimir Putin Says Liberalism Has 'Become Obsolete,'" *Financial Times*, June 27, 2019, www.ft.com/content/670039ec-98f3-11e9-9573-ee5cbb98ed36.
3 Sharmila Devi, "COVID-19 Exacerbates Violence against Health Workers," *The Lancet*, 396 (10252), p. 658, September 5, 2020, www.thelancet.com/journals/lancet/article/PIIS0140-6736(20)31858-4/fulltext#%20.
4 Rachel Hatzipanagos, "How Online Hate Turns into Real-Life Violence," *The Washington Post*, November 30, 2018, www.washingtonpost.com/nation/2018/11/30/how-online-hate-speech-is-fueling-real-life-violence/.
5 Shannon Bond, "Just 12 People Are Behind Most Vaccine Hoaxes on Social Media, Research Shows," *NPR*, May 14, 2021, www.npr.org/2021/05/13/996570855/disinformation-dozen-test-facebooks-twitters-ability-to-curb-vaccine-hoaxes.
6 Musadiq Bidar, "Lawmakers Vow Stricter Regulations on Social Media Platforms to Combat Misinformation," *CBS News*, March 25, 2021, www.cbsnews.com/news/misinformation-extremism-hearing-google-facebook-twitter-watch-live-stream-today-2021-03-25/.
7 Max Fisher, "Disinformation for Hire, a Shadow Industry, Is Quietly Booming," *The New York Times*, July 25, 2021, www.nytimes.com/2021/07/25/world/europe/disinformation-social-media.html.

8 Romain Dillet, "French Constitutional Authority Rejects Law Forcing Online Platforms to Delete Hate-Speech Content," *techcrunch.com*, June 19, 2020, https://techcrunch.com/2020/06/19/french-constitutional-authority-rejects-law-forcing-online-platforms-to-delete-hate-speech-content/.

9 Jenny Gathright, "Kenya's Crackdown on Fake News Raises Questions about Press Freedom," *NPR*, May 19, 2018, www.npr.org/sections/thetwo-way/2018/05/19/612649393/kenyas-crackdown-on-fake-news-raises-questions-about-press-freedom.

10 Dan Glaun, "Germany's Laws on Hate Speech, Nazi Propaganda & Holocaust Denial: An Explainer," *PBS Frontline*, July 1, 2021, www.pbs.org/wgbh/frontline/article/germanys-laws-antisemitic-hate-speech-nazi-propaganda-holocaust-denial/.

11 Natasha Lomas, "Germany Tightens Online Hate Speech Rules to Make Platforms Send Reports Straight to the Feds," *techcrunch.com*, June 19, 2020, https://techcrunch.com/2020/06/19/germany-tightens-online-hate-speech-rules-to-make-platforms-send-reports-straight-to-the-feds/.

12 Tackling Fake News, the Italian Way, "Resource Center on Media Freedom in Europe," www.rcmediafreedom.eu/Tools/Legal-Resources/Tackling-fake-news-the-Italian-way.

13 Dashveenjit Kaur, "India's New Social Media Rules Explained," *Techwire Asia*, June 1, 2021, https://techwireasia.com/2021/06/indias-new-social-media-rules-explained/.

14 Sheikh Saaliq and Krutika Pathi, "India's New Law Would Restrain Social Media. Are Rights at Risk?," *The Christian Science Monitor*, July 15, 2021, www.csmonitor.com/World/Asia-South-Central/2021/0715/India-s-new-law-would-restrain-social-media.-Are-rights-at-risk.

15 Karan Deep Singh and Paul Mozur, "As Outbreak Rages, India Orders Critical Social Media Posts to Be Taken Down," *The New York Times*, April 25, 2021, www.nytimes.com/2021/04/25/business/india-covid19-twitter-facebook.html.

16 Joseph Menn, "WhatsApp Sues Indian Government over New Privacy Rules—Sources," *Reuters*, May 26, 2021, www.reuters.com/world/india/exclusive-whatsapp-sues-india-govt-says-new-media-rules-mean-end-privacy-sources-2021-05-26/.

17 Shannon Van Sant, "Russia Criminalizes the Spread of Online News Which 'Disrespects' the Government," *NPR*, March 18, 2019, www.npr.org/2019/03/18/704600310/russia-criminalizes-the-spread-of-online-news-which-disrespects-the-government.

18 Library of Congress, "Russian Federation: New Law Enables Restrictions on Digital Platforms," February 22, 2021, www.loc.gov/item/global-legal-monitor/2021-02-22/russian-federation-new-law-enables-restrictions-on-digital-platforms/.

19 Reuters, "Putin Signs Law Forcing Foreign Social Media Giants to Open Russian Offices," July 1, 2021, www.reuters.com/technology/putin-signs-law-forcing-foreign-it-firms-open-offices-russia-2021-07-01/.

20 Anastasiia Zlobina, "Belarus Escalates Crackdown on Independent Journalism," *Human Rights Watch*, December 7, 2020, www.hrw.org/news/2020/12/07/belarus-escalates-crackdown-independent-journalism.

21 Reuters Staff, "Egypt Targets Social Media with New Law," *Reuters*, July 17, 2018, www.reuters.com/article/us-egypt-politics/egypt-targets-social-media-with-new-law-idUSKBN1K722C.

22 Ruth Michaelson, "'Fake News' Becomes Tool of Repression after Egypt Passes New Law," *The Guardian*, July 27, 2018, www.theguardian.com/global-development/2018/jul/27/fake-news-becomes-tool-of-repression-after-egypt-passes-new-law.

23 Darell West, "How to Combat Fake News and Disinformation," *Brookings Institution*, December 18, 2017, www.brookings.edu/research/how-to-combat-fake-news-and-disinformation/.

24 AP, "Nicaragua Approves 'Cybercrimes' Law, Alarming Rights Groups," *Associated Press*, October 27, 2020, https://apnews.com/article/legislature-legislation-crime-daniel-ortega-cybercrime-ce252ed4721a759ed329798a7e2e30db.

25 "Computer Crimes in Iran: Online Repression in Practice," Article 19, 2013, www.article19.org/data/files/medialibrary/37385/Computer-Crimes-in-Iran-.pdf.
26 "Freedom on the Net 2020: Iran," *Freedom House*, 2020, https://freedomhouse.org/country/iran/freedom-net/2020.
27 Farieha Aziz, "Pakistan's Cybercrime Law: Boon or Bane?," *Heinrich Boll Siftung*, February 14, 2018, www.boell.de/en/2018/02/07/pakistans-cybercrime-law-boon-or-bane.
28 Raphael Tsavkko Garcia, "Brazil's 'Fake News' Bill Won't Solve Its Misinformation Problem," *Technology Review*, September 10, 2020, www.technologyreview.com/2020/09/10/1008254/brazil-fake-news-bill-misinformation-opinion/.
29 Anthony Boadle, "Brazil's Bolsonaro Would Veto Bill Regulating Fake News in Current Form," *Reuters*, July 2, 2020, www.reuters.com/article/us-brazil-politics-fake-news/brazils-bolsonaro-would-veto-bill-regulating-fake-news-in-current-form-idUSKBN2433FN.
30 Júlio Lubianco, "11 Laws and Bills against Disinformation in Latin America Carry Fines, Prison and Censorship," *Latam Journalism Review*, December 16, 2020, https://latamjournalismreview.org/articles/laws-and-bills-against-disinformation-in-latin-america/.
31 Shawn Lim, South Korea puts proposed "fake news law" on ice after backlash, The Drum, October 4, 2021, https://www.thedrum.com/news/2021/10/04/south-korea-puts-proposed-fake-news-law-ice-after-backlash
32 Laura Lederer, "What Are Other Countries Doing in Media Education?," Excerpted by Center for Media Literacy, www.medialit.org/reading-room/what-are-other-countries-doing-media-education.
33 Emma Charlton, "How Finland Is Fighting Fake News—In The Classroom," *World Economic Forum*, May 21, 2019, www.weforum.org/agenda/2019/05/how-finland-is-fighting-fake-news-in-the-classroom/.
34 Hannah Denham, "These Are the Platforms That Have Banned Trump and His Allies," *The Washington Post*, January 14, 2021, www.washingtonpost.com/technology/2021/01/11/trump-banned-social-media/.
35 Em Steck and Andrew Kaczynski, "Marjorie Taylor Greene Indicated Support for Executing Prominent Democrats in 2018 and 2019 before Running for Congress," *CNN*, January 26, 2021.
36 OLAFIMIHAN OSHIN—Twitter Bans Conservative Author Alex Berenson, The Hill, August 29, 2021.
37 2021 Online Antisemitism Report Card. ADL, www.adl.org/resources/reports/2021-online-antisemitism-report-card.
38 "Failure to Protect, How Tech Giants Fail to Act on User Reports of Antisemitism," *CCDH*, https://252f2edd-1c8b-49f5-9bb2-cb57bb47e4ba.filesusr.com/ugd/f4d9b9_cac47c87633247869bda54fb35399668.pdf.
39 "Failure to Act: How Tech Giants Continue to Defy Calls to Rein in Vaccine Misinformation," *CCDH*, https://252f2edd-1c8b-49f5-9bb2-cb57bb47e4ba.filesusr.com/ugd/f4d9b9_dbc700e9063b4653a7d27f4497f3c2c2.pdf.
40 Shannon Bond, "NYU Researchers Were Studying Disinformation on Facebook. The Company Cut Them Off," *NPR*, August 4, 2021, file:///C:/Users/Owner/Documents/persuad3/Facebook%20Boots%20NYU%20Disinformation%20Researchers%20Off%20Its%20Platform%20_%20NPR.html.
41 Doha Madani, Andrew Blankstein, and Ben Collins, "California Dad Killed His Kids over QANON and 'Serpent DNA' Conspiracy Theories, Feds Claim," *NBCNews*, December 10, 2021.

INDEX

9/11 Truthers 115, 116

abortion 13, 28, 48, 62, 106, 117–119, 169
Adams, John 1, 2
ad hominem attacks 17, 62
Akin, Todd 62
aliens 91, 95
Allsides 46, 71, 140
Annenberg Public Policy Center 40
Antifa 58, 111, 112
anti-vaxxers 3, 104, 117, 119, 120, 158
authority, arguments from 8, 15, 17–18, 62, 88, 105, 115, 129–130, 154–155, 162, 169

Barr, William 56
bee apocalypse 81–83
bias: intentional 149, 152, 154, 155; unintentional 147, 149
Biden, Joe 1, 23, 24, 37, 42, 49, 88
Bill Gates 105
Black Lives Matter 29, 97, 137
blame avoidance 23, 25, 26, 128
blame diffusion (diffusing blame) 26, 79
blaming the victim 24, 112
blind peer review 51
block grants 134
blogs 9, 20, 51, 75, 95, 112, 164–165
Breitbart 166
Brookings Institution 70, 73, 172

Calling Bullshit 171
carbon capture 83–84
censorship 7, 129, 176, 185
Center for Countering Digital Hate (CCDH) 176, 185, 186

Center on Budget and Policy Priorities 71, 134–135
cherry picking 8, 18–19, 61, 72, 81, 85, 91, 97, 98, 117, 133
China 12, 24, 26, 78, 99–100, 106–107, 177
Christopher Blair (Godfather of Fake News) 51
climate change 1, 4, 77, 84, 90, 106, 173
Clinton, Hillary 14, 23, 51, 107, 112–113, 119, 150–151
Collins, Susan 13
color words 12, 109
comments on stories 162
community guidelines 160
Conservative Treehouse 112
conspiracy theories 14, 49, 104–121, 150, 151, 164
context 13, 30, 43, 62, 91, 101, 126, 143, 146, 155, 164, 180; lack of 13, 65–66, 67, 84, 96, 127, 130–131, 135, 145, 152, 153
Conway, Kellyanne 6
credit taking 26, 57
Crowdstrike 112–113
Cruz, Ted 29

Daily Kos 12
deep state 14, 112, 151, 164
delegitimizing 14, 15, 87, 88, 107, 108, 152
democracy 1, 4, 5, 28, 42, 159, 186
denialism 25, 97, 128, 158
disinformation 175–177, 183, 186
distortions 1, 5, 7, 18–19, 23, 49, 52, 152, 157, 158, 162, 164, 165, 178, 186, 187

INDEX

distraction strategy 26, 29
dog whistles 13–14, 164

Economic Policy Institute (EPI) 71, 75, 76
electric cars 71, 77–78
errors 5, 58; measurement error 139; non-response error 139, 140, 143; sampling error 139, 142
exaggeration 1, 2, 5, 23, 157, 164, 173, 186; examples of 18, 50–51, 80, 109, 128, 161–162

Facebook 40, 42, 108, 120, 159, 160, 166, 179, 184–187
fact-checkers 55, 59, 60, 70, 87–88, 130, 132, 135, 159, 160, 164, 183, 184, 186; certification 38–39; and conspiracy theories 106, 108, 111, 112–113, 115, 119, 120; and quick search 35–52; and reliability 6, 36, 39, 58; and survey questions 146–147, 151, 154, 155
fact-checking 35–44, 45, 48, 51, 52, 59, 62; fake accounts 17; going beyond 1655; reporting to sites 159
fake news 7, 11, 20, 45, 46, 50, 182; consequences of 2–5; fact checking 39, 43, 48, 108; laws against 180, 183; responding to 157, 159, 165; and slippery slope arguments 30
false advertising 2, 18, 160
false dichotomies 28, 49, 90
false equivalence 57–58
false flags 114
false websites 45
FBI 39, 56, 90–91, 94, 112, 113, 120
Federal Communications Commission (FCC) 161, 166
Federal Trade Commission (FTC) 160
filter questions 144, 150, 152
Firstdraftnews.com (fact-checking tutorial) 52
FiveThirtyEight 65, 138, 140, 141
Flynn, Michael 119
follow-up questions 64–66
Food and Drug Administration (FDA) 99, 160
Fox News 25, 41, 51, 72–73, 99, 120, 147, 151, 154, 166
Fusion GPS 149–151

Gabbard, Tulsi 59
Gates, Bill 105
Gateway Pundit 108, 109
GIGO (garbage in, garbage out) 134
Giuliani, Rudy 6, 26, 49, 184
Graham, Lindsay 15
Grassley, Chuck 100

Harris, Kamala 36, 59
Hogg, David 108
The Hyde Amendment 118
hydroxychloroquine 2, 25

IFCN (International Fact-checking Network) 38, 39
illogic 20, 30, 54–58, 64, 95, 104–106, 114, 116, 119, 132
immigrants 1, 26, 46, 93, 135, 167, 176; blame shifting for mistreatment of 79; counter arguments 60–61; scare tactics about 90–91, 95, 106; stereotyping 16, 20; surveys about 144–148
impeachment 41, 124, 150
Infowars 108
Ingraham, Laura 99
Instagram 160, 179, 185
Ivanka Trump 19, 88

January 6, 2021 1, 176, 182, 184
Jones, Alex 108

latte liberal 14
leprosy (Hansen's disease) 91, 167
letters to the editor 9, 162
libertarian position 70, 71, 74, 75, 99
lies 1, 2, 5, 7, 17, 23, 45, 52, 157, 158, 162, 164, 165, 173, 177, 187; accusing opponents of 179, 181, 186; examples of 19–22
lukewarmer 90

The Manhattan Institute 71, 77
margin of error 143, 144
marijuana 18, 59–60, 71–72, 132, 169
McConnell, Mitch 15
measuring the wrong thing 95–96, 132
Media Bias/factcheck 38, 39, 45, 46, 71, 72, 108, 112, 119, 140
media control laws 177–183
media literacy 181, 183–184
memes 14, 42, 48

INDEX

Meyssan, Thierry 115–116, 120
minimum wage 132–133
misinterpretation 87, 90, 99; of surveys 138, 154
mistakes 6, 26, 35, 38, 52, 92, 95, 130, 140
MMR (measles, mumps, and rubella) 117, 119
MS-13 58
Mueller, Robert 56, 150
name calling 15–16, 58, 163, 169

Nancy Pelosi 14, 15, 185
Newsome, Gavin 158–159
New York Post 12, 133–134

Obama, Barack 6, 12, 13, 24, 25, 36; and conspiracy theories 104, 106, 119, 151
Ocasio-Cortez (AOC), Alexandria 3, 14, 41, 152–153
One America News Network (OAN) 111, 112
on-line surveys 142
op-eds 163–164
opt-in surveys 142, 146
out-migration 49, 95

panels 141–142, 149, 165
Parkland mass shooting 108, 110
photo checkers 39
Pinocchios 41, 58
Pizzagate 107, 119, 120
Planned Parenthood 118
police killings 97–99, 131
Political Ears 20
post hoc ergo propter hoc 57, 132
poverty programs 72–73, 133–135
Poynter Institute 36, 39, 43, 44, 48
protests 29, 44, 97, 109, 166, 180, 182–183
push polls 149
random sample 142

rape 24, 62–64, 95, 118
Reason Magazine 99, 100
reliability 35, 39, 45–52, 109, 138
ruling out options 27–30

sanctuary cities 144–147
Sanders, Bernie 14, 93
Sanger, Margaret 118

Schumer, Chuck 13
Sean Spicer 6
sex discrimination 74
shibboleths 22–23, 61, 98, 172
silver bullets 21–22, 78
slippery slope 29–30
social media 94, 162, 182; abuse of media control laws 179–181; fact-checkers 39, 42, 44; fighting back on 158–159, 161, 165; self regulation 9, 175–179, 184–186, 187; spreading fake news and conspiracy theories 3, 11
Soros, George 13, 20–21, 106, 109–110, 185
stereotypes 8, 16, 18, 38, 60
surveys 7, 8, 83, 137–155, 165, 171; survey companies 138, 141, 142

taxes 21–22, 47, 49–50, 60, 61, 65, 96, 101, 105, 158, 159
Ted Dabrowski 49–51
test case 62, 96
think tanks 70–71
time series 8, 19, 82, 83, 131–133
Trump, Donald 1, 5, 6, 12, 14, 21, 22, 23; ad hominem attacks 17; claiming the victim role 25; and conspiracy theories 104, 109, 112, 113, 119; covering for 56, 127, 150–151; credit taking 27, 128; distracting from a charge 26; diverting blame 24, 79–80, 111, 112; effect of his rallies 93–95; and exaggeration 18; false dichotomies 28; guessing his motives 66–67; his policies 137, 145, 154–155, 157, 168; illogic 57–58; and lies 19–20; misinformation 64; misleading with numbers 124; misquoting people 88; and name calling 156; rebuttals to 162–164; reelection 1, 110, 153, 176, 182, 184–185; and stereotypes 1; subject of fact checks 36–37, 39, 40–42
Truth Brigade, The 167
truth decay 2, 167
Twitter 15, 58, 88, 158, 161–162, 166, 179, 184, 185

vanity presses 52
the victim role 25
voter fraud 39, 64

192

wage gap 71, 74–76
Washington Examiner 71, 88–91, 93
The Washington Times 80
weasel words 11–12, 80, 100, 115, 129
WIREPOINTS 49, 61
Wordpress.org 165

YouTube 4, 160, 185

Zelensky, Velodymyr 88
Zuckerberg, Mark 176

For Product Safety Concerns and Information please contact our EU
representative GPSR@taylorandfrancis.com
Taylor & Francis Verlag GmbH, Kaufingerstraße 24, 80331 München, Germany

www.ingramcontent.com/pod-product-compliance
Lightning Source LLC
Chambersburg PA
CBHW061348300426

44116CB00011B/2042